STRINGER

STRINGER

ANJAN SUNDARAM

A REPORTER'S
JOURNEY IN THE
CONGO

Atlantic Books
London

First published in India in 2013 by Hamish Hamilton, an imprint of
Penguin Books India.

Published in Great Britain in 2014 by Atlantic Books, an imprint of
Atlantic Books Ltd.

10 9 8 7 6 5 4 3 2 1

A CIP catalogue record for this book is available from the British Library.

Trade paperback ISBN: 978 1 78239 247 7
E-book ISBN: 978 1 78239 248 4

Printed in Great Britain

Atlantic Books
An Imprint of Atlantic Books Ltd
Ormond House
26–27 Boswell Street
London
WC1N 3JZ

www.atlantic-books.co.uk

To the family that welcomed me in Congo,

to Nat

CONTENTS

STRINGER

PART I

LINES OF DISTRESS

1

I was already feeling perturbed. There was something perhaps about the bar's large parasol umbrellas, lit starkly by the hanging naked bulbs. Or it could have been the figures flitting behind them, beyond my view.

I had sensed his presence, his curt movements. But they did not seem malicious. Then he lunged for my table, and I found myself running in the night. I ran with all my force. And I would have said I was faster than him. But I might have imagined my own speed from the people who passed me by like pages in a flip-book: mamas with bananas on their heads, vendors carting cages of birds and monkeys, the crocodile-leather pointy-shoed bureaucrats. They turned to stare at me, the whites of their eyes stabbing the darkness and piercing my face, my side, my back. Who are you looking at? He's the thief, stop him!

I squinted to keep sight. His form was like an illusion—feet leaping off the earth, driving up plumes of dust. His hands pulled at his falling shorts; and when he looked back to see I was still running he screamed in surprise, showing dull teeth, and turned into a narrow passage.

We regressed from the city. The alleys amplified the darkness and my shallow breaths filled the spaces between the walls that rose on either side—gray walls high and long between which I ran blindly, without thinking—until we came to a field. And for a moment I lost sight of him.

I turned sharply, feeling a panic rise.

"You!" He appeared, empty-handed—and jeering at me, almost as if he wanted to play. A sickly chicken of a boy, with limbs extending like antennae from his belly. "You have my phone!" I yelled. "*Té!* I refuse!" The ground was wet and yielding, covered in waste, cans, wrappers. The smell was rotten. It was like nothing I had known. A landfill in the middle of the city. Of what was I afraid?

"I'll give you money."

"How much?" He wiped his shoulder over his mouth; his face was covered in sweat.

A group of children skipped toward us. I reached into my pocket for my notebook and wallet. The boy turned, and I saw a wound on a hairless part of his scalp.

"Keep the phone"—I pointed into my palm—"I only need the numbers inside." He smiled, as if smelling a trick. I felt frustrated at my carelessness. I didn't have money to hand out, and those numbers were precious. I was new in the country and had few friends. Most meetings had been gained by chance, in the street, at the odd conference, in a waiting room or at a bar; they had not been planned, necessary, or even particularly friendly. And yet they had taken on, in my mind, a great importance.

Kinshasa, when I first arrived, had felt giant, overwhelming. The scenes on the roads, the people moving from here to there, the languages, gestures, stares—the smallest rituals had seemed imbued with meaning and purpose, and the city appeared as a collusion of secrets only the locals shared. But these strangers I had met—journalists, businessmen, minor politicians—had become bearings from which I navigated the confusion. With them I constructed a sense of place, and for moments felt part of the mystery. So the phone contained my personal map; and without it I felt lost, as though I had newly arrived for a second time and was again without connection. The bewilderment was now greater. And having exhausted the initial excitement of the new place, I now found the city distant, hostile.

My sigh came out heavy and sharp; it startled the boy. Already he was stepping away. I half tripped forward and yelled, "How do I find you? What's your name?"

"Guy."

And, making a cackling noise, he ran behind a mound. I felt suddenly strained.

I could not tell the way by which I had come—so I picked a nearby narrow street and followed it for a mile or two. The walk was not unpleasant. We were in the middle of a brief rainless period, in the summer; and there was a slight breeze. But even in this season the climate was humid and hot, and in such conditions everything grew quickly: the nails, the hair, the plants and insects. All attained giant or copious proportions. I stopped to inspect a falling banana tree. Its top was sappy, and crawling with red ants.

The city also grew daily. It was a center of migration for the region, like São Paulo or Calcutta, and already black Africa's largest capital—a collapsed metropolis, unable to assure even the survival of its nine million people. But still the dispossessed came in floods from the villages.

I passed some women sitting on their porches, washing down their children from canisters of soapy brown water. They looked up. *Bonjour,* I said. Slowly they repeated the word, as though they had not expected it.

The main road was unlit and cars streamed past. People stood in packs, frantically waving their hands and rushing to each slowing taxi. I made a circle with my forefinger pointing at the ground and twenty minutes later found space in a minibus going north. My house was to the south, but it was the end of the working day and I was commuting like the masses. This was my way of finding a free seat.

I trembled incessantly—as did the bus's plywood floor. The metal chassis around me was covered in the dents of countless collisions. The driver took us to the city's commercial area, cruising along the street edge and gathering passengers. A man hanging on the back of the bus constantly yelled our route. People swelled toward us like a oon. We sat in an old Volkswagen whose twelve cushioned seats had been pulled out and replaced with wooden benches; soon we were more than thirty inside, cramped side by side, hands between our knees. We squeezed more for the woman who brought in her drooling infant. The windows were sealed shut, so there was no breeze, and inside it was suffocating. The human smells engulfed us. But I looked through the glass and saw the movement; and this perception of the wind gave some false relief. We came to the harbor, with its broken heavy machinery. And the two- and three-story buildings stained with long black stripes: algae, rising from within the cement and blooming in the open. One imagined the decomposition that lived hidden within. The city seemed to be falling apart, building by building—structures crumbled so slowly they seemed almost to melt. At a roundabout we circled a brick monument—black, as though burned. The statue of the Belgian king had long been toppled, leaving two pillars framing an empty space. Lining the roads were heaps of garbage, glowing like embers and giving off black smoke.

The collapse, the crisis. It is how the world knows Congo. Death is as widespread in few places. Children born here have the bleakest futures. It is the most diseased, the most corrupt, and the least habitable—the country heads nearly every conceivable blacklist. One survey has it that no nation has more citizens who want to leave.

And now we come to the mouth of the Boulevard, the city's

artery. The bus, shivering, accelerates in the wide lanes. On both sides old trees with majestic green crowns and high-rises pass quickly. They still inspire awe. Not far away is the Congo River, opening into a pool and curling around us. One is reminded that this place, even in Europe, was once called the Beautiful, *La Belle.*

The Boulevard is soothing in a way—this part of the city, one feels, has a certain vision, and was made with care. Buildings eighty and ninety years old are still intact, with porches and pillars and triangular eaves. Walls show traces of ocher. Old floors are of fine red and black oxide. The city is well planned, and traffic is congested only because wear has thinned the roads' drivable widths and because of modern neighborhoods, haphazardly constructed. The boulevards are enormous, like in few African cities. The lampposts are tall, solid, evenly spaced. And the railway station has a monument in Latin, declaring the colonial project for which this city was made: *"Aperire Terram Gentibus"*—"To Open the Land to the Nations."

Congo was then opened like a wound. And the world, continually seeking modernity, still consumes the country. A Belgian king committed genocide during the automobile revolution to pillage Congo for rubber—the world needed tires then. Mid-century, the Belgian state initiated a war over Congo's copper, to wire the world for electricity. Congo's recent conflicts were heightened by the world's growing demand for tin, to make the conductors used in almost every electronic circuit. We currently live in what some say is the Fourth Great Pillage—others call it the Fifth or Sixth. The world now needs cell phones, and Congo contains 60 percent of known reserves of an essential metal called tantalum. It is the curse: each progress in the world produces some new suffering. And a succession of Congolese leaders have tried, in their ways, to reclaim their land—first Lumumba by expelling the white man and gaining independence from Belgium; then Mobutu by reviving the old Congolese idea of kingship; and finally the father Kabila, with his half-Marxist ideas of liberation. But even now the country gives the impression of being possessed by outside powers. Kabila's son, the president, seems himself overwhelmed. Much of the country is without government. The wealth has brought out the worst in man: greed, corruption, great violence.

These four men had defined Congo's history. Patrice Lumumba, the fiery politician who united the Congolese and remains the country's only true hero. Then Lumumba's onetime secretary, Joseph Mobutu, ruled as dictator for more than thirty years, with Western help, after having Lumumba assassinated in 1961, just six months after Congo's independence. The rebel Laurent Kabila—the father Kabila—in 1997 toppled the cancer-afflicted Mobutu. And when the father Kabila was himself assassinated four years later, it was his son, the relatively unknown Joseph Kabila, who was installed, and still presided over this naturally rich but ravaged country.

A Congolese legend has it that God, tired after creating the world, stopped at this part of the earth and dropped all his sacks of riches. Gold, diamonds, oil, silver, uranium, zinc, cobalt and tungsten. Such is the wealth—they say you only have to dig and you are sure to find something, though you may not know its name. And it seems somehow significant that this wealth, which another culture might have interpreted as a divine reward, is described in Congolese legend as an accident. God only happened to be at this place.

The minibus turned in to the Avenue des Huileries, the Avenue of Oil Works—we were now only a few miles from the journey's end—where the bus had to share space with the pedestrians, and slow to their pace. As we shed the colonial structures, the past, buildings on the roads grew small and clustered, reflecting the country's anarchy. And against this backdrop the sluggish walkers appeared almost magical, like the survivors of a cataclysm. Men wore suits and fat-knotted ties, yellow and pink; women,

frilly fancy dresses. The shoes stepping in the mud were well polished, of fine leather. Rings of wetness showed under their arms
on the satin. So laboriously beautiful—the people had an air of
character, defiance.

The north and the west of the city were affluent, particularly
along the river. As the bus plunged inland, on every side opened
up slum-like neighborhoods, vast, featureless, without light. We
moved through one of these murky areas, and entered a busy
market, with roaming figures. The sides of our bus began to be
thumped. We were gently rocked. Suddenly our bus was mobbed.
Children's wide-eyed faces pressed against my window. I drew
away. "Give me money," said the shapes of their lips, round as an
O. "*Pesambongo.*" But it was useless—our windows were fixed,
and they could not even sell us their cool drinks, shoe shine or
melting candy. Their desperate small hands stained the glass
with wet palm prints. And they passed by like slow-motion pictures, glaring at us.

We at last arrived at the roar of Victoire, my neighborhood—
and one could feel the chaos become acute. It was a place of raw
cement. Few buildings were even whitewashed. Occasionally a
low wall would be made of brick, adding a touch of color. But
Victoire was legendary in Africa—revered, almost as a site of pil-
grimage. Already, at this hour, from all parts of the city people
would be coming; and beginning at 11:00 p.m., when Kinshasa's
lights had mostly extinguished and the regular families had
retired, here the vitality would resurge, creating an experience
of almost pure pleasure and excitement. The music and meat
grills would go all night. Saxophones would sound from terraces.
Dancers would move like water: slow hips, tempting. The city
would live a second life.

But now it seemed to oppress: the street of wooden stalls lit
by kerosene lamps, where I alighted—the stalls crooked, winged
insects gathering around their glows, the earth pushing against
their walls in chimneyed piles. The feeling, I knew, had some-

thing to do with the house, around the corner. I tried to delay getting back by running some errands.

The shop I made for was just down the road, but people and cars flowed incessantly: I was forced to move, and often against my intention. To be still anywhere was to be in the way.

And at the center of this disorder, beside a pile of garbage being eaten by dogs and shrouded by flies, I arrived at a table of electrical goods. Shops in Kinshasa, especially in this part of town, had moved into the open to escape rents. The vendor was reading a stained small-format magazine, and looking disconsolate. I said I needed a fan. "I have a new ventilator," he declared. "High quality. I give you the best price." *Best price* meant there were other prices and I should negotiate. A large pedestaled machine with blue blades was produced.

"I don't want Made in China."

His salesman demeanor vanished. "Okay, I know the fan is no good, but *you* pay only thirty dollars. Made in Japan I have no stock. And why should I? The fans last too long and no one buys again." I relaxed. Now we could talk freely. Outbursts augured well in Congo—one only had to expose the initial theater, I found, and people were generally up-front.

We agreed on the terms of sale, including a one-week guarantee, which the vendor scribbled on the receipt and signed. He meticulously wrapped the fan in cardboard, while I observed the people, the street. Near me danced a stout man, alone, holding a portable radio to his ear; in front of him a butcher massaged a block of meat.

This area around Victoire was called the *cité* (pronounced with a spit, as opposed to the gentrified *ville*, spoken gently), and here for the most part one saw only Congolese: Victoire had a reputation for gangs and disorder, and expatriate and embassy workers (whose money made a substantial part of the consumer economy) were prohibited even from visits.

"Who wants those foreigners anyway?" said my supplier of

phone cards, Anderson, who operated one street from my house. "Their interest is only to rob this country, not to help us small people."

"All right, all right." I had heard this speech before. "I need a telephone," I said, knuckling his wooden kiosk. "Mine was stolen by one of those *schegués*."

When Anderson smiled his face became boyish. Otherwise, with his gapped teeth and balding head, he appeared very serious, and sometimes frightening. He always dressed simply—in a T-shirt, trousers and sandals—and he made a living selling cell phone credit. Two old telephones sat on his countertop, which was made of scrap wood. He sometimes talked about replacing the kiosk, but it seemed to have made its place: long use had formed depressions in the gravel, at the edge of the open gutter, where Anderson sat outstretched, surveying the street. This was his territory. He was a respected member of the Opposition Debout, an outspoken political movement headquartered in Victoire. He was also my antenna to Radio Trottoir, the underground news network.

"So you met the president," he said to me.

I put a finger to my lips. Not so loud around the opposition! "He wouldn't see me."

"But that's good, my friend! That's good!" Anderson raised his voice. "You are one of us. No use meeting those clowns."

"But the clowns have the power. And the news."

"You want news? Just wait a little. My friend, this country is going to blow up."

"If the country explodes you procure phone cards for me, eh? Ten dollars won't do anymore."

"When this country explodes *you* take care, my friend. We'll kill all the foreigners and burn this city." His phone beeped. "Let's talk later"—he winked and flashed me a thumbs-up—"Don't worry, you're one of us!" And I picked up my fan-in-a-box and made the short march home, feeling sick.

I entered a grid of obscure and ruined streets that stretched away from Victoire, and I followed a group of children playing soccer. The ragged ball, of plastic and string, rolled toward where I lived, on Avenue Bozene. I passed a boy doing his schoolwork, and men huddled over low tables crowded with one-liter beer bottles. Inside gated compounds women chattered, slapping their plastic slippers against their heels. Cracked walls rose from the ground, smelling of moss and crowned with glass shards. The ball fell into a gutter; a boy reached in with his hands and threw the ball in the air; sewage scattered from above. The game passed in front of my compound, which carried no name, just the number 32.

My house was a one-story structure with dirty white walls ringed by blue paint at the bottom. An iron gate led into the courtyard, and first I passed the landlord's identical dwelling before, at the back of the plot and near a set of toilets, coming to our metal-grill door.

I stepped in and tried to smile. Nothing had changed. The bulbs waned, the cistern hissed, Bébé Rhéma slept in her crib and Jose and Nana sat at the table, napkins tucked in. The living room was long and divided into two areas: close to the door was the dining table, near some low cupboards against a wall. At the far end was a television surrounded by khaki sofas. The plot was connected to water and electricity, and also had a septic tank. These were the important things, and they made our house nearly middle-class. (In Congo there was no middle class: there were the sprawling bungalows and the serviced apartments, with their maids and armed guards, and there was this.) I rented a room from Jose and Nana, themselves renters.

Jose's eyes were droopy, and he stooped over his plate. He was a mild man who worked in the city tax department and wore only designer shirts, mostly secondhand. He was over fifty but had married only two years earlier. Nana was a housewife, though she had a certificate as a nurse and was constantly saying she would soon return to a clinic: it was one of her frustrations. She was tall and heavy boned, and her short-sleeved blouse amplified the thickness of her arms (she had swelled after marriage, as the wedding photographs on the mantelpiece showed). "You are late," she said, and then squealed: "What a beautiful fan!"

I had wanted to be alone that evening, but I did not expect it to happen—there was, it seemed, always someone around in the house; always some commotion.

"Look, it's a new one!" Nana chewed twice, then reached for the box. "Let him eat," Jose said. Nana retracted her hands and hurried off, her heavy steps resounding on the cement, to find me a fork and a plate. At the end of the corridor she shook the cistern handle. There was a gurgle, and the tiresome hissing stopped.

I had rarely dined with the family—our routines had seldom coincided—and I had still not learned their ways. The stew was in a large casserole, and a ceramic bowl contained white rice. The place mats had drawings of fruits on them. Nana passed me the bowl, indicating I was the guest. I served myself a spoon of rice. Then Jose heaped a ladle of rice on his plate, protecting the falling grains; his fingers tickled the air. He hummed contentedly. I tried to pass the bowl to Nana, but Jose's hand reached again. Grains tumbled from the bowl. Then Nana tipped the dish over her plate and shook it empty, banging with her spoon. Jose mumbled a prayer.

"Amen."

The family ate only one meal a day. Jose called it lunch; Nana called it dinner. And it was custom to serve oneself all at once, without expecting the food to pass around again. A small grilled fish was produced. Nana gave me a piece of tender meat, picking it off with her hands. We ate at a rapid pace—as though the meal were a stress and had to be consumed quickly, so that the house could return to its regular, foodless state. I finished my plate still hungry.

Jose said, "You met the president?"

"He was in meetings all day. An ambassador visited unexpectedly."

Jose took a moment to chew. "Where did you buy the fan?"

"Here at the market. Twenty-five dollars."

"Good price."

His few words lifted my spirits, and after dinner, in the living room, together we unpacked the box.

Soon the fan stood on a tall metal pedestal with its plastic blades housed in an enormous cage. It looked magnificent, and Jose circled it excitedly. Nana was outside, telling the neighbors. At this time in the evening the neighbors were usually out and about, drinking beer and chatting up the ladies, but as word of the fan spread, our living room filled. People took turns putting their faces against the wind and delighted at having their coiled hair stretch behind like stiff wires.

"The twenty-first century has come to Bozene," proclaimed Jose. And if the neighbors didn't seem jealous it was because Bozene shared all material possessions, especially items of technology. Except my computer, which, I had made clear to a perplexed Nana, was not for use by her nephews or friends. On that evening, however, everyone seemed to forget my foreign ways— and I was Mr. Popular during the half hour for which the fan spun and spun. I stood beside the fan, talking up my purchase. Until suddenly the house was plunged into darkness.

The neighbors moaned. The fan slowed until it hardly moved; it stopped completely. The neighbors squatted, as if it was as much their business as mine to wait for the power, to protect the fan and make sure Made in China survived the electric modulations. In the dark the appliance looked like a dead bird with caged wings; beside it Jose was sprawled on the sofa, half-asleep, his sweat-beaded head over his shoulder. From inside I heard Nana, *"Tapé tapé tapé,"* trying to distract Bébé Rhéma from the heat.

"Jose," I said, testing if he was awake.

"*Ouais,*" he drawled.

"You know they say the riots happen around here."

"Hmm."

"Where do these riots start?"

"Around Victoire."

"Where, exactly."

Jose rolled in his sofa, licking his dry lips. "You know where Anderson sits? . . . But now is not the moment for riots."

I turned the fan's cage from side to side, making it move as if it were working. "The current will come," he mumbled. "Don't worry." The evening passed like that, until the neighbors lost interest or tired of waiting.

My room was in the middle of the hallway that led from the living room. Across from my door was the master bedroom, next to the bathroom-cum-toilet. The kitchen was at the end of the hallway. My room was small—about ten feet by five—and it had been made, but the sheets were thrown, without tenderness, over the bed; the rug on the floor was askew; papers were stacked untidily in the corner; the curtains were tied up near the rod. The welcome had been brief; the warmth was now gone. I felt only accommodated.

Lying in bed I looked at the ceiling, at the disfigured panel of patchwork plywood. The grain on the sassy wood—ash black, insect resistant—had expanded in the cycles of rain and heat, twisting its surface and making the panel sag like the skin of some large animal. Above my face the wood had rotted and split. I wondered if it could crack open, and if the roof would then fall.

Two weeks before, I might have moved my bed. But I had realized the futility of worrying in such a place: the threats were too many. And I took my new indifference as a sign that I was settling in.

I lay awake, thinking. Guy and his place had seemed so strange; the feeling of loss returned.

But at midnight the church bells sounded and the sopranos began at Bozene's evangelist choir; and I could no longer think. Mosquitoes buzzed my ears like little biplanes from a World War I film. I tried to swat them but hit myself. The fan stood beside my face. I pushed its plug harder into the socket, hoping to see the blades rise into action. Nothing. My head dropped to the pillow, and I heard my lips flutter as I softly blew air between them.

Sometime at night I went to the kitchen. Rats banged through the metal pots when I turned on the bulb. The fridge was empty but for fungicide creams. I wet a towel and draped it over my pillow, to keep down the dust and provide temporary coolness. The sopranos sang all night, without rest, and by morning I knew their songs so well that I hummed them in the cold and brown-water shower I made by emptying a bucket over my head.

The night had made me restless. I wanted to get out.

2

I had left for Congo in a sort of rage, a searing emotion. The feeling was of being abandoned, of acute despair. The world had become too beautiful. The beauty was starting to cave in on itself—revealing a core of crisis. One had nothing to hold on to.

I was at the time at university in America.

The professor's eyes gleamed. His gaze penetrated, even frightened. Serge Lang, a legend of mathematical theory, sat behind his large desk, a black telephone to his one side and, on the other, a wall covered with yellow hardbound mathematics classics that he had written.

He was a fiery man, bursting with vitality. He screamed at his students, threw chalk at us in class. He shouted with his nose held to our faces. "Truth! Clarity!" He pressed his forefinger into our chests in the middle of arguments. But Lang and I got along. I liked his fury and candor. And he believed in my mathematical ability. When he saw me devour his classroom material he delightedly goaded me on. He wanted me to see more. Over three years he gave me more than two thousand dollars' worth of his textbooks. I cared for them as my small treasure. I studied them in our stone department building, near his office, feeling pleasure and satisfaction—convinced that I was going to become a professor.

But on this day it was with those same yellow books, piled high in my arms, that I stumbled into his office. The professor's gaze set on me. I put the books on his desk. Lang frowned—he had understood.

"What happened?" he said. The anger was gone. He looked distraught. I felt as if I had betrayed him.

It was for the beauty that I had stayed. The beauty of the world in those symbols. The mathematics I loved was inspired by nature's exquisiteness: in crystals, corals, snowflakes; and by nature's grandeur in stars and oceans. It was the purity of the work that appealed. One was devoted to revealing the meaning of the symbol as well as the beauty of what was signified beneath. And my work at the best of times seemed an almost spiritual pursuit, for something elusive and universal—for a truth. Lang had shown me this.

In my field, algebra, we were devoted to generalization—a search for the universe's deeper rules. Our goal, indeed the ultimate triumph, was to reveal different things to be the same. And for this purpose we drew abstraction from abstraction, piled cleverness upon cleverness. Three dimensions became four, and five. One had to imagine in seven, seventy, impossibility. Objects grew too complex; new languages were invented. Conventional geometries became fully explored; other geometries, less imaginable, were brought about.

This was mathematics progressing. And Lang was now taking me to a place where nature's mysteries had extinguished, where man was surpassing nature. Fresh symmetries were being discovered, more complex, profound and elegant than in the world. This new mathematics was pristine, but it offered no stimulus to the senses. Its relations to the universe were numerous, but fortuitous. It was man's brilliance and vanity at play. I started to feel lost. Our world seemed multiplied out into many worlds, like in some fantastical game. Sublime laws were substituting for life.

I shrugged at Lang.

I told him the textbooks would be better used by someone else.

I fidgeted, feeling a kind of anxiety wanting release. I was to leave university in two months. Lang had taken me far in a very short period: I should have been finishing my first degree, but in three years Lang had brought me to the point where I would begin a doctorate. I waited, not sure for what, and shuffled about.

"Where will you go?" Lang asked, staring at the wood of his wide table.

I was surprised by the preciseness of his question. "I've decided on Congo." I added, "I'm going to try to be a journalist."

"To play the fool." He said it at once.

His face was stern. But he was smiling with his eyes, brilliant. Always those eyes. I would never forget their lucidity.

I glanced for a last time at the tower of yellow books I had placed on his desk.

Some weeks later I was in a Togolese shop in New York, buying khaki pants to take with me to Africa. Lang called me from California. He always used a fixed line. The professor asked what I was doing. It was a strange call. I wondered if he was feeling lonely. But I found the shop's music too loud, and asked, "Can I call you back?"

I forgot to call him.

A month later I received a message that Lang was dead. I contacted the university, but the mathematics department would tell me nothing more. Rumors were circulating that the professor had killed himself. I suppose he had called me to say a goodbye of sorts. I was devastated, shocked. But there was little more that I could do; by then, I was already in Kinshasa.

———

I broke with America. Congo consumed me. After Lang's calm world of mathematics, I felt here only impermanence, fear. I had to constantly push, fend. Around me the crowd ground like a windmill—now loudly bellowing, now whirling in silence. A volatility seemed exposed against the black terrain. It felt impossible to belong to this place. The houses, the paint, even the brilliant goldwork of new villas appeared to announce the coming of a jaded future. But it did not shock. I felt somehow alert.

The war in Congo was the world's worst in half a century. Already more than five million people had died in it. The war was monstrous, filled with stories of rape and massacre, and so exaggerated in its proportions that it had become absurd. People struggled to find words to describe this conflict, and were now calling it—despite the contradiction in the term—"Africa's World War," to convey some sense of the number of armies it had drawn in and, more important, the scale of killing.

It was an unusual time in my life. The beauty in America and in mathematics had become cloying. I felt increasingly connected to a sense of being troubled, and I felt the need to grow into this, not escape. In America I was beginning to feel trapped and suffocated, and removed from the world.

Three strange things had happened in America to make me come to Congo. First, someone gave me, by chance, an interview with a Polish journalist, who spoke about the need to go to these wars in Africa, which he said few people took the trouble to witness, or to experience. Then I met a Congolese political refugee while paying my university bill; her husband's brother was Jose, and it was she who found me a room in Kinshasa. And finally, I was offered a job at Goldman Sachs that would have settled me for life.

The job only strengthened my desire to leave. My mother tried, naturally, to convince me to take it. She started to cry when I told her I was going to Congo. The interview with the Polish journalist kept coming back to me. And listening to her weep, strangely, I felt I needed to go.

Journalism seemed a natural choice. I felt that the profession would immerse me in the world, and take me to the crisis. The world appeared to be uneasy about Congo, to turn away from it, and write its story from far away. I wanted to experience this place I read about in two-hundred-word news reports: those tiny stories seemed to describe events and emotions that were so large. I wanted to see how people responded to such crisis, what we could become. History was unfolding in Congo, in its war—our history. But such ideas became secondary as soon as I arrived. The apprehension was immediate, and assailing. I had come to Congo alone. I needed to survive. I needed money, a job. There was an urgency about this.

Congo was an unlikely place to launch a journalism career. Nothing about it was welcoming. And the world had largely rejected the country. Few cared for its news. Reporters were usually posted to Africa after several years in the business; and even among those who chose to start on the continent, the rule was to base oneself in Senegal or Kenya: safer, more ordered countries, with regular streams of tourists, and where the major newspapers stationed full-time staff.

But in my favor was the moment. Congo's elections, due in less than a year, would be historic, the country's first chance in four decades at democracy. It was a precarious time: old tensions had surfaced. Power could again be won or lost. I could feel the people's agitation. I could sense the threat—looming—of change.

The experience of Congo's last true elections was at the root of the apprehension. That had been in 1960, when the country had elected Patrice Lumumba as its first prime minister amid the violence of Congo breaking free from Belgium. Lumumba was subsequently betrayed by his handpicked protégé, Joseph Mobutu, among those he trusted the most. Mobutu had the prime minister arrested and killed, and then installed a deeply repressive dictatorship.

There was now an additional risk. This vote was to be the final step of Joseph Kabila's peace process. Kabila had over the past three years managed to calm Congo's war, which had seen two major waves of violence. The war had begun in 1996, when Kabila's father was the front man of a Rwandan invasion that toppled Mobutu. But when the father then spurned his Rwandan backers, a power grab followed that saw another invasion by Rwanda, drew in armies from nine different countries, and engulfed Congo—as well as all of the heart of Africa.

Until three years earlier Congo in its entirety had been at war, divided between these armies. Kabila had brought together the warlords and made them his vice presidents. One of these, Jean-Pierre Bemba, would be Kabila's main opponent in this vote.

And the war still raged in the east of Congo. The main warlords had laid down their weapons, but particularly bloody militias spawned by the years of violence still killed, raped and pillaged. Adding to the five million victims, a thousand more were dying each day. And Kabila seemed more and more isolated—always seeming to fear that he would be assassinated like his father, and with few in his entourage whom he could trust. The elections would open him to attack. He was vulnerable. And there was a growing sense that the vote could cement the peace that had been gained, or again tear the country apart.

It gave me immediate purpose: I visited the election commission, a building on the Boulevard with an enormous orange voting box painted on its facade. The vision of Congo was different here: gleaming, organized, contemporary. I found the staff to be unexpectedly warm. I was given a front seat, as a foreigner, and a special-colored badge; my questions were answered graciously. Later local journalists came up to tell me the answers I had been given were wrong. They had their own explanations. They proposed we collaborate. The atmosphere here, in the shiny halls, was more subdued than in the streets. I felt a sort of inclusion.

And then at home, with its anxieties and half acceptances, I was surprised by the hospitality. Nana had apparently decided to make me more quickly familiar with local culture. But she told me nothing. I found out only later that for more than a week she had been busy making arrangements.

The girl was an important figure in Congo. She cured moods, I had been told. She conveyed pleasure. She gave life to abundant families. She was coy, rebellious; tolerated, taught to be fickle and so cantankerous that it would seem nothing could possibly appease this girl until her man drew her closer, produced extravagant gifts and satisfied the restlessness. The acting was hyperbolic and overt. The girl knew to extract the maximum.

Anderson, who was thirty-five and still womanless, told me that at any given time the Congolese girl kept five men whom she referred to as "offices." (Traditionally only men kept offices. Women had usurped the model.) Anderson had repeatedly been on the short list. The office that went the full distance, he said, was either the wealthiest or the most cunning—for the poor man could also win. Months later Anderson took me to a wedding; he was a friend of the groom, who was wearing a tuxedo and smiling toothily though he had spent his every last franc on the girl and steeped himself in debt.

But not all men were as clever, or foolish. And in Kinshasa there was a dearth of suitable males. So the outsider had become desirable; for his money, job and passport. Nana later confessed to me that families with "values" derided foreigners: as outcasts to tradition, as bearers of grotesque sexual fantasies about the African woman, and—most damagingly—as the masters of paltry families. Every child was negotiated, planned. But so dire was the situation, Nana said, that good women were sending their daughters even to such men.

When Fannie came home I didn't remember that I had met her two nights before at Anderson's kiosk. And I didn't know she was Jose's niece. It was morning, and I was shaving in the bathroom-cum-toilet when Nana clanged the metal door. I started. Some hair fell on the toilet seat and became embedded in the yellow grease. The door shook again. "Someone's here to see you."

"Who is it? Can you tell them to wait?"

I rinsed my face and with a towel wiped away the traces of foam from my neck. The mirror was cracked through the middle, in three diverging fissures, distorting my features. Carrying my shaving kit I returned to my room. Fannie was already there. She was looking at the fan with interest, touching its motor. I stepped out. Nana was holding a broom.

"I asked her to wait. But not in *my* room."

"She wanted to see the fan."

"Couldn't she wait a few minutes? I'm half-naked."

"You don't understand," Nana whispered and pulled me aside. "How do I say it?" She looked a little confused. "She *likes* you."

"What? You're joking."

"Shhh . . . Don't tell her I said." And Nana deposited her heavy frame on a chair at the dining table. "Go! Talk to her!"

"Fannie," I called out. "Nana wants you in the living room."

I crossed her in the corridor but couldn't look her in the eye. And I had hardly put on my shirt and tousled my hair and wondered what I should say when she was back. She was a tall girl, made to appear taller by pants that reached high up her wasp waist. Her full-sleeved white shirt was for men. Her features were fine, and she was of about marriageable age. She entered the room with confidence, sat down on my bed, and began to talk in a soft, melodic voice: she wanted a job, she said, but the employers were running her in circles.

I empathized, saying it wasn't easy in Kin.

"You're telling me," she said. "I have a university degree and all they say is come back again." She stressed the word *university*. There was a silence about the house, unusual for the morning, and I wondered if Nana was eavesdropping from the yard. Fannie pointed at my notebook. "What's that?"

"Some work."

"Nana mentioned. Why don't you write about me?" And she opened her eyes wide, as if she thought it were a grand idea. "You'll have to know me better, though," she said, laughing, "or you won't have the juicy details."

"Why don't you show me around Kin? I'm looking for stories."

"It's a date." She tapped her feet on the carpet and fingered her braids tenderly; she wouldn't leave my bed. Then she said, "Could you lend me a small thirty bucks?"

"What for?"

"Your girl needs to braid her hair." I must have looked skeptical. "Don't you want to write about a beautiful girl?" She waved her hair and the plaits swayed like playground swings. I shook my head. "That's too bad," she said. "Because I love you." She waited for the words to have effect. "Surely you have something to share."

"Nothing at all."

She stood up sharply and strode off like a cat, crossing her legs exaggeratedly. I followed through the corridor. She stopped and leaned against the living room doorway, not moving as I approached. I had to brush against her chest to pass, and I felt her press; she tried to trip me. Nana appeared not to notice any of it. She offered me a piece of bread and sat on the floor, breaking green beans.

Fannie moved to the dining table; she almost wafted.

I took the adjacent seat and picked at the bread. Some awkward moments passed. Then I looked at her. "I'd like your help."

She frowned.

I described the landfill to which I had followed Guy, when he had stolen my phone. "You know the place I'm talking about? It's close to the restaurant that sells whole goats."

She turned—I thought to look at me—but she only scratched the back of her head. And she spoke with skepticism. "Nana says you're important, but then how come you're so poor?"

While Fannie sat with a long face we had more unannounced visitors. They popped in and out with precise wants: a lemon slice, some tonic quinine, a cloth to wear to a funeral. The visits were regular, part of Bozene's sharing: it was Congolese custom to share both good luck and misfortune. Later I understood that I was a piece of luck that Nana had tried to share. And by asking Fannie to show me around I had given her license to make her own request; I had reneged. It set my reputation. But I was new to Bozene, and there were more experienced abusers. The street had a very definite structure; it operated like a tribe: an urban clan of village and city, of assorted languages, religions and cultures. All this had coalesced here into a Donut Society, with the family at the center, and the clan (the street) as the ring. Outside this ring the world was chaotic, without clear rules or enforcers. At the center it was much the same—family was excused no matter the gravity of the crime. But the clan was society's best-organized unit: here the rules were strict and the punishment was severe. Disobedient families had their credit extinguished—which meant they could starve—for errors that outside Bozene or within families would be considered minor. The severity showed in the wounds on their dwellings: gates falling from hinges, iron frames exposed on crumbling walls. Nana said they slept sixteen in a room, mat beside mat, arms and legs over one another. Theirs were always the darkest houses, voids among the lights; and in the morning they lay empty, quiet. I never knowingly saw the inhabitants. "Better keep away," said Nana. Bozene tried not to talk about the wretched. But lately there had been some chatter about the neighbors. And it was one of their boys who now shook our door and peered through the grill. His face was small between the painted bars, his eyes dark and fearful. Nana heaved harshly, "What is it?"

"Sugar."

"Only sugar?"

The boy lowered his face. Nana stood and straightened her dress, spilling the blackened ends of the beans. She grumbled all the way to the kitchen. The boy waddled around the living room, the shame apparently forgotten. He skipped wantonly. He deposited himself at the TV. A musical skit was playing. Fannie, now ignored, played with the saltshaker. I heard Nana move pots and bags. The mood in the house was dull. I lay my face sideways on my arm and the plastic lace tablecloth made an imprint on my skin. A light breeze touched my feet.

I didn't mind the moment of quiet.

Before she left Fannie answered my question. She had not been to the landfill, but knew it as the 25th Quarter. It had an entrance from a main road, she said, avoiding the need to pass through the alleys. That's what I should tell the taximen. They all knew the 25th Quarter.

I asked around. Most people didn't seem to know the place; some had heard of it; others only "remembered" after I probed. The more I learned about the place the more I became intrigued. The 25th Quarter, I found out, had once been a cemetery.

But I did not go until the next day, until after a knock sounded on our door and the tall figure of Mossi, a journalist I had met at the election commission, strode in. "Why the hell are you not picking up the phone?" he said, throwing his cap to the table like a Frisbee.

Mossi Mwassi was a refugee from South Africa. He had a short crop of gray hair. Nana didn't like him—she said he had the bloodshot eyes of someone carrying hepatitis. But Mossi enjoyed being an irritation: he stretched his legs on the chair, though Nana had told him not to, and he put his arms behind his head and dug at his back tooth with his tongue. His face screwed up when he saw Nana. But Mossi was undeniably helpful: he knew all the journalists and also which stories were hot—he recalled news expertly, without pause, as if reading from some mental ticker tape.

I told him how my phone was stolen.

"Oh, good," he said. "I thought you were avoiding me. The president is giving a meeting tomorrow, are you going?"

"I wasn't aware."

"His protocol must be trying to reach you."

"Can I call them?"

"No, they have to call you. It's a big meeting. He doesn't talk a lot, this president."

"What's he going to say?"

"They're changing the constitution. Rumor has it they want to reduce the minimum age for a head of state so Mr. Kabila can run in the elections. Can you believe it? He's too young! It's causing an uproar. The opposition is saying he's illegitimate, weak, this, that. Tomorrow will be a sight. You don't want to miss it. Get your phone, man, there's still a chance. The protocol will probably make another round of calls in the morning. Pay the boy off! Fifty dollars usually does the trick. Show him the cash. Yes, that's how it works in Congo, you pay twice, three times for your own things!"

I did not need more convincing. At another time I might have shown more prudence, I might have interviewed more people and thought through the plan another day. But Mossi gave me reason to go that night. And his nonchalant confidence ("only fifty dollars," he now repeated, waving a hand) revived a buried hope that I might retrieve my phone. So I hurried.

The timing was perfect. It was late afternoon and the children, known to sleep during the day, would now be waking. Nana tried to dissuade me. "Those boys are fetish." It meant they had connections to dark powers. "They become monsters at night.

And the girls, they seduce old men. Make fools of them." She put a banana on the table. "At least talk to the boy at the grocery store. He'll tell you what's what." The insects chirped outside the bathroom window as I washed my face.

I purchased a packet of milk biscuits at the Bozene corner store. They were crushed. The shop boy cracked open a new Britannia carton and asked casually, "Visiting someone?" I told him; he grimaced. "Don't buy biscuits." Gasoline or glue would be better, he said, but his kerosene stock was finished. He helped as best he could, and at the end my cargo pants were stuffed with sugar, a canister of Baygon insect repellent, a handful of *stems*— long cigarettes—and two samples of pastis, a strong liquor made from aniseed.

"I used to live on the street," the boy said. "You'll see. It's a place God doesn't visit."

Before I left Victoire I again tried calling Guy. But my phone had been switched off.

The twilight began to fade as the taxi progressed. The roadside gutters grew wider and greener, the heaps of rubbish higher; the air felt more laden with noise and the fires to our side grew more frequent. Our car seemed an absurd addition to the environment. I amused myself by imagining our form seen from high above, our dim headlights slowly turning among the ruins. Some children ran along the walls; a couple drank from a puddle in a place where the sidewalk had caved in.

The taxi deposited me at a stretch of sand and left at once. Two mounds of waste formed an entrance to the 25th Quarter. A path led in between and curved out of view. With two steps I was inside. Instantly I felt apprehensive. In front, in the field, dozens of empty car frames were silhouetted against the sky, making shapes like large tombstones. The garbage rose as mounds and arches, rolled over pipes and fell into pits. The ground splintered as I walked. The boundary with the city was lost; there was no boundary. The garbage seemed to grow in an expanse around me and consume the city as one gigantic slum.

Cautiously I circled the first mound. Behind it stood a boy in a pit of water. The pool was black, like some juice secreted from the surrounding decomposition. He froze when I said, "Guy?" Then he shouted in high pitch; the sound carried beyond; I heard children call: isolated calls. It was as if my presence had become known. I took a seat on a brown-brick parapet while the boy splashed himself, eyeing me like a sentry and scratching his wiry thighs. And perched there, under the force of his stare, I gained a sense of composure. I smiled. The boy babbled something.

The landscape felt deceptively peaceful. From time to time there was the cawing of birds. And the hustled motions of children. Tinny voices could be heard. They seemed distant, and I felt disregarded, separate, that the Quarter didn't perceive me as a threat and continued its regular business. A large crow fluttered and landed on the ground; its horny beak picked at the garbage and scraped against plastic and metal. Two feet together, it hopped about.

Some moments later I heard a sound from behind. I turned. Guy was dragging himself across the field like an old man, his brow furrowed. He looked small, ruined. In both hands he held brushes that began to clack, each hand in succession. *Clack clack.* The noise seemed to resonate inside my ears, and it mixed with the anticipation, sounding strangely weary.

He swooped over my feet, mumbling, "White man," as if in some trance, and not responding when I said his name. He ripped the cover off a can of watery shoe polish and began to paint, acting out the scene like a formal ritual, as if this was a necessary interaction between the street boy and the foreigner. I waited uncertainly, still: a brightness rose through the leather. Guy brushed with vigor. But the intention seemed foolish, and thoughtless, and at the end the solid black of the polished shoes only jarred against the waste. His lips stretched in a smirk. On his face was a look of triumph. *"Pesambongo!"*

"No," I said, imitating his urgency. *"Moyen té!"*

He laughed at my usage of Lingala. Then he hit my shoulder with the back of his fist. He jumped back and jeered. "White man. Give me money."

"Guy. Where's my phone?"

"Phone?" He paused. "Gone." His French was labored.

"I have money," I said.

"Give me money!" These words came easily.

There was nothing to be done, and I let it go. I had known all along, I thought. I had known better than Mossi: this gave me some solace. And I think how I didn't get angry, and accepted his word, I think this surprised Guy. He held my arm and took me into the field. I felt he thought that I somehow understood his position.

We ran into a group of boys but Guy shouted and they fled. Then we came to a gray car frame. All the glass was gone and the chassis was dotted with barnacle-like clumps of orange rust. Guy looked left and right and climbed in. The ceiling was too low to stand under—we sat on the ground. On the dashboard were arranged liquor bottles. Guy handed me one, pulling out the stopper, while he upturned a nearly empty bottle over his mouth. But the liquor smelled like laboratory alcohol; I pulled out my pastis. He broke into a smile. I only sipped, and when Guy finished his bottle he drank from mine, with its orange label and yellow lettering: "PASTIS. For Export Only. Made in Nagpur, India."

He sucked the last drop with a whistle. He gave a long gasp, stretching over the mud.

We went out again. I felt his wrist. "Come," said Guy, opening his arms, as if showing me some monument—in his tone I thought I caught a sense of his pride. We walked over the fields. For the first time I saw graves. In places I saw offerings: food

tins, prized open and empty, fruit peels, empty frames for photographs. The city used to place its dead here, but garbage, it
seemed, had simply been piled on top; and then the cemetery
had been reclaimed for new purposes: for waste and unwanted
children. We came upon a large agricultural clearing, lined with
rows of carrot and cassava; so the cemetery now provided the
city with food.

As night fell children materialized from the cars like mice,
carrying bottles and blowing puffs of smoke in thick, mysteri
ous clouds. One saw us and cried: a big-boned but skinny boy, he
skipped over, rubber slippers flapping, followed by a girl whose
blouse barely reached down to her waist. She stopped at some
distance and pulled the bottom of her tight black shorts over her
thigh.

The boy and Guy pushed each other, quickly becoming violent. "Thief! Thief!" Guy accused. The boy raised his hands and
hit back. "Confession!" screamed Guy. "I refuse!" They pushed
each other for a while; after this the boy looked at me vacantly.
His name was Patrick.

The girl came around, dirty but pretty, with brilliant eyes
large like leaves. Her name was Sylvia, and she looked older than
the boys. All of them seemed in their mid-teens. Guy and Patrick stood at attention. "Confession?" Guy said. Sylvia scowled.
From his pocket Guy drew out a joint that he lit with a match.
He smoked with compressed lips. Sylvia looked around appearing bored and suddenly pulled the roll from his mouth; she put
the joint in her nose and inhaled it to half the length. Her eyes
had turned red.

The boys fell upon her, pinching her body. She rolled, laughing.
They fondled her breasts, felt in her shirt. She pulled away. Guy
produced another joint but Sylvia snatched it while he searched
for a match. She stuffed it into her bra and took two steps back.
The boys didn't pursue her.

I wasn't sure if I should be shocked: it seemed natural,

innocent—merely play. Guy now showed Sylvia something on his palm. Patrick lay on the ground. The sky was dark. The breeze had stilled. Worried the taxis would stop running, I announced that I would leave. To where? Sylvia asked. Victoire. How? By taxi. She suggested we take a ride. The boys agreed. Patrick disappeared, all jumping, and returned pushing a two-wheeler. The motorbike looked new—and almost certainly stolen. Guy pulled me on, between him and Patrick, the driver, in front of whom stood Sylvia. We pushed with our feet over the garbage, rolling out of the Quarter. What about gasoline, Sylvia said. I gave money for one liter, which we bought at a garage.

Too heavy to move fast, we trundled through the main road, dark, and then through a street colored caramel by wicks in kerosene. My legs sweated from dampness in the air. The night felt ripe. An occasional taillight reflected in a red patch on the road. It seemed provocative to engage Kinshasa so directly and in the company of its outcasts; it felt reckless to enjoy the wind against one's face. Patrick drove steadily. We had covered almost the full distance home when we passed the tall iron gate of the Stadium of Martyrs. Suddenly the bike swerved. We're going inside? I didn't hesitate. From here the house was only a walk, even if at night I would be less sure of the way.

Behind the gate we passed a fire that a homeless man sheltered by cupping his hands. The fire was small, about the height of my ankles. A child slept beside it. They could not take refuge in the sentry post, a cement cabin with grilled windows that was vacant but locked.

The stadium loomed: a giant coliseum with tall archways and corridors wide enough for tanks. The immensity of the place—pillars thicker than my body, the towering roof—felt like the presence of a government. And so our trespass produced a perverted excitement, as though we defied the highest authorities. We climbed the flights of stairs, wide, and made of concrete. Patrick grabbed my hand, and with the other I held Sylvia's. Guy stumbled and fell and scrambled to his feet. We pulled each other up, as a chain, toward the end of the corridor that opened to the sky.

Circle upon circle of seats we climbed on all fours until we reached the topmost row and the stairs became a wall. We turned. The stadium seemed impenetrable, totally black.

Joints were rolled and passed around. It was as though we had reached a summit; there was that kind of exhilaration. For a moment I wondered if we could be seen or heard. The children chattered, insensitive. And Patrick killed all my inhibitions by screaming into the blackness.

The echo came garbled. Patrick mimicked it by mumbling. The air felt heavy, liquid almost, as though it rippled. He bowed like an orator. Sylvia clapped. He pointed in the air; Guy laughed. Patrick spit above himself, saying, *"Congo na bísó! Ezalí bosóto!"* He stepped forward and backward like in his own private theater; he screeched; he shouted at Guy; he turned on me. His face seemed charged with anger and bitterness; the boy seemed consumed by some interior emotion. His mouth opened and saliva stretched between his gums. With a cry he fell over Guy. *"Fou!"* Sylvia yelled.

She told me to ignore him, saying he had lost his mind during the war.

Patrick slammed Guy in the chest. "No!" Guy shouted, reeling, but he laughed, then punched Patrick. They hit each other. Suddenly their laughter seemed unreal; it transformed into cries and screams. The violence grew; the boys seemed unhinged. Guy buckled. Patrick coiled his arm and hit him on the back so hard that his head hit his knees. Patrick punched the air. I stepped away. He punched like a madman. He would not stop. Guy leaned toward the stadium and shouted, "Congo!" Patrick stopped, waiting for the echo; "Oo . . ." They laughed.

Patrick became still. The boys calmed down.

We sat in the stadium's silence. Our breaths made fog in the air, from the cigarettes. From time to time Sylvia would say something to the boys; she spoke in long phrases, properly enunciating words. She had been educated. The boys mostly communicated with motions of their heads, in rude bursts.

Our silence was sometimes broken by a cry from the city; when it was a dog you could tell by the barking that followed: one bark after the other and then a chorus. But sometimes it was like a woman's screech: unaccompanied, piercing.

Sylvia sat cross-legged, folding her long legs and exposing her satin-covered crotch. She drew the joint from her brassiere and had it lit. It passed from her to Guy to Patrick to me. "Do you live at the cemetery?" I asked. "I live with the boys," she said. "And sometimes with white people."

After some time Guy crawled over and lay on her lap.

The ride home was short. The motorbike started uncertainly but found its rhythm, bumping over the mud roads near Victoire and veering dangerously. This was the city that had rejected the children—and in turn the children had rejected it. I reached Bozene between night and morning and banged on the door and stamped out the joint, which they had given me "for the road." It glowed before dying out. I had never been up in Kinshasa beyond zero o'clock, as the Congolese called it. I went to the back room, past the public toilets outside the house, and hissed. "Jose!"

He fumbled with the padlock. I apologized, staggering into the house in a daze and falling over my bed. I writhed on the mattress, succumbing to all the aggressors: the heat, the mosquitoes, the stabbing bedsprings. The choristers started again. I felt I had collided with reality.

At the time what struck me was the freedom I had felt around the children—they were free to seek pleasure; and they did, in sex and intoxication. Their lives were unbridled by the constraints and the repression of society. Yet almost every journalistic report, NGO statement and academic paper I found perverted their expansive lives and obvious pleasure, depicting everything as a wretchedness. It was important to me that the children be able to express themselves, in terms near their own, and not be described by a moral or even sympathetic prejudice imposed on their experience.

I would experience such incongruity repeatedly: in miserable places I would find the most exuberant *joie*. It seemed to me both extraordinary and implausible, and at first I imagined it to be cosmetic cover-up, a mask worn to hide the suffering, or to help overcome it. That may have partly been true. But I also felt that the Congolese in their delirium truly forgot the misery, that they spoke in verse and caricatured their misfortune in genuine comic spirit and not for farce; it was their way of taking distance, I thought, of suspending the destruction of time. To a degree that exceeded any people I had known I found the Congolese able to isolate the present, and be satisfied. Theirs was a sort of amnesiac solace.

"Fockoff! Fockoff!" The children's last words to me kept coming back.

I woke up scratching the blisters on my shoulders. They had bled. The night had been a frenzied experience, and all morning the nostalgia lingered, making the house seem dreamlike, dreary, looming, like a part of the Quarter, or as though I were still there. That was my first adventure. Good morning, Kinshasa.

3

After this, Nana changed to me. Bébé Rhéma had been woken by my door-rattling in the night. Jose had escaped to the living room but Nana had been forced to stay up and feed her. Angry and tired, she reproached me at the dining table, in full view of the courtyard. The neighbors listened. I apologized. But Nana's irk seemed to run deeper. Whether she now thought I was infected by a diabolical spirit or if it was simply that I had been irreverent and naive, she became morose and began to behave as if she needed to prove that evil lurked in children.

Her behavior was unusual—for she had a child and a nurse's training. But this belief in evil seemed to be something Nana was taught not to reason with, and in which she believed so powerfully that even having a child did not change her.

The new frustration showed one day as I watched a cartoon. It was a Portuguese production dubbed into French about a schoolboy who turned into a superhero and saved the planet. But to Nana it was proof of her convictions—for the boy, transformed, could fly and laser blast a giant octopus. From behind my sofa she hissed, "Turn that off, it's fetish!" But I stayed at the television, watching cartoons, until Jose came home and switched to the news channel.

Nana took me aside and told me tales about her nephews and cousins and the children of her friends—a cast of characters who had caused miscarriages, orchestrated poisonings and magically dissolved marriages by infecting fathers with lust for girls. Nana had experienced the evil when she was young. She said children could grow large at night, into giants, and come and eat us. I asked questions—she answered excitedly, as though hoping I would agree with her. Then she overheard me discuss the Quarter with Mossi. She loudly snorted. I began to ignore her remonstrations.

But the standoff was broken one week later when Nana found an opportunity to make a scene. It was a day on which I had woken late and then spent an hour in bed. As I walked to the front of the house, passing the tiny storeroom extension, I saw Nana's two nephews and Corinthian, her preacher cousin, ironing socks. How nice of her to give me a full room, I thought. But I decided not to thank Nana for as long as she was displeased with me—in case she took it away. Then the neighbor's boy, who was again waiting in the living room while Nana grumbled about having no money no sugar no milk, was found eating her hair cream.

The boy seemed in some ethereal happiness. His fingers were covered in the pale-green fluid and he smelled the cream pot, smiling, as though pleased with his discovery. And ignorant of the danger approaching he turned about, hands in the air, searching, presumably for a cloth. Nana came into the living room, her hair undone, stiff, scattered like the rays of a sun. And her eyes opened large with satisfaction. "There! Look at him!" In a shrill voice—urgent and authoritative—she summoned Corinthian.

The preacher appeared: calm, humming a choir song. His

clean white chemise was buttoned to the top so it pinched the skin on his neck. Corinthian gave sermons at the Bozene Evangelical Church, and Nana often nudged Jose as if to say, "See what a benediction my family is to this house." Corinthian had no place of his own, as I understood, so he spent his days at the church, a tall brown building at the street's entrance, and shuttled between families grateful to harbor a man of God.

"He was *eating* my hair cream," Nana said. One could sense the merriment in her vindication. "Just see and you'll know, Corinthian. You know these boys."

The child seemed unsure of what the fuss was about. He smiled stupidly and appeared to enjoy the attention—he looked at us one by one, as if someone might give him a candy.

Corinthian kneeled to the level of the boy's face and quietly asked if the child wished to confess. All at once the small face contorted. The smile vanished. And the boy recoiled and looked around the house as if he was trapped. His mouth opened inertly, speechless. Nana nodded. "That's right." And in a sweet voice she said, "Come now. Uncle Corinthian wants to help you." With wide eyes, a terrified expression, the boy concentrated on Corinthian.

In Kinshasa troublesome children often confessed. The evangelists recommended it on the radio, and Nana faithfully listened—the noise expelled all peace from the house. The sermons were screamed and replete with warning: "The devil is among us, we must protect our infants and our families!" "To go to heaven we must climb, but the path to hell is a slippery slide!" The pastor would wheeze hallelujahs. His anger would seem unending. And at the end he would call for the faithful and their families—especially the troubled souls—to be purified.

There was a trick in this, for the signs of the troubled soul need not manifest in the soul itself. They could appear in the parents, in an aunt or uncle, even in distant family. A misfortune—of which there was no shortage—could therefore be imputed to almost anyone in the family. The only way to certify a person's purity was by ecclesiastical examination.

When a mother brought her child before a pastor it often marked a rupture within her family, but also in her society and in the child's life. Many children on Kinshasa's streets had been seen by a pastor—sometimes even in a famous church. The stories surfaced only years later, in radio reports and from the city's few orphanages. Courageous children related how the pastors had beaten them, deprived them of food, water and sleep and psychologically manipulated them until they had confessed to working for the devil. Once the evil was confirmed, with the community's approval, the child was beaten more by the family—so as to render the rupture complete—and then usually intoxicated, trussed like an animal and left in a place far from home. The child knew not to return.

Of course, the treatment could also be less cruel. It depended on the gravity of the mother's accusations and the depth of the family's misfortune. But the exorcisms happened all the time, in the *ville* and in the *cité* and on Bozene, even in the best households.

If Nana had acted from an impassioned desire to prove a point—or from some past anguish—she succeeded in ridding herself of the boy as well. He bolted off, startling Corinthian, into the sunlit street. Never again did he come asking for sugar. Nana seemed satisfied: "You see?" Corinthian claimed to be concerned for the child. But he refused to let me witness his exorcisms. He first said they happened too late, then that I was a nonbeliever, and finally that my presence would need approval from America.

And ever since, when the sopranos begin each night, I wonder for whom they sing.

4

The following weekend I made a brief trip outside the capital. Before coming to Congo I had made contact with a student conservation group protecting rare mangrove forests. I wanted the environment to be a theme of my reporting, and the students were enthusiastic to show me their fieldwork. But more than anything, I was curious to get out of the city.

The coast was not too far away: we traveled most of the way by bus, passing forests and market towns, and then made a short ferry ride, until we came to the gushing mouth of the Congo River. The ferryboat curved around the continent, and to the port of Banana.

We lodged at a defunct resort on the beach. The rooms only provided shelter, without beds or electricity. Water had to be fetched from a nearby village. I walked with the students along the mangrove forest, with its stunted trees that seemed raised on stilts. We waded in the rivulets that flowed into the ocean. The students showed me some grunt fish that the locals hunted for food. In the evening we sat on the sand, watching the sun set over the waves. And at night the horizon seemed dotted with several suns—appearing almost as bright as during the day:

Congo's minuscule twenty-five miles of coast was rich with oil;
the lights were the flares of oil rigs.

Each morning on the beach I watched a dozen fishermen push
out their boats. By evening, when they returned, their fine nets
had caught pebble-sized juveniles and discolored adults coated
in black film.

It was for these sights that I had come. I conceived of this,
my first trip outside Kinshasa, as an exploration of the context
surrounding the capital: the sprawling grasslands, the ghostly
villages, the gushing river, the giant Japanese suspension bridge
ordered by Mobutu, the ships at the port cities (an American
naval vessel was docked at one), the heavily guarded oil company
premises (visitors were not even allowed to stand nearby). And
already I felt my notion of Congo expand: the city had swamped
the senses with its movement and noise, but the countryside
had an intellectual, less accessible complexity—for whom had
the Americans come? There had been no news in Kinshasa. Was
the ocean being poisoned, emptied of fish? How much had the
petroleum company paid the oil minister? Here the machina-
tions seemed beyond the scrutiny of the people and able to pro-
ceed in silence, secrecy.

It would have to be from the city outward that I would grasp
Congo. The excursion ended too quickly: the weekend was
barely over when we left for Kinshasa. The students piled into
the bus with boxes of specimens. We rumbled up the hills. And
as much as the trip had progressed in friendly atmosphere, the
journey home was marred by misunderstandings: the students
had assumed that I, as the foreigner, would pay for their hotel,
food and bus tickets. Worse, they believed I had promised. After
several arguments—which effectively ended our friendship—I
agreed to pay half.

We approached the suburbs of Kinshasa and passed through
them one by one. Each seemed a separate city, with a different

vibe: cordial, lazy, tumultuous. Our bus traveled alongside container trucks bringing food and merchandise from the ports. There were the tankers, spilling what seemed like gasoline in a trail from their bottoms. On the tall trees hung black balls like pendulums—weaverbird nests. We drove beside rows and rows of pylons that brought electricity from the massive river dams, and we followed the wires into the city.

The reception at home was cool. Jose and Nana were preoccupied with paying the electricity bill and the rent. Corinthian was hardly around, passing his nights at the church compound. There was some news: the Opposition Debout had marched peacefully on the Boulevard, to which the government had sent riot police. It created bad sentiment in the neighborhood. At the bars, the corner shop, and around the kiosks the discussions centered on the new wave of government reprisals; and like everything at the time the authorities were also blamed when it emerged that a financial crisis had hit Victoire.

The trouble, only now apparent, had begun about a week earlier when overnight the Congolese currency had inflated by 5 percent. That had been attributed to rumors. But after the fourth and fifth days of further rises the crisis could no longer be doubted. Inflation was not new to the *cité*, but now the elections were suspected. There was proof: the Opposition Debout leaked information that the president was printing thousands of bills to fund his campaign. The street's economy was paralyzed.

The *ville* hardly noticed—the dollar prices at its expatriate restaurants barely budged. But our neighborhood was in turmoil. There was a rampage of purchases, and the extra cash accelerated the inflation. Nana, trying to keep up, constantly needed money. Common sense was lost: vendors sold goods by auction. Exchanges were set up between parts of the city to profit from arbitrage. By the time the frenzy cooled I had bought several crates of water and toilet paper. Nana had bought so much rice the storeroom resembled a small granary.

Our neighbors from across the street visited, but I had to refuse them funds. Jose advised I keep my money somewhere else. "Not to scare unnecessarily, but I don't want you to have a bad experience in my house." Nana began to leave her phone when she left for the market. Jose no longer wore his Yamamoto watch.

The city's most credible bank was in the *ville*. It was called RAW. An Indian family ran it and the manager, a short man with thick, oily hair, welcomed me with special warmth. He asked where I came from, and about my family. On the wall, a gilded plaque boasted of an affiliation with Citigroup, next to a map of India and a garlanded picture of one of the owners' ancestors. I felt reassured, for I had come with a problem: RAW required a ten-thousand-dollar minimum to open an account. The bank catered to diamond dealers—and reputedly to Avi Mezler, an Israeli notorious for dirty dealings. The manager patiently listened to my case and then picked up the phone. At the end of a quick deliberation with his chief he said for some reduced wire-transfer privileges he would be able to make an exception. I thanked him profusely.

The next day I combined some errands with the trip to the bank, to make the initial deposit. It was a relaxed day, and after an interview with an NGO boss, I was near the Chanimétal shipyards, waiting for a taxi. Then, without warning, the road filled with honks. A 4x4 with blinking taillights roared past, followed by two others. Suddenly a convoy of black jeeps. It was the president. But tailing him—almost harassing his convoy— was a rattling car drawing a long opposition banner. People were being called to march against Kabila. Pedestrians cheered at the passing car. Demonstrators would soon block the traffic; I would have to hurry to the bank and hurry again to reach home.

I waved my finger vigorously. A white hatchback stopped at the curb. The driver leaned out, "Boulevard?"

The two passengers in the backseat squeezed me between them. The driver wore a felt bowler hat. The car was in good shape: the seats were clean, our feet rested on rubber mats and the dashboard dials seemed to work. From the rearview mirror hung a miniature penguin. The travelers smiled at me as if they wanted to make friends.

One of them handed out a bag of licorice candy, and soon all of us were holding the thin red straws between our lips. I passed on the bag, careful not to touch the melted syrup on the plastic. They sucked, slurped and ground the licorice to pieces. The bag was emptied.

"You like our country?" the driver asked, chewing.

"Very much. I just came from the coast; it's beautiful."

"Is it? I've never been outside Kinshasa."

"You've never seen the sea?"

"Only on TV."

The driver smiled, looking at me in the rearview mirror. My gaze shifted to the road, then back to the mirror. The driver pulled the licorice from his mouth and held the soggy strand, licking his lips before speaking; there was a gap between his front teeth and though he wasn't fat he had a double chin, which was unusual for a Congolese. "Have you had a chance to see our monuments?"

We passed a wide gray building, some ten stories high, covered with laundry whose dripping had over the years made vertical lines on the walls. "Look at how the army lives in that hospital." A decapitated tank covered in ferns sat in the courtyard. "It's been this way for a long time," he said mournfully. And at that moment the lined gray building looked as if it wept.

The blue presidential compound appeared, with its giant iron gates and battalion of guards. The driver's teeth were now red; he seemed in a daze, looking at the guards and talking in a flurry—

then ranting, like the opposition: "Congo could be the greatest country in the world. If they shared just a little of our wealth. But our leaders only think about themselves. Egoists."

It was a familiar grievance in Kinshasa. I didn't feel qualified to speak.

Our car sped through the streets, through slums and beside rows of misshapen dwellings made of corrugated tin. Women stood with colored plastic buckets in long lines at water pumps. The tin reflected the light and the roofs appeared brilliant, blinding.

"This city is a pile of rubbish," the driver went on. "Look at the garbage on the road. They sweep and pile it up but then leave it for the wind and the rain. What is the use?"

We had reached the Boulevard. It was midday and trucks were in town to deliver goods—their dense exhausts clouded the grim crowds huddled atop each vehicle, their legs reaching over the trucks' dusty tarps and bouncing against the metal sides. Our taxi followed the slow traffic, repeatedly jerking to accelerate and brake. We came upon an orange edifice—the Ministry of Migration—and now the driver completely lost his head.

"I used to work there, but they threw me out," he said, pointing to his side. "It is the Ministry of *Méchant* [Malice]. They should make it a prison. No need to move anyone."

The other passengers laughed. I looked around. The worn condition of their shirts betrayed that they were of the poorer classes, from the *bidonvilles*, the suburban shantytowns. They probably headed into the city for some minor commerce: to pawn a trinket or as day laborers; the going rate was eighty cents for eight hours of work, but that would pay for a roll of bread and a Coca-Cola, and perhaps something for the children. An urge overtook me: I wanted to show I cared about them though I was a stranger—that despite my relative health and riches I sympathized with their condition.

"That ministry stole two hundred dollars from me at the airport," I said. "Even though I had a valid visa from New York, they threatened to lock me up until I paid a bribe." I pointed accusingly at the orange building behind us. "That place is full of thieves!"

The driver stopped nodding and he frowned in the mirror, the edges of his face now contorted. The passengers began to shake their legs. Feet rapped against the rubber mats; air whistled through a gap in the window. We passed a street policeman. The driver shook his head, slowly, like a metronome. He became pensive, drumming his fingers on the wheel.

"Thieves," he murmured, so softly that he seemed to whisper, and then his tone was frighteningly hysterical: "*Thieves*? You are who to be talking like this?"

We suddenly accelerated. The driver firmly shifted gears. And when the car swerved off the Boulevard I realized I was in trouble. "I'll get off here please."

"Calm down. I'm taking you, aren't I?"

I leaned forward with an effort—the passengers had wedged me tight. "I've changed my mind. I'll get off here."

"*Tranquille*." The driver pushed me back with a firm hand. The backseat men pinned down my shoulders.

The man to my left plunged his hand into his pants. Oh, f——.

He fumbled with a black revolver whose handle was misshapen. Deftly he ejected the magazine. "See?" It was full, stacked with shiny bronze bullets. He reloaded the gun, cocked it with a click and pressed the barrel against my temple. His eyes were like two bulging onions. His arms were thick and venous.

I screamed. He pressed his fingernails into my throat. I gasped. I screamed louder, without thinking. His nails cut into my skin; it made a piercing pain. "Shut up or I'll shoot," he hissed.

"Don't do this. I'm a friend of the Opposition Debout. Ask Anderson!"

"Who?" The driver's stained lips made thin red lines like arteries. My vision went blurry. I felt disconnected from the world.

It felt as if there had never been a connection. I was completely betrayed. I closed my eyes. I squirmed as I felt their hands move up the insides of my legs and down the small of my back, over the lining of my underwear and in every crack and crevice they could find. Their rough hands, sandy, coarse. They pushed me open, pulled me apart. Their fingers were powerful. I was immobile, helpless. I gave in, only wanting them to stop.

They dumped me near the river, in a wealthy neighborhood. I fell on the ground and rolled to the side. The door banged shut. The hatchback, speeding away, didn't have a license plate.

It screeched around the corner. All around me the walls were high. Alerted by the noise, two guards came to a peephole in a gate. The people here would not help. They were people who lived in big houses with big cars and big money. You should have robbed *them*! The words screamed in my mind. *Why me?*

And I'd lost the deposit money—thinking the cash would be unsafe in the house I had taken nearly all of it; and now it was gone.

"Police! Where do I find the police?" I shouted, stretching my arms down the street in either direction. The guards shut their peephole. A finger rose above the gate. That way.

In that moment I felt the need for pity, and my frustration came out in this terrible way. My body lurched forward instead of walking; enervated, I wanted to fall. At the Boulevard the beggars were waiting. I heard them first. Moneymoneymoney. Young, old, hunchbacked, stunted, hairy, bald, they ambushed, grabbed. I turned to run but they had made a ring and converged. Suddenly surging I pushed away their heads, shoulders, muscular chests; my hands felt the dirt on their bodies and I started to slap them, jolt them, hit them hard. They scattered: behind cars and buildings; in the shadows of doorways. I was alone, and it was like after a sudden storm. Cars honked and rushed past. The breeze flapped my shirt.

As I traversed the long Boulevard the Congolese faces blurred into one another. At every corner I became apprehensive; all the figures seemed to resemble the robbers. And on the narrower roads I felt watched. I became conscious of the strange sight I made: the walking foreigner. I kept my distance, careful not to brush against the pedestrians. Physical separation was my small way of escape; but it was ineffective. In my alarmed state I stared at each person, scrutinizing the face; they returned my stares; and I felt angrier, but shorn, small.

The roads had no sidewalks so I had to compete with the traffic for the uneven graveled street edges, ditched and crammed with equipment: generators, barrows, pumps, piping; the taxibuses I used to travel in now nearly hit me, careening, honking drumbeats, preventing me from crossing streets. The wayside shops were grouped together by type: on one street were automobile spare-parts garages and on the other only furniture stores. Chairs and coatracks spilled onto the driving areas. I passed photography studios, paper boutiques, and rows and rows of dark houses. It took me two hours to reach the police station. I arrived tired and thirsty.

I had imagined the station as a place of authority, like the ministries, or the presidential palace. But it was a simple oblong compound, guarded by a single sentry. Inside the gates was a long tree-lined courtyard. To each side cadres trained and played football. At the far building I was made to register at a desk and then ushered into a waiting area—a cramped room with a few chairs and a mass of silent people who stared. I felt guilty at once.

I was made to wait like the others, without privilege. An hour or so later my name was called. A policeman led me to a room that was airy but bleak: the windows had no curtains, the hanging bulb was without shade and the table's only chair was positioned across from the officer—like in an interrogation cell. The officer wore square gold spectacles that accentuated his sunken cheeks. His navy-blue uniform was regular, thin at the waist and swollen at the limbs. He smiled sinisterly. A white page graced the table. He drew columns on it with a ruler and abruptly began: "Dead or alive?" His tone was irreverent, even for such a question.

He asked for my parents' names, dates of birth and nationalities. He sneezed. A soiled handkerchief appeared from his pocket and ran over his hands. He asked where my parents worked, which school they went to and if they were Catholic or Protestant. "Hindu?" It seemed unacceptable. "Fetish?" he asked. I said no. He wrote "Other."

He said, "Spectacles?"

"Yes, both of them."

"No, no. Versace? Armani?"

He pulled out a pair (Nina Ricci) and positioned them on his head—he now wore two pairs. Adjusting himself in his seat he asked where I lived, where I had lived and the names of all the countries I had visited before Congo. He sneezed again. The page was spotted with droplets. With his handkerchief he held his nose; his finger probed inside his nostril. For two minutes he cleaned it. Then he asked what I had studied, and where, how I spoke French, for whom I was working. "No one?" He said suspiciously: "What *are* you doing here?"

He squinted at me and slowly returned to his paper. But there was an error in the spelling of "journalist." He sighed. With the ruler he crossed out the word and from his cupboard lifted two small bottles that were shaken spiritedly; the erroneous word was smudged with white paint. He blew over the page at an angle. We waited for it to dry. Then he wrote again, slowly, in clean schoolboy cursive, pen rolling over the paper. He sneezed. The wet handkerchief appeared. He brushed the page and wiped his pen. My patience wearing, I interrupted the ceremony.

"Monsieur Officer. I'm in a hurry, please—those robbers were on the Boulevard two hours ago. If you move quickly you could still find my money!"

He looked bemused. "But there's a process to be followed."

I stood. "What process? Have you ever caught anyone?"

He huffed. A framed photograph was produced from his drawer. Against a red Peugeot leaned four Congolese men, wearing sleeveless jackets, shades and pointed leather shoes. They looked like criminals, but this was the elite unit. "Team Cobra," the officer said. "The country's best." He held the photograph in front of his chest like a winner's plaque.

"And what did they recover?"

"The red car!"

For a moment I considered it. And then, after a little discussion, I discovered the catch: their search could take days, weeks, even months; and all the while I would be paying. "Only business expenses," said the policeman, sensing my apprehension. "Cobra will be working for you full-time."

I closed my eyes and sighed slowly, feeling the last of my hope evaporate. The chair clattered as I pushed it away. The policeman said, "*Ei!* The report costs ten dollars!" Again he sneezed. I stepped into the evening. "Who do you think you are, eh? This is the process in our country!"

The traffic had eased, and I walked intentionally slowly. I was simultaneously thinking about if the money was truly lost— if I had forgotten some possible solution—and assessing what that loss would mean: immediate concerns, of food and rent, mixed with a broader, numbing anxiety that I could not place and that pervaded every possible future I could imagine. It became too much. I stopped thinking. From the outside for once the house seemed settled. Its light spilled into the courtyard, making the mud glow orange. Jose was wiping down the music system with a white cloth. "*Ça va*, Anjan?" He looked up, his expression tender.

"*Très bien*, Jose."

Nana had sprayed my room with mosquito repellent, as a favor. But I felt nauseous inside. Squatting in the corridor I waited for the smell to leave, and I felt my neck where the robber's nail had pierced the skin. The wound was inflamed; it hurt to the touch.

Only when I lay in bed and looked at the overhead wooden beam did I feel the full horror. The scene of the taxi kept resurfacing. I spent hours picturing how I had entered the taxi. If only I had noticed how strangely the passengers had squeezed. The driver's smile now seemed too friendly. I regretted that I had felt pity. I despised my good intentions. In the last visions just before I fell asleep I invented new scenarios that had me catch the driver unawares and beat him up. I seemed strong. And now *I* was able to hold a gun against his head.

It was early morning when I called Mossi, the journalist. I had not told Nana or Jose, and even to Mossi the words did not come out: "Two thousand six hundred and fifty dollars." The shock was still present. The crime had been like a violation that made me, the victim, feel ashamed that it had happened—it was as though not only my body but also my experience, memories and mind had been sullied.

I decided to press on with my journalism plans. The decision didn't require much thought: I had not prepared for any other kind of commerce, and I needed money. There was no time to dally now—I felt I should act, and that this would somehow soothe the growing anguish.

When I told Mossi I'd had trouble he only said, "What do you need?" I was grateful for his discretion. I said I needed to find a story, something I could sell quickly. He paused, then said, "I'm interviewing a drug manufacturer. About bird flu. Don't tell anyone, it's hot-hot. He's a fabulous man, a real magnate from India. Maybe you'll get along." I had expected him at best to give me a second-rate lead. This was a generous offer.

I dressed in a hurry and ran water through my hair. And now the house seemed lively. Metal scrubbed dishes. Flames crackled. A bristled broom scratched cement. The neighbor's chicken clucked in the yard. Bébé Rhéma gurgled on Nana's hip. The baby's nose dripped; Nana pinched out the mucus between her thumb and forefinger and flicked it to the ground.

At my request Corinthian came to the taxi station and had a word with the driver. "I'll need to be back in the evening," I said to Corinthian. "May God bless you," was his answer. He promised to come get me. It felt comforting to shake his hand. And everyone in the taxi saw that I was friends with the pastor.

Mossi was outside the café, carrying a worn-leather bag, heavy with papers. He had brought a range of pens as well: blue, red, green. "Journalism is like art," he said. "Sometimes even these colors are not enough." For Mossi had his proper vision of the journalist life. He refused to own a car. "We should be close to the people. In your car how will you feel the pulse of the city?" He advised me to be thankful for my dingy room: I would live cheap, move like the locals and discuss the issues that mattered to them. "You are the High Representative of the little man," he said, writing *High Representative* and scribbling extravagant messy circles around the words and all over the page.

I felt overwhelmed by Mossi's energy, and by the interview preparations as a whole: we had stacks of papers to read, questions to formulate, the story to draft; without resistance, feeling directionless and dazed, I was swept into the process; and I momentarily forgot my situation.

Mossi said everything had been arranged for our meeting with Satwant Singh. But the office receptionist, a stern Congolese, twirled on her chair and said, "I am not aware of your appointment." She wore a dress with a picture of the president painted on her stomach. Around the image were inscribed the words "My Husband Is Capable." She looked at me starkly; I stopped reading her belly. She said, "Wait over there," as if speaking to a child.

Mossi and I sat on an old leather sofa between two men holding VIP briefcases who leaned against the back wall, mouths open, exhaling hot air onto curls of peeling wallpaper. On the wall was a picture of Satwant, in gray turban, shaking President Kabila's hand. Satwant looked elated; the president bored. They stood before the building we waited in, half of which was the "Head Quarters," according to a sign, for Satwant's pharmaceutical facility. The other half was his house.

Satwant stormed in and banged heads with Mossi. He was in black turban and black suit. We banged heads as well—it was the formal Congolese greeting (and because none of us was Congolese, it showed a special intimacy). The secretary glowered.

The magnate escorted us inside, taking purposeful strides. A brass plate announced his house: "Shantinivas—Abode of Peace." He shouted for his wife. She appeared, edging forward in a hobble. "Arthritis," said Satwant. I didn't know whether to believe him, because a friend had pointed out to me that in Punjab women are still fattened with milk and glorified in poems:

> With silver crescents in their ears
> The two women walk the village path
> Like vermilion-painted elephants
> Graceful and swaying.

I had begun to feel buoyant. The interview was unfolding perfectly—Satwant was treating us with warmth and sobriety: as important guests, not as common reporters. My respect for Mossi swelled. And I regained some of my curiosity, my previous enthusiasm; again little things amused, offering relief.

"Please," said Satwant, indicating a low table adorned with flowers. The wife served coffee and "ordinary cake" (as opposed to cream cake, but she said this cake was "extra ordinary"). Satwant moved his hand over the hairs of his forearm, delicately, as if feeling their softness. Mossi began expertly, giving the industrialist the stage: "Bird flu, Mr. Singh. Hype or serious issue?"

"Oh, very serious." Poker face. Satwant didn't blink.

"Is Congo prepared?"

"No."

Mossi and I exchanged an appropriately grim look. We were onto something. And Satwant was talking. I raised my pen and asked, "How bad could this get?"

"The first cases of human-to-human H5N1 have already been confirmed. It is only a question of time. When the bird flu hits Congo it will cause a catastrophe."

"Millions?" I asked.

"Easily millions."

Mossi hummed and noted the word. He underlined it. I created a provisional headline: "Millions at Risk from Bird Flu. Government Unprepared."

The interview went so well that we stayed two hours. Mossi read from a list of pandering questions but soon Satwant ignored the script and started on a monologue. He had traveled from India to Uganda and Tanzania before coming to Congo. "This country is Africa's biggest hope. As a businessman I have never seen an economy with such potential. Only two problems: corruption and bad hygiene. Please write this in your stories. I have factories to make medicines but no one wants to buy. It's the NGOs. Only American medicines, they say. They don't want to give Africans jobs. I'm telling you, I used to work at Novartis."

It was mentioned that I had recently arrived in the country. Satwant was surprised, then effusive. "You came to find your potential. That's like me." He promised to organize a dinner for the three of us; and then he stood. I gathered my things. But Mossi had planned the meeting's conclusion. "The camera," he said, gesturing like a surgeon.

Under Mossi's direction we moved to the study room. It was floored with green linoleum and decorated with some shelves of books. The industrialist was made to sit behind the glass-topped desk. Mossi adjusted Satwant's hands on the table. Behind him he positioned the Congolese flag.

"Three, two, one," Mossi said.

Satwant smiled at the camera and raised his chin. Through the viewfinder, his body looked stiff and tiny, but his head seemed large. I clicked.

Mossi raised his hands to his head. I sensed disappointment even from Satwant, who looked around senselessly while keeping his arms flat on the table. "Do it again," Mossi said. "Open your *flash*."

Satwant shook the ruffles from his sleeves. The camera popped like a fused bulb, like a magician's trick; I took three rapid shots; Satwant kept a stupid grin. He looked dizzy, dazed from the rapid bursts of light in his face. Mossi clapped his hands. "What a picture. What a great picture!"

And the industrialist smiled, looking pleased.

I polished off a Coca-Cola while waiting for Corinthian outside Satwant's office. Mossi said he had to leave—to chase other stories. I watched him turn the corner. This used to be an industrial part of the city—few industries now functioned. The roads were wide, the buildings low and large. Some workers walked by, carrying muddy shovels on their shoulders. A child stooped under the weight of a cement bag. The world—with its drab people and trucks—seemed static in contrast to the charge of the last few hours. I waited inside the gated compound, between the silent office and the menacing city.

A taxibus swerved onto the road. From a window waved Corinthian's hand.

I sat out the afternoon glumly on my bed. As much as I had been motivated in the morning, now, waiting for the heat to pass and for Nana's meal of the day, I felt captive to inaction. I listened to sounds, scrutinized the room. Everything seemed remote, new; I felt suspicious of my surroundings. Any familiarity I had felt was gone. And I was taken by an urge to clean.

The room, whose clutter I had learned to ignore, suddenly

seemed a mess. The books on the shelf became especially intolerable. I pulled them down. The books were old, of literature and for self-training in computer languages. There were faded magazines of the intellectual variety: *Jeune Afrique*, *Le Monde Diplomatique*. I restacked them by size. I moved to the curtains, shaking them of dust. With my hands I picked the carpet clean. And as I uncovered the sheets and stacks of cloth left by Nana (my room was used for storage) I discovered odd items: a large black box I hadn't known was a speaker, a set of French vinyl albums, a Flemish Bible, and some wigs, sparsely haired. Soon I stood in a cloud of dust and my skin, normally dark, had turned a luminous gray. Nana appeared at the door. "Someone's here for you."

My first thought was that the police had come with good news. But Nana giggled.

Frida was Nana's niece. She was more forward than Fannie. "I love you very much," she said, shutting my door. Her blue jeans were short, revealing porous-shaved skin at the bottom of her legs. Her top was fashionable and strappy. Her frizzy hair was pulled back and smothered down with gum. And she would have been a big girl even without her four-inch heels.

"I'm sorry. I like someone else," I said.

"Who? A whitey? In India?" A smile. "But she is there," she twirled her finger, tinkling her metal bracelets. "And I am here. You need someone here to keep you happy."

What is this? The girl was clearly trouble, and more so because she was family. Opening the door, I said, "Wait for me in the living room." But she stared. I went to fetch Nana.

Her smile was warm.

"Ask Frida to leave."

Her eyes dipped. "What happened?"

"Nothing happened. I just want Frida to leave."

"But what if she loves you?"

"I don't care."

Her face shrank into a ball. "Ask her to leave yourself."

"I did. She's your family. Do something." I stood tall over her, and she looked down at the table. Frida was called. I returned to my room, happily remarking its new cleanliness. I peeled off the plastic wrapping from a new soap. I felt inside the pillowcase with my fingers. I lifted the mattress against the wall. One by one, I shook everything on the bed. I don't know what came over me, but I felt Frida had taken something. I returned to the living room.

Frida stood by the door. She looked away when I appeared, and she then smirked at the wall. "Nana, Frida took something from my room."

"That can't be. Why don't you check your things properly?"

"I want you to search her."

"It's not right to accuse people without knowing," Nana said.

Frida looked surprised, as if she had just tuned in. "Something happened?" She adjusted her bangles. I said, "Give it to me and I'll buy you something." Frida didn't reply. All the emotions of the robbery returned: the uncertainty, the sense of being violated. But now, in front of me, I had my perpetrator. I bristled uncontrollably.

"I don't want to see Frida in this house. Get out," I said to her. "Get out."

Nana clicked her lips. "Who are you?" She addressed me facing the wall. Her voice was filled with loathing. "*You* are not family." I went up to her and pointed, close to her face. "I'm going to tell Jose."

"Tell." Nana smirked, and she loosened and tightened the cloth around her waist. "If you want to live in a better house I understand."

Who said anything about a better house? And why is Frida smiling? Nana looked icy. I fled to my room, and turned on the radio. There was something about Tony Blair, and about the elections. But I did not listen: I felt helpless. The distress rose sharply, as if it might choke me.

I hardly ate at dinner though it was my only meal that day. Nana served cow stomach. We usually ate the ribs or thigh. I didn't know one ate stomach. "It's a specialty," she said. I tasted the meat's fingerlike projections; they tickled my tongue. I chewed on a piece for a full minute. It was disgusting. "I'll eat something else." Nana pulled the plate from under my nose, muttering: "Whatever you like, monsieur."

I knew I had been rude: I had transgressed the rules by blaming family (the rules of the Donut Society). And this time, unlike with Fannie, the punishment was harsh. I was also riven by doubt: about Frida's guilt, and about the force of my mad reaction. A trust between Nana and me had been broken. *Better house* I knew was a threat to have me evicted. I felt sorry, and suddenly scared. Jose too became cold to me—it hurt more; he had taken her side in the battle.

I called Mossi. The line was heavy with static. He was at a meeting on the other side of town. "What for?" I asked uncertainly.

"Local stuff. The chairman of a local coalition is changing. Did Mr. Singh call you?"

"No." I checked my phone.

"He's invited us to a party at the Château Margaux. You should go."

"You're not coming?"

"It's on the weekend. I have family responsibilities. But you should collect business cards for us."

The Château Margaux was a posh restaurant in town. The party was sure to end late; taxis would be difficult—I wasn't sure. I had really wanted to talk to Mossi about all that had happened—to buy him a drink and spill everything. But he seemed rushed and scattered; and I felt a request for a drink that night would sound too much like a plea.

I could not bear to stay inside, so I left the house. The stars had surfaced. Warm air swirled over my face. At Victoire the multitudes sat around a white pillar with a hand at its top: a monument dedicated to the proletariat. Physically I felt liberated. The agitation in my mind began to lull. The crowd made me anonymous, unnoticed; the people were busy, animated; they made me feel secure.

It was odd that I should find myself under this pillar. The father Kabila had erected it after deposing Mobutu: the hand was to show that the people had won, over Mobutu's corruption, over his destruction. And as with each of Congo's previous uprisings—for independence, for Lumumba, for Mobutu—the Congolese had hoped this victory would bring improvement, and they had vigorously celebrated the father Kabila's troops storming Kinshasa in trucks.

Africa has a history of using geography as symbols: cities are named Freetown, Libreville; arterial roads are called Liberation, Victory; countries are named and renamed as Democratic and Free with each revolution, coup d'état and election. Congo bears these physical scars of its many upheavals, each of which had been seen as a liberation. But, and almost unbelievably, each regime was worse than the previous. Every change worsened life. It created a distrust among the people, and a perverse nostalgia, an idealization of past dictatorships and colonial regimes that, as punishment for poor labor, cut off hands and brutally massacred. This past was not only repressive, it was shameful; so the nostalgia, which gave so much comfort, simultaneously degraded the Congolese self-worth. At times, I felt it had crushed the people.

The nostalgia was public. In Kinshasa it was the "correct" attitude to have, especially before the foreigner: Congolese would readily sink into cloying soliloquies about Mobutu and Lumumba and the Belgians. The abuses, on the other hand,

were only awkwardly acknowledged, and usually with sullen-
ness, humiliation, self-pity. So the two were kept separate: the
disgrace in one consciousness was not allowed to taint the ideal
in the other. And this is what crushed society: this constant need
to switch between two worlds, the impulse to deny what had
happened.

The distrust was a private phenomenon. I saw it in Nana's
reflexive defense of Frida. The Congolese confined themselves to
their Donut Societies and evaded the capricious, lawless world.
For this world had possibility: it had a future. The Congolese,
having learned to distrust the future, retreated to their families
and clans.

The society that resulted seemed intellectually stagnant, half
emerged from its history and only reluctantly moving forward.
Only around Anderson, so far, had I got an idea of the Congolese
potential. In his dissidence and rebellion he seemed to have a
notion, a conviction, of how the future ought to be. But he was
in a minority.

Congo's history is particularly repressive. And dictators can
be hard to shake off. I grew up in a dictatorship—in Dubai—and
I recognized in the Congolese elements from my own society:
a certain acquiescence, a cloistering within small ambitions, of
business and family hierarchy; a paucity of confidence in oneself,
and an utter belief in the power of one man.

It startles me how steadfastly I believed, growing up, that our
dictator was just, good and wise. I was never told anything to the
contrary. The media only carried good news. I did not know that
the slick British newsreaders could be censored; I did not know
that the opposition had needles stuck in their noses. Out of fear
my parents did not speak. My father, in the middle of conversations, would press his finger to his lips. But because the dictator
gave my parents jobs, they chose to live in that society.

Congo, I sensed, was a victim of the dictator's myth. It is what
I had experienced as a child: the indoctrination that holds up

the dictator as a savior, a sage, as all-powerful. Until recently this myth usually invoked God, a divine right to power. These days dictators have less need for mysticism: they use the tools of liberty—elections, business, schools, art, the media. The successful dictator creates at once a terror of his presence and a fear of his loss. But his myth, which can so profoundly shape society and is indeed shaped by society, is as destructive as it is powerful.

The father Kabila ruled for only four years before he was killed. His reign did little to improve Congo's condition. He began by professing his Marxist intentions, promising to restore to his people their riches. But he ended up spending most of the rule fighting off Rwanda, which had installed him as president. He attempted some economic reforms. But he had inherited a country so profoundly wrecked by Mobutu that it would take years to undo the damage. The father Kabila was an idealist: he had spent thirty years in the bush writing Marxist speeches. Heightening the sense of urgency, Rwanda invaded Congo again in 1998. Impatient, but able to achieve little, the longtime guerrilla fighter became confused, irrational and depressed. He lost his grip on the country and the economy. His allies defected. Inflation and corruption mounted. The story goes—and perhaps its truth is less important than its symbolism—that the father Kabila was assassinated with his hand in a bowl of diamonds, in the act of corruption. So the leader who once symbolized hope for this country was insulted even in death, the most sacred of life events to his people.

I have not lived through a dictator's fall but the Congolese tell me it is like malaria that ravages the body. It pierces the nation's consciousness. And the people, at the end of such upheaval— many times over in Congo's case—can be left quite broken, empty of belief.

The Congolese now mock Kabila's monuments, one senses, from bitterness; for by the same token they mock themselves, and their raucous cheers for Kabila's rebellion. The pillar under which I sat had, after all, come to commemorate not a victory but regret.

Something darted against my leg: a lizard with a black tail snaked through the sand. I bought a boiled egg from a boy loitering nearby. The shell peeled easily. I scattered the little pieces on the ground, and in the evening light they took on an unearthly gleam.

I trundled back, and the feelings from the day returned. I hoped Frida had left. My escape from the house had been fleeting, but now beyond its walled confines I clearly saw the greater problem: with practically no money I would not last long. I did not want to dwell on this sense of defeat. A solution, I told myself, would come tomorrow. But the streets, the people, Victoire, all seemed resplendent; I had the heightened awareness of details that comes from knowing one may soon be gone.

5

That night I went home and thought about the time I was still in America, preparing for my journey to Congo.

A strange thing had happened to me then, I recalled. The closer I had drawn to my departure, the more I had needed to eat. Breakfast didn't last until lunch anymore; I ate again mid-morning. And my purchases at the supermarket became calorific: cream cakes, donuts, snacks of processed cheese. I didn't force myself to eat; I was just constantly hungry. There was a surprising physicality to my apprehension of the journey.

This happened in near loneliness. It was summer and New Haven was empty. I saw few people. My friends had all left. It gave a hermetic quality to my days: reading, note taking, packing. I put myself on a trial of mefloquine, the U.S. Army's preferred antimalarial, but my dreams disturbed. And my anxieties were promoted by Annie, the bank teller who processed the last of my educational loan payments. She was black, and she spoke with an accent.

I asked where she was from.

"Zaire," she said, using Mobutu's name for the country.

I was stunned. "What a coincidence. I'm going there."

Annie looked annoyed. "You can't just *go* there." She glanced at me derisively.

"Could I ask for your help?"

She paused, without looking at me, before again processing the checks on her table.

I visited her the next day. And the day after. Once I bought her lunch at Dunkin' Donuts. Annie wouldn't leave her desk—every hour was money. By 4:00 p.m. she was done at the bank, and she jetted home to check on her children; at 6:00 p.m. she was at her night-shift kiosk, guarding a parking lot on Chapel Street.

One night at the kiosk she dug into her voluminous handbag and drew out a photograph in which she had pinned up her hair. "What do you think?" she asked. I took a second. "Not your style." She agreed. "That's what I thought." That weekend Annie took me to a Congolese party on the Upper West Side of New York—she told me to dress well, for the party was at the ambassador's house. I made an effort but still failed: the men were all in three-piece suits. At the dance in the basement I hid among the last row of chairs, but a large woman in purple lipstick came over and swept me off the ground. We joined the dancing circle, shaking our buttocks. Annie later told me the woman was a Congolese senator. After that I became Annie's companion on errands: I shuttled food to her cousin, accompanied her children on a lawyer's visit. I met her husband, who wore a Subway hat and asked if I could landscape their garden. They were building a house on a plot near the golf course. Annie took me once. On the upper floor she showed me a rectangular hole in the ground, and I chose the Jacuzzi tub to be placed in it. Her master builder lay on the grass, a Jamaican with his palm on his tummy. He chewed a piece of straw. Rolled up nearby was a manual on plumbing. Annie had been twelve years building her house.

On these various drives Annie told me stories: about her youth in Kinshasa, her family, the coup that toppled Mobutu; but the vast majority of her stories were useless. I think she couldn't get past thinking of me as an outsider. The stories were all shrouded in mystery and fear. They only occurred in the dark. The one happy story I remember was about when she first kissed her husband, on top of a Kinshasa hill near the old nuclear reactor. That too had happened at night. I thought perhaps Annie was trying to put me off: "It isn't easy to get to America," she would say. "You have a bright future. Why are you throwing it away by going to Zaire?"

I found it hard to answer her at the time. It was not easy to explain the feelings within me.

At one of our last meetings Annie said, "You'll be staying with my family." Jose was her husband's brother, and she called him at once to inform him of my arrival and instruct them to take care of me. But I noticed, once in Kinshasa, that Jose and Nana seemed hardly to mention Annie. I later asked why; and I learned that the last time Annie had visited, she had found the dirt at Bozene so unbearable that she had taken a room at the Grand Hotel. Annie, who had been the family's pillar and matriarch during the Mobutu dictatorship's violent end; who had been seen as a true Kinoise. Her betrayal confirmed Bozene's misery, its suppressed desire for escape. But the family only said, "That *Annie*, she's become de-Congolized."

In the summer of 2005, a week before I left for Congo, Annie dug into her handbag and produced a letter. It was an invitation from the U.S. government. "I'm becoming a citizen," she said. We celebrated with a Dunkin' milk shake. She told me not to share the news in Kinshasa. "They'll want me to sponsor the whole family. Where will they stay? My house will become a camp."

The days that followed the robbery were hard, as I was still trying to find employment. I started them early, waking to the 6:00 a.m. news bulletins, blinking open my eyes as I took notes. At noon

I visited Anderson to check on Radio Trottoir. The bird flu story was written and pitched to several newspapers. No replies came. I began an account of the 25th Quarter—I knew it would be a more subtle report, harder to sell. Life slowly became restricted. I curbed my eating—it saved only a few dollars but it helped create an assurance that I was doing the maximum—and drank bottles and bottles of water, especially at night, when the house was asleep and I worked in the dark.

And at 32 Avenue Bozene, we seemed to sink together. Jose had begun to stay at the office longer, to try to "find" more money. Nana was no longer able to stretch her rations the full week. Meals became poor (more stomach); the condiments on the table diminished. But it wasn't until Jose's big misfortune that Nana cited the evil eye. It was looking, she then said, straight at us.

The cousin of Jose's director had needed a position. We were, after all, in a year of elections, and god knew who would have power after that—someone else's cousin. The shuffling that ensued shunted Jose near the airport, to a quarter called Massina. The shops there didn't pay taxes, least of all to a man in a suit. Jose was too polite to extort. And Nana silently scolded him for it. Each evening when Jose came home, fatigued, she would ask what he'd found; he would not answer. She would say to the ceiling, "If we only had a few francs for the baby," and retire to the bedroom. The couple lived in this muted tension. Nana didn't have it easy either: inflation had risen again, all Victoire was hit. She told me the family of four next door had started to take turns at lunch; each day one of them ate and the other three scavenged.

In all this my troubles showed no visible end; the house and the street gave no respite. So it was a surprise when something good happened.

6

I t came to pass on the least likely of days: Sunday, the *jour de repos*, on which as per tradition the family rose together for breakfast and Jose played high-decibel devotional songs. Pedestrians outside sang to our music. The street had a lazy feel: People ambled; they did not walk. Even the dogs seemed to sit quietly. Men and women gathered in clumps along the road. They discussed the events of the week past: a fortunate few mentioned what had gone well; this gave everyone hope; most wished it had been better. There were those who openly prepared for the week ahead: mamas fried stocks of beignets; the neighbor's boy read his textbook. And for a few hours in the morning people seemed to set aside their troubles and make an effort to look their best. Jose wore his flappy brown suit on that day, and Nana a long red dress; Bébé Rhéma floundered in a blue frock. And the family joined the slow-moving procession of churchgoing people, all dressed like Christmas-tree ornaments and looking radiant.

I had decided to leave. Slowly, quietly, I was beginning to prepare. Sometimes I felt as if I had failed. It wasn't my fault, I told myself.

And the slowness of the Sunday helped to soften the feeling.

I rolled over in the bed and flipped the radio switch. The headlines: A governor committed to reducing power outages before elections. Some workers complained about transport to a copper factory; the cycle-taxis had raised prices, citing the cost of oil. The Belgian ambassador magnanimously announced a new aid program for the colony his country had once ravaged. Then an intermission of pop music; but the beats were weary; even the jockey seemed to have just gotten out of bed.

Seeing everyone in their fancy outfits made me want to wear something nice. I hadn't had a clean shirt in a week. Nana normally did the washing, but since our fight she had left my clothes soaking in a bucket. Clothes were important to the Congolese: people were judged by their dress, and I was no exception—I had noticed that my simple, crumpled clothes were not appreciated by the bureaucrats and politicians. But they helped me navigate Victoire: when vendors saw my Mexx shirt, so obviously purchased at the secondhand market and with stitches over its little tears, they did not bristle; some even treated me with deference.

I squatted between the pail and the toilet. The water was murky. I drew a shirt and started to scrub it between my hands. Then scrubbed with more vigor on a sock. But no matter the hardness of scrubbing I could not make suds. The detergent sachet was new; it seemed Unilever didn't sell the same Omo in all countries. The "clean" clothes I hung from the showerhead, over the sides of buckets and over my shoulders and neck while the rest I washed; the detergent dripped; and my skin itched. As I strung all the clothes on the line outside a sock fell on the dirt. I rinsed it under the yard tap and pegged it with a clip. I stood there, sweating. The socks and underwear dripped. On the ground I noticed a small pit where a pipe was leaking sewage, the pressure of the liquid slowly digging into the mud.

I had asked to meet Mossi that day—ostensibly for him to look at my bird flu story and see how to make it commercial. "Selling to editors is a marketing job," he assured me. "Completely different skill set from reporting." I had not told Mossi of my decision to leave. I merely wanted to spend a little time together—I believed it could be one of our last meetings.

He was late, however, and it being Sunday, the internet café had not opened on time. I walked over to Anderson's.

He sat like a stone. Perhaps it was part of the new persona: he'd obtained a new red kiosk, with Celtel mottos on all its sides. On the front he'd had a painter scrawl "Celtel Center" in cursive. The sassy wood was gone. Anderson had become an official agent—he was moving up. With a little money, he said, he would order a street cleaning, to give his business the proper ambience. "Look at the mess," he said, pointing. Papers littered the ground. I saw the previous day's edition of *Le Phare* with a headline about illegal uranium mining. The yellow cake was apparently being excavated with bare hands for exportation to North Korea and Iran.

Drawing a chair to the kiosk, I asked Anderson what news.

He showed me an Opposition Debout pamphlet, a cheap printout with smudged ink. Corruption in the ministries, political prisoners, angry threats to the government. "Same, same," I said. He shook the paper so it stiffened. "Look." At the page's bottom was a report that some Americans would be visiting for a gorilla conference.

I said, "Conservationists."

"No"—his gaze searched me, and he sounded patronizing—"the CIA. They think they can wear straw hats and khaki and pretend to talk about apes? Fools." He drew a plastic sachet from under his kiosk and unwrapped a mayonnaise sandwich. "Every few years they come, always on time," he went on, "to give a man a suit and call him our president. The elections are no coincidence." He swallowed a piece of bread and rubbed his palm over the back of his pants. "But they won't stop *us*."

"The riots."

"More, monsieur. An inferno." His lips twitched.

And somehow it was easy to imagine our street, the houses and the cars in flames; the scene—of people sitting before broken walls and gates hanging from single hinges—seemed disjointed already, like a Guernica foreseen.

"Do you know *The Matrix*, Anderson? The movie?"

"I don't like Hollywood, monsieur."

"You'd like this one. You look like one of the actors."

He mumbled embarrassedly, as though not knowing how to digest the compliment.

The internet café had at last opened. It was empty but for two workers dusting computers with yellow feather brushes. Four dirty fans, on long stems, circled slowly above my head, with the subdued hum produced by low voltage.

I took a seat and waited for the data to stream over the satellites and cables. It seemed a miracle that we had the internet in Congo, when it worked—which seemed another miracle entirely. Often at the cafés the power would die, and one would wait for hours, not leaving the computer for fear of losing one's seat. There were also risks· Nana said the keyboards carried hepatitis. Her words always came to mind as I began typing. The internet was finally up. The image swam on the screen, as if it might slide off. The *Guardian*, the British newspaper, had replied.

I felt a wisp of hope. And then a sad relief. It was, like the others, a rejection. Mossi appeared in the chair next to mine and without asking began to read from my screen. When he finished he was frowning, shaking his head. "They have just two journalists for the continent and say don't bother sending stories? They are not serious, these people." I felt as he did, that they were at fault—and that we were on the margins, and did not matter.

The internet café boy Stella came by with his hanging macaroni hair and 501 Levi's. I placed four hundred francs on the table. He scribbled a receipt. I could not yet confirm it, but something in his eyes gave me the idea that he was swindling the café.

I quickly went through the news: there were a handful of stories about Congo, none about bird flu, and nearly all from the four big agencies (the AP, AFP, Reuters and the BBC), written by the same four reporters. I leaned back. Mossi squinted at my flickering monitor.

"That one writes in the *Guardian*, I think," he said. "Yes, quite sure."

"Who, Bentley? You know him?" He was an important correspondent—I had seen his reports in the press.

"Not at all. We only met once."

I nodded, and perhaps spoke only because Mossi then stayed quiet. "Nice guy?"

He shrugged, as if he did not know.

But in that moment of inertia, and hopelessness—it seemed something of an audacity on my part—I decided to go meet the correspondent. Mossi had his number. Bentley said he might have time, if I came at once.

The taxis were tardy. They were also unusually full: I had to let two vehicles pass. It was getting late. A minibus slowed, and a crowd gathered—I ran to the door and grabbed a piece of the handle, attaching myself to the moving vehicle. Men and women pushed and crushed me but I held on, head inside, legs running outside the bus; then a woman let go, creating a space. I hauled myself in. The taxi had never stopped; it had only slowed long enough to fill itself with people.

In the relatively spacious Westfalia with windows that opened a fraction and old carpets draped over the seats, we sat face-to-face, our knees touching; the man hanging on the back of the bus screamed, "Gront Hotel! Gront Hotel!" And I began to hope in a small way that Bentley might be able to help me. Perhaps he would call the *Guardian*'s editors—and perhaps they would then accept my bird flu story, and also the one about the 25th Quarter. It might help me to stay in Congo a few more weeks. And this hope, this expectation that Bentley might solve some of my problems, made me feel as I did before a job interview. I worried about how I would introduce myself, and whether Bentley would like me. That he could help seemed beyond doubt; but would he?

The meeting was to happen at Bentley's residence: the 422-room Grand Hotel, an epicenter of Congo's wealth and the very antithesis of Victoire. The hotel owed its name to the father Kabila, who after deposing Mobutu dismissed its American owners and claimed the hotel for his "grand country." It was a place associated with many grotesque stories —many of killings—but also loved as a national icon. The taxi took us to the northwest district—to a point about equidistant from the railway station and Victoire, just before the president's house—and left me at the foot of an imposing gray tower. The air inside was icy, and came in a blast as the sliding doors opened. A chandelier glittered on the ceiling, dripping with crystal. Waiters wore stiff jackets and carried bread baskets. The hotel seemed something like an oasis in the city. I made straight for the toilets: my biggest stress in the house. I washed my face purely for the experience of running hot water. I inspected myself in the mirror, and saw dirt gathered around my neck. A sullen Congolese handed out white towels. Upon exiting the toilets one came into curved marble corridors lined with boutiques where attendants stood beside bags of leather, fur, rings and bracelets of diamonds and lesser gems like emerald and ruby, and figurines of ivory that the staff would proudly point out as their last pieces—the sale of ivory now being illegal.

I explored the halls in a stupor and arrived at the outdoor café, where Bentley had asked me to meet him.

The foreign correspondent wore a white shirt, brilliant in the bright light. His sleeves were folded up to his elbows, revealing pale and stout forearms with little hair. He was beefy and wide breasted, and as he came through the doors he wiped sweat from his forehead; he carried a notebook and two large telephones in the palm of his hand. I felt the nervousness come up.

He offered me a beer. It seemed an appropriate drink. And almost as soon as we took our seats, I was jealous. He seemed too certain. Of course he did: he lived at the hotel. He hardly had to move to find his sources; he had air-conditioning; he surely slept well. "Do you know anyone who might buy my work?" I asked, hopefully. I mentioned the *Guardian*. Bentley frowned, as though thinking. Around our Swedish picnic table the space was nearly empty. In the air was the beginning of the afternoon warmth; one felt on the skin a picking sensation, as though one's forehead and arms were being baked. Bentley idly cast his gaze about, and up and down the waitress. It became evident that he would not reply. I asked for advice, but he would not extend any. Only when I offered myself as his lackey—it was the most exploitative form of journalism—did he raise his head. I felt small. I imagined him as a buttery toad: with his small slit eyes, even when he blinked he seemed to stare.

He waved at two burly men who approached the next table; they threw heavy keys that clacked on the wood and took their seats, crushing the tails of their fine jackets. The waitress bent exaggeratedly to receive their order. With their buxom chests, expansive walks and sweeping gazes one felt those men occupied a space much larger than their physical limits. Bentley went over; he cupped their fingers delicately with both his hands. They talked with an affected friendliness, and I found their hearty laughs distressing, painful.

Bentley returned, ignoring me. He looked at my drink and grimaced: his glass was nearly empty but I had barely touched mine. He rocked the last of his soda from side to side; a piece of lime stayed afloat in the middle. The cutlery began to shiver. He was shaking his leg. Again he smiled at the other table. And now he seemed weak: supplicating before those men but eager to exploit me, to make me submit. As though I were some proof of his stature. It gave me an idea that he was himself under duress, frustrated, abused in some way.

I did not ask more questions. And I made to leave—and it was perhaps this silent expression of defeat that prompted Bentley, as he glanced at his watch, to relax, and drop his guard.

He said it impersonally. "Why don't you try the AP? Their correspondent recently quit."

I froze. Had he really said that? And though later I would wonder if the look on his face—the way he trained his eyes on me—showed a regret, or loathing, for having let slip that information, at the time my mind was in a flurry; my cheeks felt hot. We both got up.

At Victoire, with the internet café boy Stella looking over my head, I sent the AP a message. "You found a job?" Stella asked credulously. And he decided he wanted to be a journalist as well. Almost immediately I received a call—it was the bureau chief. He hardly let me speak before launching into an onslaught of questions: "Yes, yes, of course we need someone, but who *are* you? And why the *hell* are you in Kinshasa?"

I became the AP stringer—without official contract or salary, or even proof that I worked for the press. But the editor had agreed to look at my stories. I could perhaps earn enough to live. Most crucially I could for the moment stay in Congo—when I thought about this the excitement rose like a current in my chest; at home I locked myself in my room and hopped about, boxing the air.

"*Ei ei ei*! Who's making such a racket?" Nana shouted from her bedroom. My job would calm the nerves in the house, and go some way to resolving our animosity. There had been such a paucity of good news of late that without money, without proof of success or any outcome, this hope was enough. Nana gave me a hug, and I realized she hadn't smiled at me in more than a week.

Mossi could not be convinced to come to Satwant's soiree. "Are you sure?" I pleaded. "Come celebrate, man. It wouldn't have happened without you." But Mossi had promised to be with his family. "Go have fun," he said. "It isn't every day that one has such luck."

I wanted, at that moment, to be around people—many people. And this was also why I went.

As the taxi progressed toward the *ville* I tried to take stock, but I was moving so quickly from one thing to the next, even that morning seemed remote. I felt I had lost the thread of events; and the emotions of the day seemed blinding.

In such a mood I arrived at the Château Margaux, the party's venue. A double-storied colonial mansion, it was the sole source of light and noise on that tree-lined boulevard. Baritone voices boomed from its upper floor. One climbed the stairwell—and at the top arrived at two golden-colored rooms. All seemed to glitter. Two gowned women, bare shouldered, glanced at me, then smiled, then looked away; it produced a feeling of remote arousal.

I tried to plunge into the crowd and feel in the thick of things. The party was mostly of white people, with a smattering of Congolese dressed in their usual loud colors. In a corner stood a group of Indians, inspecting everyone, sipping ice water and soft drinks. The ambience was made intense by the elegance of dress and the liveried jazz band, too large for the space. The maître d' looked on impassively as servers in black waistcoats casually posed with their platters. I picked a glass ("Riesling," came a whisper) and was almost accosted by a lanky bearded man who was smoking frantically and saying we had met before. Who would deny? I took it as part of the day's luck. Stefano was Italian and new to the UN, and seemed to take an instant liking to me—he mentioned a junior post vacant in his department. "We have interesting stories," he said, ignoring the gray cloud over our heads and lighting another cigarette, its flame flirting with his dense manicured beard. He introduced me to his friends. Soon I felt immersed in the crowd and, separated from Stefano, again began searching for a place to fix myself.

When I first saw her I did not take particular notice. A doctor was telling me about preventable death, speaking calmly, but in moments betraying a hypertension. He made me a list of viruses; they were underreported, he said, only because African People were dying. So the African Doctor, deprived of funding and medicine, had become a promoter of African Disease. She was a tall woman, long-legged and with fair hair. She looked this way again.

And now she drifted in my direction. From the outset she looked disquieted—as if she wanted to say something, or needed help. Her pants and shirt, short sleeved with many pockets, stood out among the Château Margaux dresses. Without any sort of introduction she said, "You seem to know everyone here."

"Not really." I showed her my cache of business cards. "I'm on duty."

"And drinking on the job." I didn't respond, feeling it was small talk. She said her name was Natalie. I waited for her to say something substantial.

But she took her time. We picked fresh glasses of wine and watched people mingle. I learned she was from Quebec, and worked as a radio reporter tied to the UN. The men around us had now loosened their ties, and many of the women, whose light summer dresses showed freckled backs, were visibly intoxicated. They stood body to body, the communication laden with sexuality. The band also seemed worked up; the music was restless. I looked outside, to a yellow square of light that our window projected on the road. Two sentries with Kalashnikovs walked across the illumination, talking, smoking *stems*.

And suddenly their chatter seemed no longer idle. They appeared to be plotting. Look how they talk. In whispers, exclamations. The charm of the party warmed my shoulders again. Natalie lightly touched my back.

She had sensed the feeling. "You probably heard that Kabila received new tanks from China. For the elections." Anderson had mentioned it. "Everything is hot now," she continued. "Kabila is growing nervous. My staff as well. Every day there are little disputes ... but you know when you can tell something deeper is behind it all?"

"My family wanted to throw me out," I said. "I think they're worried. If a riot breaks out, I'll be a target."

"Your family lives in Kin?"

"I rent a room with a Congolese family. At Victoire. You should come."

"I don't know where that is."

She handed me her card. "For your collection." And as she turned away I caught a gentle expression on her face, and noticed the feather-like hairs on her arms burnished by the light.

The conversation had felt mysterious; it seemed to have promised; suddenly I longed for a connection. I fingered her card. A musician blew his trumpet thrice and stopped playing. I looked around. Stefano was gone and I hadn't seen Satwant. I was among the last loiterers. The waiters looked lazy and ready to pack up; the band members hoisted off their heavy liveries and gathered their instruments. I pattered down the stairs. The sentries leaned against the gate. I lifted my chin at them, "Taxi." But the cars had all been taken.

I walked down the empty road, aware of furtive sounds and movements in the bush. Long drains stretched along the roads in this part of town. Leaves around me dimly reflected stray light. The crunching sound of my feet carried. I reached a restaurant but there were no taxis. Three Congolese teenagers crouched over the hood of a pickup truck. They rose hastily and searched me with weary stares. I lifted my palms in greeting and asked if I could have a ride.

"Victoire?" he said. "Hop in the back."

Two teenagers joined me on the pickup's flatbed. The sky was covered in moonlit popcorn clouds. We backed out of the parking lot and sped into the city. The roads were empty. I held on to the vehicle's sides. One of the boys flicked a match alight; he huddled over the flame so it wouldn't extinguish. He offered it. I waved a hand. No, he said, it's a joint.

"Party?" I asked.

"Tupac."

The boy was a rapper, and his friend a drummer. They played gigs at upscale restaurants, wearing dog tags with engravings and 50 Cent shirts. We arrived at Victoire and I jumped off. They gave me their business card; I said I'd surely visit.

There was no light in the toilet and I spit into the darkness, listening for the plop of liquid on liquid. I tried to throw up but drew nothing. I stumbled away from the commode and sat.

7

Almost immediately I ran a string of stories for the AP. I had never written a news story before, but my acquiring the job coincided with a spate of Congolese airplane crashes. I became proficient at reporting such deaths, identifying the type of near-antique aircraft, the often illegal cargo, the usually drunk Ukrainian pilots, and the number of unfortunate passengers. I kept close tabs on Bentley—as soon as he published a story I too hunted it down. So I was never first to report the news. But it was a way for me to learn my job.

I progressed to other kinds of news—which stunned me for appearing in a hundred newspapers across the world. It was a thrill not only to see my name printed but also to feel that Congo was suddenly getting more press. One story I wrote was about a moving army battalion that had contaminated twenty villages with cholera. And another was about Congolese soldiers kidnapped by Rwandan fighters hiding in the forest.

Almost every element of news I first heard on the UN radio station that employed Natalie. It was the country's best. Sometimes I found myself waiting to see if I would hear her voice. I never did. I tried to imagine what she might be doing.

And I started wanting to go to the war in Congo's east, the center of this region's crisis. My mind was there constantly. It was the main subject of almost all the news on the radio. It was perhaps the deadliest place in the world. It was there that a thousand people were said to be dying every day from the war and the resulting humanitarian emergencies. The violent cities of the east—and a town famous for its massacres called Bunia—started to seem half-familiar. I imagined I could soon visit. I started to dream of the journey. The desire to penetrate deeper into the conflict began to grow in me.

I received my first payment. It was a happy moment of sorts—I collected $340 from a neighborhood Western Union. I got home and paid Nana my share of the rent. She said at once that it would not be enough. Jose was still making nothing and the family would soon be broke. I would have to pay a greater share. I watched as she took the money from my hand. "Is this all they gave you?" Nana asked disbelievingly. She said we would not survive. I felt the pressure build within myself. I made the calculations. She was correct. Despite all those stories I would just barely be able to keep the family and myself going. The climb had gotten steeper—the challenge was in a sense only beginning.

I was becoming attached to the family, and feeling tangled with their fate. It was because, despite her harshness, Nana was counting on me so desperately. I could not simply desert her. And the job had made my possibilities entirely different. I started to wonder if I needed to take some sort of risk—to leap out of this rut.

So when I learned the Indian community in Kinshasa was going to hoist the flag for India's Independence Day, I decided to go. I thought I might find others like me, might find a way out—or some support.

The bumpy journey reminded me of a pebble road near my grandmother's house in India, where I had spent a few childhood summers. Just a few hours earlier, in the morning, she

would have stood salute in that house, facing the television—
the national anthem set very loud as the army marched past the
prime minister, a small man under a large red umbrella.

I stood in single file with sixty Indians in the embassy garden. The men wore white topees. The women were few, perhaps
five. They covered their heads with hoods, to be modest, both for
the national occasion and in front of the men. A large flag hung
above us, limp on the pole. As I stood surrounded by country-
men, the songs conjured old sentiments; and the scene, though
in an alien country, felt comfortingly familiar. We chanted the
anthem solemnly, without tune.

After the singing was over the women, all married, with bin-
dis on their foreheads, huddled in a corner and held their sari
ends around their waists. The men talked in groups. Several
pants slipped down the slopes of bellies and were strapped on
with tight, thin belts. One older man, less rotund than the others,
held his stomach with both hands, as if in mimicry, and came
over. "What are you doing in Kinshasa?" he said, with the air of
the old-timer assessing the newcomer.

I said I was a journalist and he touched his head—his tone
softened, and he even thought he might have seen my name in
the press. "The AP? Oh *my*. We don't get many literary people in
our community." His name was Bobby, and I saw from his card
that he ran a store. I asked what he sold. "All and sundry" was
his answer.

I inquired about the other Indians standing idly around us.
Bobby was dismissive: "They're all into business." It surprised
me; I thought he could have had a dispute with Kinshasa's Indian
community, and I became wary of being seen as his friend. But
in his tone, and his comment about literary people, I also caught
an idea that Bobby thought himself cultivated, and above the
trader. The flag, meanwhile, had picked up. A heavyset Indian
showed some guests into the embassy, presumably for cake and
coffee; we were not invited.

Bobby offered me a ride. My address gave him a shock. It seemed to jar with his idea of my success, and he spent the drive trying to convince me to move out. "Locals have no culture, no civilization. Okay for business, but how do you *live* with them?" He knew an apartment block that provided meals of Indian food in tiffin carriers. I imagined a squalid setting, and stared glumly out the window. The car stopped—it was his shop. He asked me to get out; he was locking the car.

We were at a cement plaza, not wide on the street but stretching long into the neighborhood. Bobby hurried in, ringing the doorbell many times. His daughter appeared through a curtained doorway; without consulting me he told her to make *chai*. So I became the Indian guest—though I had been more or less kidnapped—to be fussed over.

I thought it must be a storeroom: the place was so dark, with a counter in front and boxes at the back, battered boxes strewn between artifacts: woodcuts, dirty boots, old radios, tins. Black and red cables covered everything; bulbs hung on wires from the roof. I was shown to a small clearing around a coffee table, with two high-backed chairs whose leather was pinned back by large metal buttons. The girl brought us tea.

Bobby crossed his legs affectedly and sipped. And I felt he was acting out some private fantasy. He didn't stop asking questions: about the UN's success, the purpose of the war, my travels. Feeling I had to live up to his expectations I related anecdotes from my trip to the beach. Minor information was a good way of demonstrating deeper knowledge; Bobby nodded, often as though not quite understanding, but always certain of my intelligence and keen to prove his intellect.

I wanted to take a taxi home but he insisted on driving. And just as he pulled in to Victoire's Shell gas station two street boys jumped on his rearview mirrors and broke them off. Embarrassed, I apologized, as if also to blame; it showed that I felt abnormal for living here. Under his breath Bobby cursed the boys. He said we should have dinner, and his words sounded hopeful, not like mere pleasantry. I got out.

Over time I grew used to such regard. My job changed how people saw me: Nana now commented if my shoes lacked polish, if my shirts were not pressed. Bozene turned to me for opinions about society and politics.

And as people opened up it changed my view of them. Jose introduced me to his friends, pro- and anti-government, for lengthy night sessions over beer. I was often quiet, listening; and even when they became emotional and stammered, when it would have been natural for them to switch to Lingala, for my benefit they stayed with French. I found in Jose a special calm, an ability for defusing tension; he was a natural mediator. Nana too revealed new facets. I gained a sense of her independence—I learned she wanted to start a cooperative for nurses—and of her rebellion: she supported a different politician from Jose despite his pressure. I experienced that period as one of intensity, of expression, of self-assertion—and I felt I began to see the personalities of Bozene in the way that other Congolese saw them.

Then the emotions peaked one day. There was unexpected joy and all else was forgotten. Bébé Rhéma began to crawl, and earlier than the doctors had expected. How Nana squealed on the day of the first sighting: "Jose! Bébé Rhéma! Jose! You have to come!"

We rushed to the living room, wondering if something was the matter, but no: Bébé Rhéma breathed heavily and showed her two buckteeth and, scrambling over the cement, tried to make her way across the hall to her pacifier. The baby cried. Jose and Nana hugged. The baby rolled over and looked at all the people staring. She smiled, and she was gorgeous.

"Bé-bé!" Nana cooed.

Jose flung Bébé Rhéma in the air and caught her in his

arms. He rubbed his nose on hers. Gurgling filled the house. I remember Nana in the kitchen on that day, the towel draped over her shoulder and her face covered in sweat; but she smiled, she laughed thankfully; amid all her troubles and crises, Bébé Rhéma seemed her constant source of comfort, happiness and pride.

That evening Jose and Nana had friends over for rice and chicken. To this modest dinner I contributed three corner-store sausages. And when everyone had come we must have been nine at the table and on the sofas, anticipating the moment. But Bébé Rhéma only played with her doll; she would not crawl; she chuckled, as though mocking us.

Jose was roundly teased. "You called us over for *this*?" "What a hoax." "This is like a Kabila project." And Nana's chicken was praised.

8

At first I thought hard work would find me a solution. Propelled by the needs of the family, and my own hopes of going to the heart of the crisis, I doubled down, looking for every story, writing as much as I could, harassing my editors.

And with the hot season having officially arrived in Kinshasa the house became like a radiator. Outside was worse. Nana advised me to travel only in the morning and evening. "The heat hits your head like a baton," she said, "you could faint in the road." In the shade of my room, but sweating, I listened to the bulletins. The headline one afternoon was of women protesting abuse. Gathered before a UN base they had scuffled with the guards and tried to get in; the gate had nearly toppled.

"Four hundred rapes and the UN hasn't acted," I told the editor. "One woman says she was raped on the road by six policemen but no one was questioned." Hundreds of women had protested, I explained. There had been a spate of human-rights violations in Kananga.

"Where?"

"Kananga. It's near the middle of Congo."

"Was there any shooting?"

"No."

"Any fighting, clashes?"

"No."

"Any violence at all?"

"Not that I know of."

"So no dead."

"Correct."

He paused.

"Nah, not interesting."

From the outside, as a reader, the world of news had seemed orderly, confident, authoritative. But on the inside I felt disoriented, lost. I could not understand why none of the following qualified as world news. It seemed half the country was going unreported:

Excerpts from my notebooks

Young girl killed by "savage mob" in Goma. Stones and pieces of wood were thrust into her vagina. No one in village able to say what she had done.

City of Butembo has plunged into "great psychosis." According to the mayor, population is patrolling the city to combat would-be vampire.

Laurent Nkunda, dissident general, raided eastern village. Huts were pillaged and burned; some eighty people fled; three elderly found dead.

Drama in the Park of Virunga. A fifteen-year-old girl was seized by a hippopotamus. Park guards ordered to attack pachyderms. Girl is presumed dead.

Twelve children survived a rebel attack on Sunday. The children lost their parents and are still in shock. One boy is in coma.

Thirteen-year-old girl, deaf and dumb, was killed by
two men in their twenties. According to the victim's parents, the men drugged the girl and raped her.

Death, as a rule, had the best chance of making the news. And
in a country torn by war one might imagine such news would
be abundant. But in Congo so many people died that, farcically,
mere death was not enough: I needed many deaths at once, or
an extraordinary death. A raid on a village—with a hundred
people displaced—was only important if it involved the army or
the UN. Rape was too frequent to be reported even six at a time.
And the constant fear people lived in, if mentioned at all, was
either in the penultimate paragraph of a news story or on the
opinion page.

Then a sensation broke in Liberia—Charles Taylor was caught
at the Nigerian border trying to flee—and it became impossible
to sell Congo. The AP didn't take a story for more than a week
(and since I was paid by the word, during this time I made no
money). I heard three miners died digging a tunnel, and then
that a rebel group was planning an attack, but after ten days of
my incessant calling with such news the editor laid it out to me: I
wasn't to phone unless it was serious. "We're busy," he said. "And
I don't have time to explain why we're not taking this."

The editors had their own hassles. The bureau in Dakar covered twenty-two countries, and every day was a grind, a competition to beat the other agencies, to pursue tip-offs from dodgy
sources, to edit and translate from patchy language, to identify
what would be important to customers—for the AP, primarily
Americans. "Think about what my grandmother in Wisconsin
would want to read," an editor told me. They were three in Dakar,
working in shifts like prison sentries, toiling in front of computer
screens . . . and the constant news of rape, death, child soldiers, it
must all have blurred.

Lying in my bed I took copious notes, trying to make sense

of the bulletins, for myself and for the outsider. My notebooks
filled up. I would become overwhelmed, and pace around the
room, unable but to imagine the scenes. They made me numb.

The narrative that formed in those notebooks was disconcerting—for though it was broadcast across the country
it remained strangely silent inside homes: Congolese didn't
vocally acknowledge it; they didn't transmit or hand it down.
They listened, quietly assimilated it and returned to their rituals;
and when Nana told Bébé Rhéma a tale—the baby would stare,
wide-eyed—it would be about a heroic Congolese warrior or the
defeat of an evil king, or about a princess who sought a kind husband; her stories were about valor, hope, love. The news seemed
divorced from the world Nana created for her child, from the
world the Congolese inhabited.

Thankfully the tragic bouts of news were followed by music,
and the BBC ran a nightly classical segment to which I often listened in the dark, lying in bed. In the evenings, after the sun had
set but while the day still carried light, I would sit at the corner
store with a glass of cold milk. Sometimes I saw Fannie there,
buying fertility vitamins (Nana had told me, very casually, that
she had found a British boyfriend). And I usually wrote at night;
occasionally I frequented a bar on the main street; I found the
beer helped me sleep, especially when the night was warm.

On one of those idle evenings I invited Mossi. We met at
Bozene, in front of the house, and as soon as we started to walk
Mossi slapped my back. "What, eh?" he said with a cheer. I smiled
at my feet and basked. He walked with long, slow steps, taking
his time. Mossi had just returned to Kinshasa from an assign-
ment, and it was our first meeting since I had gotten the job. Sitting at the bar, we poured for each other from large bottles of
frothing Primus and talked about his hometown, on the coast
of South Africa, and how his family, opposed to the government,
had needed to flee—to seek asylum in Congo, of all places.

Mossi frowned at his glass, sipped, gasped with contentment

and sat back in his chair. And I noticed how the gray hairs rose on his face in prickles, how they moved like a wave when he licked his teeth.

It was the first time he allowed me to pay for the beer. We walked back together, and he dropped me off near the church building, at Bozene's entrance.

I was relaxing in the living room. Music was playing, but beneath the melody I could hear Jose tell Nana about his boss at the tax department; he was tired of workplace politics—he had tried everything, he said. But Nana didn't seem to be in a sympathetic mood. "Why don't you ask to have your old post back? Just pose the question, that's all I'm saying." Jose looked uncomfortable. Our eyes met and I felt I was intruding. I retired to my room, washed, changed into my pajamas and was about to catch the bulletins when Jose poked his head around my door. "Can I borrow your fan?"

"Of course. What for?"

"The funeral." A boy in the neighborhood had recently died—crushed by a piece of cement that had fallen off an old building. Jose unplugged the fan and twisted the cable around the pedestal. He carried it with care through the doorway. "Remember to bring it back," I called out.

"When the funeral is over," he shouted back.

I followed Jose to the living room. "When will it be over?"

"In three days."

"But I need the fan for the night. It's too hot."

"Maybe you can buy another?" Nana muttered from the floor. It was the third time she had mentioned it.

"But we already told them," Jose said.

"They need it at night?"

"For the preparations."

"I thought this boy was fetish." There had been accusations of occult happenings around the boy. "Why are we giving him my fan?"

"Electronics don't catch fetish," Nana retorted, as if I couldn't know anything about such matters. Then she looked at her husband and said, with equal annoyance, "But someone at your office is talking against this house, Jose, and you're not doing anything about it." The accusation seemed to take Jose by surprise and he stared, then grimaced. He threw his hands in the air. "*Why* do you want to provoke me?" His gentleness was gone; he marched into the corridor, and the bedroom's door shut with a thump. Nana looked unnerved. It was the first time I had seen them fight openly.

The baby coughed and Nana patted her back. She coughed again, and Nana slapped harder, and with a rhythm, as if beating the coughs out of the baby's chest.

The next morning Nana was still agitated. I woke early, and as I came out of my room stole a glimpse into hers—I was surprised to see her ready to go out. She stood in front of the mirror, picking at the shoulders on her dress, which glowed a resplendent yellow all the way to her ankles and was decorated with floral brown motifs. She hooked studs to her earlobes, looking tired, baggy-eyed, and reached for the counter, where small white boxes contained puffs of cotton. She lifted a wig. Over the black knots on her scalp she placed this piece of hair, which was dull red but shone brilliantly where it caught light. Her face was covered in talc, giving it a sheen. She straightened and looked in the mirror; briefly, she smiled; her shoulders sagged. She gathered her things; a box fell to the floor and pieces of metal rolled out. She clicked her lips and bent over, muttering.

I waddled into the living room, where the television blared. Sitting almost against the screen, Jose flipped between news and sports channels. It was the day of club football—and of two much-awaited matchups. All week Jose had been anticipating this day.

He raised his voice to salute me. "*Ça va un peu.*" "It's going a little" (always "a little" in Congo, never just *ça va*). He had not shaved or changed out of his pajamas. It seemed he had forgotten the fight. But Nana, without addressing him, brought in the writhing baby, and taking the seat next to Jose she started to sing: "Bébé Rhéma, please don't cry / If you cry, so will I / Bébé Rhéma is a good girl / Then you and I will be happy." The baby turned to hear her name called in Nana's gentle voice; she searched her mother's face.

The nervous song mixed with the excitement from the television. And Nana announced she would be going to the clinic— the one across town because it was the best, even if it cost a little extra. The baby had suffered all night. She would be late. Jose didn't respond. Nana turned to me and said there were groceries to be bought; the neighbors would send a boy who knew the place. She gave me a list. "I want you to help him carry the bags," she said. "Tea is on the table."

The thermos lid was wound too tight. It came off with a struggle, making a spill. The ants had found the sugar again.

It was in the middle of the afternoon and while I was reading a magazine that the neighbor's boy came bounding down the street. Look at him jump, I thought, as if we're going to the circus.

The streets did not seem unusually loud or quiet. We took a shortcut off Bozene and reached the main road, where the boy began to walk briskly. The wideness of the road made it seem empty though trucks and cars zipped by. A gentle breeze shook the boy's pants. On both sides of the road were sand and low dry bushes; the wind raised the sand and moved it over the road like snakes. We reached a bar and heard cheers. Men stood in beer-drinking clusters, fixed on a screen. The boy turned.

"Nana will be angry," I said. "Let's go to the market and come back."

"The market is just here," he protested. "Can we only take a look? We have so many hours and later the game will be finished anyway." He mumbled, "It is my favorite team."

It *was* the biggest match of the season, almost a national event to the Congolese. "Ten minutes," I said, and the concession reinforced my sympathy. We entered the bar.

The game was screened on a small television on a high ledge. The play was scrappy. A goal was scored. A man drinking beer asked whom I supported; he slowly explained the history of the teams, why the match was so crucial. At any small thing in the game—a trip, an off side—he would turn to give me commentary. Until a woman appeared on the pitch. There was a movement, and it was hard to tell, but she seemed to drop something. "Fetish!" the bar roared. The stadium seemed to combust: one half erupted in cheers and the other exploded with fury. Bottles were thrown on the pitch. Play was halted. Referees grouped the players and took them aside one by one. A newspaper would quote the losing goalkeeper as swearing he had seen the fetish. But the referee would say he could only call what he saw. And now the disorder—which seemed a greater entertainment than the game itself—had become too much. The men at the bar were raging, shouting over each other. It did not seem that the game could end normally. I had forgotten to keep an eye on the time. I called the boy.

The bright headlights of an oncoming car blinded me; the road led straight ahead and we had some distance to cover.

The boy said it was better to try a neighborhood shop; he had looked at the list and we would be able to get nearly everything Nana wanted. We now headed back the way we had come. And I felt he had played me for a fool. I tried to sound stern. "Hurry, okay?"

The first sign that something was wrong came at the shop. At
the counter a group of women were harassing the vendor. They
jostled for space and clutched money between their fingers; candles and oil flew from his hands. The vendor struggled to hear
the shouted orders: "Give me the milk," "I came first," and "Why
aren't you helping me? Can't you see I've been standing here for
so long, old man?" He lost his calm. "Go manage yourselves!"
He shut the windows that covered his shop. The women banged
for him to open.

We walked more. All the shops were shut, rows of them.
Metal shutters reflected the last light and bounded the space like
cracked mirrors, extending it in haphazard angles and making it
seem to stretch beyond, to the garden, the commune headquarters, the churches and over the roofs of houses, the disco with
the metal grill, beyond the plastic-sheet-covered lopsided stalls.
All this emptiness, it suddenly made one alert.

"Hsss," a lady said, drawing our attention. "There is a riot!"
And she ran away clumsily.

We followed her, keeping close to the walls, searching for signs
of a noise, until we turned for Victoire. And we saw them at the
end of the street. It was a mob. They were street boys. I immediately felt sympathy, thinking of Guy. But the boys climbed
over cars and perched on the walls; on the road they appeared
as a jumble of hands and legs. They could have been forty or
fifty, but the chorus of cries made their group seem larger. I saw
gangly figures rattle the gates of a house and call to residents
inside; boys climbed the gates and jumped into compounds and
chased stray chickens and goats onto the gravel, clapping after
them; they smashed car windows with rods and fell inside. My
sympathy turned into fear. The vehicles were stripped of radios,
gearshifts, and seats. The boys laughed wildly and danced down
the road, jeering at the barred-up people. They tied the livestock
at the feet and dragged them along the dirt. We needed to find
a way out.

The streets around the mob were silent and settled. The neighbor's boy ran into a narrow lane, at an angle to the wreckage. He was fast; I gave chase, apprehensive about our environment, feeling that around any corner the boys could suddenly come at us. We reached the monument at Victoire, strangely lonely without the throng. Bozene was equally silent. The house was locked. I banged on the door and Jose warily divided the curtain. He let us in.

I asked what had happened. "This is not the worst," Jose said. "Sometimes they are one hundred, the Kata-Kata." It was the term the Kinois used to describe the mobs of boys—which were said to decapitate people to kill them. Some claimed that the boys possessed sinister powers. Jose latched the door and turned the key. Then he paused at the door. "Who knows what really happened. The boys have nothing to do. It is so easy to start a riot."

Jose pulled the curtains shut and took a seat, his baggy shorts covering a portion of the sofa well wider than his legs. The television was showing the post-match coverage. Nana stacked empty plates on the counter, wiping each one with a red-checkered kitchen cloth. I crept behind her and to my room but she followed me to my doorway. "There's no more food," she said, calmly.

"No problem," I said, trying to make light of it and to sound reassuring. "I'll go tomorrow first thing."

"Don't you understand? There is no food for Bébé Rhéma." And she waved her hand at me, as though slapping me through the air. She seemed overcome. I felt dreadful. I felt she did not say more because I was paying for the house.

I returned to the warmth of the living room and sat on the broken sofa. I swatted the mosquitoes on my legs. Jose still seemed light-headed, somehow detached from Nana's suffering, and the house's plight. He smiled weakly and said, almost mourned, "An era is over." His team had failed to make the play-offs, and for the first time in years. All of a sudden the bulbs sparkled. The television tube in the dark glowed green. Appliances stopped with a rumble. I heard the irregular clicks of circuits breaking. For an instant there was silence . . . the chatter resurfaced. Jose said the match had eaten the city's power, so the districts each took turns to go without, the poorest first.

9

News had fallen to a paltry level. The airplane crashes had stopped. I was filing less and less. My income was squeezed. Jose as well was finding no solutions. The family would not make it past the month. It was then that I came upon a chance to go to the east—to the mines, and the war.

I was in the Grand Hotel. Anderson's CIA agents had arrived—hundreds of them. The hotel was graced with posters of silverback gorillas. It was a meeting of the Great Apes Survival Project. I was here to try to find news.

From the conference registration desk I spotted Richard Bentley, chasing a red-bearded man who looked important. This man was surrounded by people. I waved hello—maybe Bentley could get me in, I thought. I raised my hand higher, trying to be seen. Bentley looked in my direction but didn't wave back.

"Isn't that guy a prick?" a man beside me said. "He always makes me feel like I'm wasting his time. *Such* a prick." He looked about himself. "Want to grab a drink by the pool? It's bloody freezing in here." He gave me a card:

KEITH LEPER HALE
War Correspondent & Investigative Reporter

I had so far pursued ordinary stories. It had little to do with a lack of seeming opportunity: reports about uranium smuggling for instance were all over the press; but they felt too remote, too fantastic. As did the revelations on Radio Trottoir. They told you something of the environment of fantasy that people lived in; but the stories themselves—one had the impression either didn't exist or would kill you.

Keith Leper Hale, *Time* magazine correspondent and erstwhile Congo reporter, pursued *only* such stories. And in a single sitting he expanded my ideas of Congo's possibilities.

I followed the direction he had taken, past a set of glass doors that opened to the swimming area. I spotted him at the far end of the pool. He was bare-chested on a reclining chair and he wore a pair of swimming shorts. The day was hot and sultry; I wished I had brought my trunks.

The plastic chairs were full so I sat on a side table. All around us women in bikinis lounged about, pretending not to notice the men. A group of Congolese women with heavy gold earrings rubbed suntan lotion on their chests and contentedly lay back among the foreigners, looking like a row of piano keys. They slowly rolled over. Some slipped into the pool. All of them looked serious.

"Are you down with malaria?" Keith asked.

I said I was tired, and by way of explanation I mentioned that I lived in an African house.

He smiled. "Gonzo-style. That's the way to be."

No, actually, I thought; I'd much prefer a nice bed and air-conditioning. But I wondered what made me seem so beaten down.

Keith was an old hand in Africa. And he was writing a controversial book: Part 1 was going to be standard fare, he said—what the AP might publish. Part 2 was to be more "hard-core." Mainstream press might publish it, but only an adventurous editor. Part 3, he said, nobody would touch. "It's the *crack*."

I asked what was in Part 3.

He smiled. "See? You're already interested."

He ordered a waitress to bring chocolate cake. Though the light had faded he lifted a pair of aviator sunglasses from a hard case and put them on—it was popular fashion in Congo. The glasses were called "anti-night." Keith twirled his pen. The cake was brought. Quickly Keith hacked into it with a spoon. "Did you know George W. Bush has a stake in Congo's pillage?"

I shrugged.

"The proof is hidden in the jungle, on the border with the Central African Republic. Tons of wood are being transported by boat. The logging company is three levels down, a subsidiary in a petroleum conglomerate. No petroleum on those trucks. They're raking down half a forest on a daily basis. And Bush sits on the conglomerate's board."

"Sounds like you're all over the story."

"That's nothing," he said. "Listen to this."

Keith lifted his sunglasses and smiled. "You know the famous uranium mine? No? Let's go way back. World War II. Hiroshima and Nagasaki. Little Boy and Fat Man?"

I nodded.

"That uranium came from Congo. The mines are dead. Right?" He bit on the cake, staining his hands. He spoke while chewing. "*Wrong*. The mines are not dead. Have you been to Rwanda? You'll see American planes. Not little Cessnas. We're talking Hercules and transport craft, large enough to carry Abrams tanks and platoons of Special Forces. What are they doing there?"

Keith sniffed and leaned back in his chair. He stretched his legs and with a hand massaged his thigh, shaking the muscle briskly.

"The UN has seventeen thousand soldiers in Congo. But not

a single American, Brit or Canadian. Know why? They're too scared to send their men to this hell. It's not worth it to them. But go down to Katanga. That American military base has maximum security. It's the uranium they're after. Check any public reference: the army, the navy, the White House. That base doesn't exist. What *are* they doing here?" He paused for effect. "You know they've discovered a new nuclear deposit."

"Where?"

"It's top secret, man. This place is *full* of stories. You just eat them like a kid in a candy store."

I heard his words, but what was Keith really telling me? My mind was in a blur, overrun with ideas: soldiers, mines and smugglers crossed with the pool, the sun and the women: image upon image, they shifted confusedly. Suddenly they fell away. I felt a moment of clarity.

As if on cue Keith made me an offer. "I'm working on a new piece that goes to the highest levels," he said. "It's about a massacre at Kilwa. One hundred dead, give or take. You know who arranged the massacre? Anvil Mining. But no one's reported it because Anvil gets World Bank funding. Paul Wolfowitz knows. Kofi Annan knows. There's a UN report detailing how Anvil flew in an armed militia and gave them company cars to dump the dead in mass graves. The White House suppressed it."

"Where is Kilwa?"

"That's what I'm saying. Want to come?"

We paused to watch a girl undo her robe and step into the pool. The women had cleared from the reclining chairs. The light had faded. I could barely see the girl's face. I wondered why she had come so late; perhaps to avoid the stares.

"Kilwa is in the far east," Keith at last said. "It's remote. That's why the story is so sweet. Getting there will be expensive but we'll split it. We'll hire porters to carry the gear and supplies. I'll get started on the shopping list. Let's be talking." He tipped his sunglasses.

That night the AP confirmed its interest in Kilwa—the editor said I should pursue the story, but from Kinshasa. He would not hear about any travel: the bureau's stringer budget was apparently running on empty. I became agitated—I told him I felt the bureau wasn't supporting me. I desperately wanted a chance. "If you smell a story then maybe you should pay your own way," he said. "If it works out then we'll see. Right now I can promise you nothing."

I went home excited—convinced that I needed to take some sort of risk to escape the cycle of hardships at home, and also to get where I wanted. I felt suddenly projected outside Kinshasa—and frustrated, for the country's possibilities seemed beyond my reach. I would have to find a way to make my own luck. Entering the house I again became depressed.

10

I could not concentrate at the house. *"Ne touche pas!"* "Don't touch!" Jose's voice boomed. The commotion was around his new record. A boy from the neighborhood held his hands behind his back and leaned over the purchase, inspecting it with pursed lips. The record was in the old vinyl format, in its original cardboard sleeve; the print had faded. Jose opened a glass case and carefully placed the record on a plate. He pressed a button. The vinyl began to spin. Bébé Rhéma was brought. Jose held the baby by the ends of her fingers so she stood uncertainly and shifted her feet. The song was French, uncommon in Congo, but Jose had spent two years of his youth in Belgium and some of the customs he kept—European music, muscatel and a quiet disposition—distinguished our house, which was otherwise no taller, no wealthier and no better kept than the other cement-sassy wood structures on Bozene. The habits gave Jose a reputation for being *évolué*. And it was seen as a mark of his evolution when he made a skiing motion with his arms, jiggled his hips, and sang along to the cactus song:

The whole world is a cactus . . .

To this the little boy slapped his little bottom with his palm—a rhythmic move he had no doubt learned from the young girls who performed on television. I set aside my work and took a seat on the sofa, forgetting it was broken—and Jose added a new chorus, to which they danced with greater verve:

All of Kinshasa is a cactus!
Im-poss-ible to sit down!

It used to be an official designation, Évolué, conferred by the Belgians in colonial times to a select few families who had rejected their "primitive structures": the clan, beliefs, traditions, even dress codes and language. It was an idea of human rights: to show the African could be as civilized as the white man. A special committee was tasked with visiting the Negro home, to check the standard of hygiene, the quality of visitors, the use of cutlery, and if the children had underwear on. It was when I asked around about the cactus song that I discovered Jose was an *évolué* (and that Nana was not).

From the dining table Nana observed Jose. After a week of waiting she had decided to act. She sat with clasped hands, a figure of calm. Around her hair was wrapped a red cloth. She wore a dotted blouse. A skirt reached to her ankles, and she kicked strappy sandals back and forth on the cement. Bébé Rhéma laughed and Nana gave a restrained smile. There was a knock on the door. Jose was asked to turn off the music. He looked surprised, but lowered the volume. We observed our guest with curiosity as Nana showed him around.

He was slim, bald and wearing a suit. Prominently, he carried a shiny-silver pen that he waved like a wand at the various items Nana pointed to: the lighting fixtures, the old cupboard with plates, the deep freezer. He crouched over Nana's plastic boxes of jewelry and inspected their contents, and Nana was about to show him the television but he said he had seen enough. The man was a microcredit lender.

And he approved the loan. Nana absentmindedly straightened the chairs. Under the table were two large bales of colorful clothes. "Gym pants from Canada." She planned to turn the house into a boutique for young people. The lender smiled benevolently, and gave her some papers. Nana's hand was unsteady—as though unaccustomed to the meager form of the pencil, to the delicate task of scrawling one's name within neat rectangular boxes. The lender took the papers and left.

Jose seemed unsure, unhappy. Carrying Bébé Rhéma he walked across the living room. "I bought these for our marriage," he said, touching the jewelry. "You can't just pawn them off." Nana folded the table napkins and said she wasn't pawning off anything. It was just collateral. The terms she used: *collateral, yield, return*; they were not the vocabulary of a housewife. She fumbled with a napkin, unable to fold it correctly, and abruptly left the room.

Few Congolese would take such cheek from a wife, and though Jose was *évolué* this was perhaps too much emancipation to handle at once. He seethed, and it showed in his voice. He loudly said the next time Nana invited strangers to look at their objects she should inform him first. It was basic respect he was asking for, nothing more. After all, it was also his house. "Next you'll be pawning my music system," he said, "and I won't have it, you hear? I won't have it!" He put on a shirt and oxford shoes and, for the first time in weeks, left the house carrying his briefcase. The new vinyl had meanwhile spun past the cactus song, to its conclusion. The festivities were over.

My mind was occupied by the meeting with Keith, and how I would find the money to travel with him. I did not return to the conference—it seemed too small. Richard Bentley had written about an excursion to an ape sanctuary. The visit had been arranged by the red-bearded man. Others had gone with him. The AP was the only news outlet without the story—a fact the bureau took the trouble to point out to me. I spent the week anxiously flipping through the Congolese papers, but there was so little news that the editors had swelled the font to fill up space.

There was another reason I did not go to the Grand Hotel that day. Bobby, the shop owner from the event at the Indian embassy, had called to ask if we could meet in private. ("Do you drink beer?" he had asked—and the mention of alcohol combined with his secretive tone implied our discussion would be serious.) I said I might need to be at the conference. But Bobby insisted. I asked why the rush, and he said, with not a little exasperation, "Just come, man. My girl will cook us something good."

The drive was punishing; his neighborhood was full of traffic and the exhausts from cars saturated the air. I tried to cover my nose with my shirt but the smoke had impregnated the cotton, making my nose revolt and run in streams. Suddenly, through the chaos of smells, there was the clean, precise scent of gasoline; we passed a truck in the orange halo of station lights. Bobby greeted me at the front of his parcel with a solemn handshake and a rub on my back. And he guided me through the exterior garden facing the part of the house where we had taken tea.

The garden had not been tended. Weeds had taken over. But the little yellow and white flowers on the weeds' ends gave off perfume: it was fresh, pleasant. We arrived at a mossy corridor of his shop: plastic, grease, ink, rust; the smells were strong but powerless as soon as Bobby pushed aside the dividing curtain, for the aromas of curries came in numbing waves: coriander and bay leaves and fried mustard; rancid hot sugar, pungent garlic, sour yogurt; parsley, mint, basil; each smell layered over the other and lingered over the dining room.

The table was laid with various bowls on a clear plastic sheet. The place mats were rudimentary, of knotted jute. The table was of plywood. Glasses of lassi on the table perspired, covered by steel plates scratched from long use. The girl, who stood mute in a corner, brought us a tray with green bottles of imported Heineken. The bottle opener she used had a picture of a siren in lingerie.

She served us spoonfuls of curries in four colors: yellow, orange, red, green. Each produced a different and distinct flavor, unlike the homogeneous red pastes one got at restaurants. The *biryani* was finely spiced. It was my first Indian meal—and a home meal too—since I had come to Congo. I ate with my head bowed, almost without speaking.

The girl departed to the kitchen.

Bobby wiped his mouth and laid out the reason behind his invitation. "I have a problem," he said. "A piece of my land has been appropriated."

He had brought a folder filled with papers of various sizes and colors. There was also his deed, covered in stamps and signatures of the central and provincial authorities. Bobby's own signature was at the bottom, next to the title "PROPRIÉTAIRE." The plot was to the north of Kinshasa, in the jungle province of Équateur. It was large. It must have cost a small fortune.

Bobby claimed the appropriation was illegal. He said he had proof that powerful people were involved. But it wasn't my intention to get mixed up in politics. I was also apprehensive: I thought Bobby could be showing me a small piece of a much larger affair: maybe the land was taken for revenge, to settle some score. I said, "The biryani is very good."

Bobby smiled.

"I understand your hesitation," he said, and he let some silence pass. "But the land has become a nature park. A U.S. conservation group is now managing the territory, and the government has posted armed guards around it. Don't you think that is strange?"

Sure, it was odd. But I apologized, saying I could not help.

"You should complain to the conservationists," I said. "Or to the government. Tell them they are working illegally."

"It won't work," Bobby said. "You see, there is more." He wiped his face with his hand. "I would not have called you if it were a case of simple politics. I think there is something in that ground."

"Like what?"

"I don't know. Red mercury."

"I've never heard of it."

"It is a colloquial appellation. The rock is red when you take it from the ground. It doesn't really matter what it is called—the locals give strange names and most of the time they don't know what they talk about—but I am certain it is precious." Bobby pulled out two business cards. "See for yourself. Everyone is after my land. Even Avi Mezler." The card was for a mineral purchasing firm registered in Israel. "Mezler wanted to buy that land for seven times its market price. A businessman from Egypt was also interested. But the Americans found out. And now they are mining something while calling it a conservation project." He tucked the cards into his shirt pocket, shaking the cloth so the cards fell to the bottom. "It is a little strange, don't you think?"

"You think the U.S. government is behind this?"

He huffed. "USAID." He held one hand out, palm up. "Department of Defense." Other hand. "Don't be fooled, all Americans inform the Secret Service when the time comes."

"Like who?"

"The people at the conference . . ." He broke off, as if considering how much to say. "Some go straight to Condoleezza." His hand made a form like an airplane.

"Is it expensive to reach your land?"

"The barges leave one right against the property. It is also cheaper and better to travel like the Congolese. We can move about with less hassle."

I almost regretted not being able to clean out the curries: I felt those dishes would come back to haunt me in some future moment of hunger. But Bobby called his girl and asked her to pack it all. She poured the leftover dal into a bottle.

Tea was brought in cream-colored porcelain. Bobby leaned forward to sip, making a soft slurping noise at his lips. The cup came cleanly down on the circle of the saucer. The porcelain clinked.

"Well, take your time to think about it," he said.

I felt pity. It took courage to do business here. Stories like Bobby's were all too common, but they generally involved so much corruption that a journalist could not approach. The businessman generally feared the journalist. The fact that Bobby had solicited me meant either that he was clean, or that he had exhausted every other option.

He was part of Congo's rising Indian class. West Africa was traditionally Lebanese. Indians dominated the East African economies. Congo straddled this divide, making a natural route for migration. And among the most celebrated migrants, some seventy years earlier, was a Gujarati called Rawji, who opened a shop in the middle of Congo. For nearly all his life he had only that shop. His sons expanded, and their sons. And in only two generations the Rawji Group became a billion-dollar conglomerate. The story inspired more Indians to cross, and join the Lebanese, the Israelis, the Belgians and the politicians to form a small moneyed class that owned nearly all of Congo's GDP.

The imbalance was blatant, shameless. Outside every sit-down restaurant ragged children hoped for sympathy. Every UN jeep solicited stares. Clubs served tequila shots for fifteen dollars; a studio apartment in downtown Kinshasa cost nine hundred dollars a month, like in a big American city. But the foreigners seemed to show no compassion, and they brazenly perpetuated their extravagances.

The Congolese solution, typically inversive, was to subvert the outsider's logic, to undermine the clever immigrants. A new economics was invented, a financial order that valued cunning and hustle—skills the locals possessed—over labor and ownership. So where before in Kinshasa hardly anyone could find a job, now nobody needed employment: money passed as if by osmosis; it became a basic human right to steal from those who had more. It was why Anderson had seemed pleased when my phone was stolen, and why each rich house employed armed guards. The system of theft evolved in a communitarian spirit, and rather than embezzle in secret the politicians asked the people to join. "Do not steal too much at a time," Mobutu told the people. "*Yibana mayele*—Steal cleverly, little by little."

Some, like the Rawjis, managed the kleptocracy (they ran their business, it was said, from the golf course) and succeeded; but the majority stagnated for years in their shops and eventually became ruined by sudden devastations like this affair with the land.

And the Congolese reaction to the wealth divide, which could be interpreted as a form of social redress, has become itself corrupted, into a more primitive and instinctual form of thievery. The poor now steal not from the Rawjis and politicians but from the most vulnerable: other poor, and modest middle-class people. It is why the Congolese to the outsider appear as their bandits, and why their greed often seems as unscrupulous, incomprehensible and immoral as that of the moneyed.

Bobby asked what I, as a journalist, thought of the country's media. I spoke about the Opposition Debout; but he was impatient for me to finish. The question had been posed half rhetorically, to allow Bobby to give me *his* opinion: he had learned to read in Lingala (despite his contempt for Africans) and had come to respect the local journalists for their frankness. It was in the Congolese blood, he believed, because Mobutu—who had shaped so much in this country—had been a newspaperman. Mobutu was among the only Congolese brave enough to report the colonial killings. His writings, Bobby said, did a lot to remove the Belgians.

So the conversation, after its heightened middle, ended in a sort of theoretical peace.

We finished our teas. I handed the girl my porcelain.

She gave me the bags and bottle of food.

Bobby showed me to the door. We solemnly shook hands again.

The air outside was choking. The taxibus was covered in filth. The driver screamed at me to get in. I climbed into the mass of humans, the warmth, the bodily smells. This was how I had begun to feel in Kinshasa—always restricted, caught in a sort of interior, unable to sense the horizon.

I had an opportunity to verify Bobby's claims that same evening, when I called Stefano, the UN officer from Châteaux Margaux, to confirm Keith's story about the massacre. I was still considering Keith's offer to travel together to Kilwa, and Stefano had become a reliable informant. It was he who had supplied me with some of the stories about rape. And today he was in a chatty mood: his marriage was coming up. It would be a quiet affair, he said, with only the closest family and friends. There would be excellent food; the honeymoon would be on some island. But the last preparations were still incomplete, and his mind had been elsewhere. He had hardly had time to examine the UN dossiers. "I know, I know," he said. "You need to know about Kilwa. Hold on while I look it up."

He read me the details and I took notes in the taxi. "Any chance you could get me the full report?" I said. I heard Stefano scratch his beard. "It's complicated. We have testimonies but the report is stuck at our chief's office. Political pressure."

"I really need the report."

"Why don't you try at the World Bank? Really it is their affair more than ours. But I'll give it a try. As a favor. By the way, I didn't say anything about political pressure." I asked Stefano what he knew about Avi Mezler. "Of course," he said. "Major guy, based in Tel Aviv. The UN has been trying to indict him for years. Why do you ask?"

"He's trying to claim this piece of land from a friend."

"Where?"

"In Équateur. We don't know why."

"That's strange. Mezler doesn't go sniffing just anywhere. Listen, we're having a going-away party at my place. We have a pool. There'll be good people. Bring your friend, I want to hear more about this."

I was sitting in the minibus's only vacant seat: on a hot canister beside the driver, my legs spread to accommodate the gearshift. I pointed under my legs and asked what it was. The driver said, "Tank." I saw a pipe from the canister lead toward the engine. On the dashboard a sticker said, "Jesus Protects This Vehicle." But hardly ten minutes afterward the minibus began to glide. The driver pumped the pedal. The minibus jerked. Everybody was ordered to get out. I clutched my bag to my chest and watched the driver walk away. Passengers began to disperse. An old woman and I were the only ones who remained until the end. The driver returned carrying a half-liter bottle glowing brown.

I used the time to call the AP. I told the editor the Kilwa affair was serious. "Anvil organized the massacre. The UN is withholding the report but I might get it."

"Do you have quotes?"

I told him that if we waited a few days we would have the full report; but he cut me off. "Send it tonight. If we have the news there's no sense in waiting." The minibus reached Victoire and I rushed to the house, avoiding the garbage and gutters.

The house courtyard was empty. I locked myself in my room and began to type out the story. Stefano couldn't confirm all of Keith's details—there wasn't enough evidence, he said, though everyone knew what had happened. I wrote the hardest-hitting story I could. Then the bulbs sparkled and died. My screen waned.

Nana moved about the house like a phantom, setting candles that lit her face from underneath and made her look sinister.

I drummed with my fingers on the chair at the dining table, trying to relax among the sounds of the creatures; small shadows flashed along the wall. I had seen rats in my room the other night. Nana had promised to set traps. "How come you didn't do it?" I said.

"I had another idea," she said. "We will use poison."

I held a candle while she emptied a plastic sachet and mixed a white powder with balls of bread. Going from room to room we carefully placed the balls in cabinets, among the kitchen pots and along the walls. We put some balls around her suitcase of special-occasion clothes, and beside the deep freezer. "Put some under my bed," I said, "and behind the wardrobe. That's where they multiply." She laughed.

The AP editor called, sounding impatient. He wanted to go home and was only waiting for my story. I followed Nana to the living room.

But we were helpless against the current; we waited, listened. The initial silence was gone. Sounds from the road: murmurs from the night crowd, a dog, the resounding cry of a bird. Bars had lit generators; bulbs attracted flying insects, the intensity of lights rising and ebbing with the pitch of the motor. Stoves scraped the ground like chalk on blackboards as women dragged the heavy metal into the courtyard. They began to braise fish. Children came out and pissed over the earth, crumpling the cloth of their shirts in one hand and watching the liquid splash against their feet. The women shouted at them to go inside. The smoke from the stoves attracted large birds that circled above and observed the cuisine from electrical posts. Orange embers littered the courtyard. Sweating, I flapped a newspaper against my face.

"We should call SNEL," I said. The electricity company. Nana said it would do no good.

"Didn't they fix the problem the last time you called?"

"That was a coincidence. I had nothing to do with it."

"Can't you just call them to try?"

"You do it if you're in such a rush."

The local SNEL officer, an elderly man who had supervised Bozene's circuits for decades, assured me the current would soon return. It always did. How soon? I explained speed was imperative. He said, "I understand, but it may be sensible to invest twenty dollars. The other houses have done so." I thought he was asking for a bribe and was ready to promise payment, but then I heard our neighbor's television running. And the bulb at the next house glowed. I walked up to the gate, slowly, the realization growing: the sounds, the light, the activity of the street, the music playing on two-in-ones. "Why are we the only house without current?" I asked Nana. "Did we do something to the SNEL guy?"

"I've argued with Jose for two years," she said, "you try telling him."

Jose sat on the porch, somnolent, slumped over his hands. He said, "We're an honest family and we're going to stay honest." I looked up at the wires crisscrossing Bozene. I had seen them before but had never realized their purpose. The other houses were stealing current from alternate power lines. Why weren't we? Because Jose was trying to take on corruption in his country alone?

I filed the story from a neighbor's house using one of Mossi's tricks: by making my phone a data transmitter. It was both slow and expensive, but it worked in an emergency. Only then did I realize how exhausting the day had been. I fell on my bed. I surveyed the room. A pair of red eyes peered from under the wardrobe. I banged with my hand on the carpet. They hid, reappeared. "Go away," I said, my voice ringing. I imagined the rats nibbling at the poison, and to that image I fell asleep.

The fetish boy was being remembered in front of our house, some weeks after his death. The delay was attributed to his family's quest for finances: in Kinshasa one could die poor but one still had to be buried like a rich man. The *évolué* households sensed the contradiction: Nana told me about a boy who died of typhoid because his mother lacked two hundred dollars. Immediately relatives piled her with money—more than two thousand dollars—so the boy could have an elaborate funeral.

Likewise, the fetish boy was having a gazebo erected, and for many weeks we had seen his uncles squatting on the side of the street, setting up wooden stumps with concrete bricks at the bottom and lengths of rope; the neighborhood had come together to provide fine purple cloth to drape over the wood; a tall pole was placed at the gazebo's center to make a spike at its top.

Individual houses made further contributions. Jose was generous. Once the service began, gathered in the shade of the purple cloth was a collection of Bozene's old and weary, sadly singing. Jose's loudspeakers sounded like beating tin. The gathering swayed. An old photograph of the boy stood on a shrine-like pedestal, and on one side of the gazebo I spotted my fan giving air to a few fortunate.

The loudspeaker and the fan substituted for our house's presence; though Jose was in the *ville* no one accused him of contempt. From the house we heard the ceremony last all night and then another full day. Nana stayed at home to arrange her boutique, spreading T-shirts and track pants on the table. Frida was present. Nana unbundled a woman's top and Frida claimed it would fit her perfectly. Nana pushed it her way. Frida didn't have money. I heard the word "family." Frida picked up garment after garment and at the end Nana wrote her a receipt. Frida gave me a glare, as if to provoke. "Watch out with her," I mumbled. And Nana—even now cold to me in Frida's presence—scowled.

That I was tense on that day was clear to everyone who crossed my path. At the internet café I dropped a hundred francs into Stella's palm. "Boss, I've got something," he said, pushing a paper my way:

New System of Ravagers of the Male Sex by the Magic of a Mystic Band
    True Story in Kinshasa (Information @ Stella Ivinya)

He twitched his eyebrows and rubbed his fingers together. "Want the full information?" He looked around furtively.

I stared at the sheet, and the letters seemed to grow bigger and bigger, and they swam, floating across the page, and off it. I crumpled the paper in one motion. "Be serious, Stella."

He was offended. "What's the matter with you?" he said. "Can't have a little fun?"

The tension stemmed from the Kilwa story. It had been published but only in obscure outlets. The major papers had not picked it up. I could not understand—usually an AP story was taken all over the world. Was the massacre not important enough? Had it been suppressed? Stefano called and I answered the phone in a hurry. "I saw a very disturbing story," he said, his voice Italian neutral.

"About what?"

"I expressly told you not to quote me."

A flurry of thoughts invaded my head. "There is nothing about the politics." Isn't that what he said?

"I'm in big trouble because of you."

"What's the matter? I didn't talk about political pressure. Is there some misunderstanding?"

"I'm sorry but I don't think I can talk to you anymore," he said. "Stefano."

The line went silent, magnifying my feeling of shame. I covered my face with my hands—I had lost my best source of information. Worse, I had lost a potential friend. At home it was dark. I felt my way along the corridor and to the bed. But I could not sleep. A noise had erupted. In the courtyard water shot into a plastic bucket, making a hollow racket. "Something happened?"

"No water for twenty-four hours," Nana said.

The water company workers had announced a strike. Jose said they regularly took holidays, but Nana had heard an official was protesting Bozene's ceremonies for the fetish boy. She knew which neighbors had complained. Jose still thought it might be the anniversary of the company's founding. The speculation continued as the house took on the heavy task of preparing against the drought. Corinthian stood at the courtyard door, heaving buckets that Nana filled. Jose worked in the kitchen, preparing water vessels for Nana to boil. Joining Corinthian, I lugged a bucket from the courtyard and it swayed between my legs, spilling water in the living room. I ran faster and set the bucket down with a splash, next to the others against the wall: blue, brown, red. From the living room I heard a shout. Corinthian had slipped and fallen. "What is your problem?" Nana glared.

I was banished to my room. Corinthian and Nana continued their merry-go-round until all the buckets were filled. The house regained its quiet. At some point during the night the water system malfunctioned. The septic tank regurgitated; the toilet overflowed with a sonorous gurgle and a sucking noise, like the sound an elephant might make at a water hole. Thinking it could be trouble I appeared in the corridor holding a curtain rod. A thick green mass covered the floor. Bébé Rhéma's cries reverberated through the house. Jose and Nana had opened their door, wearing loose nightgowns. Nana looked at me as though I were responsible; she had always believed my toilet paper would clog up their tank, though Jose said it would not happen. Her expression was of distress. "I will fix it in the morning," Jose said, stretching his arms out and yawning. "Nana, why don't you clean this mess." Lying in my room, I wrapped a wet towel around my nose to repel the stink, and I listened to Nana's washcloth slosh.

The street suffered as well. The morning showed how the gutters had stagnated along the alleys and roads. There was no water to keep them running. The sewage turned frothy like detergent, fermenting and emanating a stink that was usually carried down the street, continually replaced by newer and fresher sewage, but now the rot stayed and grew. In spite of this people sat outside. It was worse in the houses, in the humidity and heat. I had not brushed or showered that morning. The bathroom still reeked; there hadn't been enough spare water to remove the grime, which had dried in black smears on the cistern and the floor. The Grand Hotel was the only place I knew that offered free water to the public—perhaps I could use the swimming pool. I put on some aftershave and a fresh shirt, but the ride was miserably hot and my clothes stuck to me in the most uncomfortable places.

I felt awkward at the hotel. I ambled about, not sure if I should try to sneak into the pool, worried about being caught. I sought refuge in the restaurant, but the waitresses became aggressive, trying to sell me a drink. The lobby sofas were occupied by black men in tapering pants and tight shirts—Africans from Europe. A breeze blew outside. I passed the sliding doors and came to the parking lot. Dust moved over the street in slow swirls. Suddenly the wind picked up. The air turned against the trees, shaking the branches. A column of air thrust down the main road, sweeping up twigs, papers and leaves, and violently scattering them. I covered my eyes under my arm and felt the cool sand whip my body. The air made a piercing noise. And as suddenly as it had risen the wind slowed to a breeze. Silence returned to the street. I moved inside the hotel and in the bathroom blew the dust out

of my nose. A man in swimming shorts pushed open the bathroom door. I splashed my face with plain water; it cleaned, but
unsatisfactorily, and I felt particles in my nose and ears. A flush
sounded from the man's cubicle, and while he dried his hands
the bathroom attendant sprayed his cubicle with freshener.

The longer I stayed at the hotel the more anxious I grew. The
staff were beginning to recognize me, to look at me strangely.
I drifted about the corridors, and the feeling came up, first
slowly, then like a spasm. A sense of internal desertion, irrational, almost humiliating. I could not stand to be alone, and I
could not bear to be around people. I walked to the back of the
hotel, to an empty spot, and through a gap in the wall I watched
a young man shampoo his head. He covered his scalp with a
chalky paste and picked at it with a blade. I watched him for a
long time, observing the curt movements of his hand, and the
chips of hair that fell away.

Two days before I had texted Natalie. I don't remember what I
had written: I had woken thinking of her, as if she had appeared
in a dream. Her presence had felt unnatural. It was the first time
I had thought of her since the day after the party. And all morning I waited for her reply, imagining how I would feel. What
would I suggest? I had no reason to be nervous. Noon came and
went. By night I had given it up. And I thought about it only in
moments—to wonder if I had said something wrong. But now in
the garden of the Grand Hotel I looked at my phone and found,
the anxiety rising, that some hours ago she had written.

The message, though long, was emotionless. Her hotel was
nearby, not grand but decent. She had to travel early the next
morning, so she could not be late to sleep, but if I would like to
relax in the few hours that remained of the day she could afford
the time. It was an offer of a quiet evening; it was what I needed.
The worry dissipated from my body; I felt relieved; I no longer
needed to inquire when she had received my message, or why I

had not merited a reply sooner. The questions, now harmless, fell away. The day so far had been searing, a stretch of disappointments. I arrived at her hotel feeling it had been saved.

I had always felt alien watching pools at night—they had an eerie glow and reminded me of hotel drownings. This one was shaped like a bean, lined with bathroom tiles and empty of people. Between the tiles the cement was uneven, as though smeared with a finger and left to dry in smudges. The water had a tinge of green. The short walk to the hotel had brought me to a sweat, and I was startled by the chill when I jumped off the pool's cement edge and plunged into the water—my head submerged in the coolness—making a storm of bubbles that rose in a brilliant stream. The water felt warm in waves, the air cold against my skin. The world acquired color again: green geckos sitting like apostrophes on the wall, the red-tiled roof, Natalie's yellow towel. She waved. I paddled with my legs and bounced. I turned on my back and floated, looking at the gray sky spread as one domed panel.

The sky was now dark, and the lights in the pool gave the water, disturbed by the wind, a vibrating fluorescence. Natalie moaned, teeth shivering: "I've missed the sun." Her sunglasses were large, like the eyes of a fly. She sipped a cocktail. The crisis of that afternoon had passed, and I was silent out of a kind of embarrassment. I was distracted. A group of muscular men and women jumped into the hazy water. They made thunderous splashes; the laughter rose. The men stepped out and dived on their chests. They somersaulted into the pool, screaming in Lingala. "It is their trauma," Natalie said. Her words sounded less enigmatic in French.

"These people?"

The men had flirted with her the week before. "They made a fortune during the war," she said, "buying diamonds from the rebels and selling in Antwerp. Then they lost their families to the violence. Every week they come here." We watched. But our conversation was cut short when almost simultaneously with the splashing of the Congolese thick drops began to dot the ground. The rain made circular ripples in the pool. Light was blotted out. We ran in the gloom into a corridor. The shower grew heavy, then settled as a steady fall. A wind picked up. Natalie wrapped her towel closer. "How will you go home in this?" Dripping, we climbed the stairs of the hotel, leaving a trail of puddles that led to her door.

She pushed me into the room. "The mosquitoes will come in."

The room had a square window. She wanted to show me the view. The window was not large, so we had to stand together. We watched water accumulate in the city. Trees shook in the torrent. Streetlights flickered and burned out. She pulled the curtains together. "It doesn't look like it will stop tonight." A few minutes later I heard water flow into her sonorous tub. I lay on the couch and closed my eyes, listening to the rain, the hush of the tap, the hum of her hair dryer. In a corner of the wall, near the floor, was a cluster of insects. And when Natalie emerged from the shower, head wrapped in cloth, she handed me a towel, as though it were now my turn to clean myself.

The bathroom was poorly planned, making it seem smaller than it really was. The door was cut out at the bottom corner so it would not hit the tub as it opened. Everywhere was pitch-black tile, even on the walls. The tub had a sunflower shower that drooped over my head, as if to bless me. My bare feet gripped scabbed crust. And I soaped under the running water. The tub filled with gray foam, the oily mix whirling as a deep funnel over the drain.

Entering the room again I felt fresh. "It's nice to have *hot* water."

"Don't remind me," she said. "I'm going to be in the east from tomorrow, and I don't know what the hotels will be like." So she was leaving—and she was going to the war. I felt jealousy, and some resentment. I wanted to leave Kinshasa, even if I could not go with her.

She lay under the sheets, holding a book. A place, where the covers were flat and taut, had been left for me. I saw the tip of her nightgown. I got in. An old air conditioner rumbled over our heads, dripping water from a corner. There was a sense of her bodily warmth. I felt her move, and my legs stiffened. I looked at the room's wallpaper, shriveled, as though too much glue had been applied underneath. Natalie's voice suddenly rang in my ear. "Why did you choose Congo?"

I paused. "My bank cashier was Congolese. I'm living with her brother-in-law."

"And you just came?"

"One-way ticket."

My fingers tingled and shifted an inch toward the bed middle. And I was transported to those initial passions, in America. It seemed a long time ago when I was in Steve Brill's office. I didn't know the man; I had found him in my university's register of alumni. He was a journalist-millionaire in Manhattan, and he was late. "I'm so sorry," his secretary said. "Something urgent just came up. I know you've traveled a long way." In the waiting room I flipped through a nature encyclopedia. The secretary returned. "I read your correspondence to Mr. Brill," she said. "And I thought you should have this." She held out some pages.

Mr. Brill finally received me. He was kind. He gave me some tips on journalism. The elevator slowly took me to the ground floor of his skyscraper office.

On the train home I looked at the secretary's pages. It was a copy of a magazine interview with a Polish journalist who had traveled extensively in Africa. This was in the 1960s, when Africa was breaking free from the colonial powers. It was a torrid time on the continent. The journalist, whose name was Ryszard Kapuściński, went from "revolution to coup d'état, from one war to another"; he witnessed "real history," as he called it, "history in the making." But on his travels something surprised him: he never saw a writer. "Where were they? Such important events, and not a single writer anywhere?"

When Kapuściński returned to Europe, he said, he found the writers. They were in their homes, writing stories about "the boy, the girl, the laughing, the intimacy, the marriage."

It was early spring in the United States, and everything was beginning to come out of the cold. I remember opening the heavy and tall library doors to a scene of boys and girls scattered across the manicured lawn. Hair flowed like waterfalls over books. Everywhere there was skin, stretches of shimmering skin, and hushed conversations about forbidden adventures. I had been reading the Pole's descriptions of the African wars. I closed my eyes; I remember how red the sun made the backs of my eyelids. I watched the translucent shapes meander across my vision, floating, rising; ultimately drifting. Natalie made a noise. I said, "Are you asleep?" She breathed, stirring her lips. The rain continued at uniform rhythm, falling at an angle. I closed my eyes and felt the softness of the cotton, the coolness of the air.

"You know what," I said. "I never thanked that secretary."

11

I had chosen Bobby over Keith. I wanted to go to the east, to the war, but I could not afford it. Bobby's proposal to travel upriver by barge had also begun to excite me. We would go somewhere that few people ever traveled to. And the story we were chasing was fantastic.

I had already started to prepare for the journey, and was under no illusion about its ease: it would be lengthy—travelling cheaply meant traveling slowly—and physically demanding. I expected to be unreachable for nearly the whole time. Planning was essential. I conducted further research on Bobby's land. Unsurprisingly, there were indeed reports of mineral riches in that area, none of them officially exploited. In the 1990s a French company had made investigations around Lake Tumba. The lake was known for being deep red, and it was conjectured that the lake obtained its color from leaky seams of petroleum. The outbreak of war in Congo ended that effort; apparently, the French equipment now rusted in the forest—perhaps they had intended to return. Roads in the region were few; the river was the main mode of transport. Équateur was only a few hundred miles from the capital but it seemed infinitely more remote. The government exerted little control on the territory. Much of it was virgin jungle overrun by nomadic tribes and animals. Large areas had never been seen by an outsider. But new visitors had recently arrived, sanctioned by the Kyoto Protocol. The developed world had invested millions of dollars to preserve Congo's forest—thus buying, under the treaty's conditions, the right for their factories to pollute in the West. Conservationists subsequently moved into the forest, cordoning off large areas and evicting tribes. With hunting deemed illegal, poachers multiplied. The police were brought in; rangers were armed. Trespassers were presumed to be hunters, sometimes shot. Numerous groups were reportedly masquerading as conservationists, secretly hiding illegal trades. In the middle of Congo, Équateur seemed like the sovereign territory of another country.

Among my sources only Mossi expressed hesitation—but he was uncharacteristically vague. I invited him for a drink to talk about it. He called me to his house. This was also unusual, not only because we usually met at a bar but also because the address he gave was in a quarter behind ours. I had been sure that Mossi lived at the foot of Mont Ngaliema, near the ministerial neighborhood. But even then I suspected nothing—perhaps he had moved.

The house was run-down and surrounded by pools of mud. Its yard accommodated at least three families. A child without a shirt played in a shed outside. Mossi's room was sparse: a low mattress, an outdated telephone, a large computer. The walls were covered in green-black moss. The mattress had craters where it was worn out. An unwashed bowl lay in one corner. Mossi sat, still, against a wall. The floor was cold. He had only a thin rug. "Come now," he said, "an old man needs your help."

He kept his hands between his legs. The exuberance was gone; his eyes contained sadness. He had not received a payment in three months, he said. But it was only a matter of time. The bank would call any day now. I remembered the grandeur with which he had introduced himself, and though I felt pity, I also felt let down. I didn't want to see this.

After this whenever we met it would feel odd: we would still get drinks at our bar in Victoire. "You're a big man now," he would say, laughing. But I always felt he also meant it as a taunt.

The gloom from that episode tainted the rest of the journey's preparations, which were done in an increasing hurry: supplies needed to be purchased, authorizations had to be obtained and we had to make final inspections before our departure. And Bobby had some good news: the barge we had been waiting for had finally anchored at port.

He had taken charge of the planning. In his office we looked over a piece of paper that he had typed up, with "ORDRE de MISSION" at the top and a short paragraph of explanation. It said we would be inspecting his land, as per the deed number and the rights of the landowner in such and such law. The rest of the writing was obscured by stamps and approvals: from the Ministry of Migration, the Federal Investigation Authority, the Transport Ministry, the Ministry of Mines, the Department of Food and Water, the Ministry of Industry, the Ministry of Environment, the Land Authority, the Department of Fish and Agriculture, the provincial government of Kinshasa, the provincial government of Équateur, the Ministry of Planning—but most important were the triangular stamps of the Ministry of Defense and the Security Bureau, with the officers' signatures scrawled over the page. Our names were clearly marked. I was denoted as Bobby's business partner. "It is good we are both Indian, they ask less questions," he said, rolling out a map of the area.

His office was barely lit by the sun and we used a tube-light table lamp to illuminate the map—a detailed copy about fifty years old, made by the Belgians. Most roads had since closed, and most cities had diminished—except Kinshasa, which had extended farther up the river, where the water was striped with long islands of sand. The river climbed northeast, narrowing and surrounded by bush; it turned into Lake Tumba, and a little higher, almost exactly on the line of the equator, afforded a view of Mbandaka, a colonial city at the mouth of the river Ruki on which the jungle encroached. Bobby's land was in the vicinity, some distance to the southeast. "All of this is under the conservationists," he said. "And there we have the mine."

I worried Bobby's hatchback would break down as we weighed it with provisions. The old Peugeot was a rattling mass. Its seats were not original and had been welded on, and the gearshift was missing: Bobby shifted gears delicately, using a metal tube the size of half a pencil. Behind the backseats we filled the car with bags: tins of sardines, rusks, canned vegetables, La Vache Qui Rit. Bobby added some dried fruits he had gotten in Bombay; I brought water purification capsules and a CamelBak water bottle. We waited impatiently at the cash counters of expatriate supermarkets, watching people buy chicken sandwiches. The essentials we bought at an Indian shop that guaranteed, on an outside banner, the best prices in the *ville*. When I told Bobby another place sold bottled water for less, he said, "Those Congolese, always undercutting prices. And then they complain that they have to live like filthy creatures."

I wanted to register at the Indian embassy, so at the end of a day of shopping Bobby steered the loaded car onto the grounds, slowly passing between the gates, the rigid suspension making the car rise and fall over the rocks. The flag from Independence Day fluttered on the pole. The guard shut the gate and returned to his spot under a palm tree. The building was silent. An African had been left in charge. He used the consul's office, a wide room with a view of the garden. "You are new here?" he said, clearing his throat as if he had just woken. The register was old, tattered and covered in plastic. He wrote the date. I listed my details while he made copies of my passport and visa; he signed my entry as an official witness. I asked if there was a number I could call should I have any trouble. He said the embassy was closed and no longer full-service.

"Is there any benefit to registering then?" I said.

"The embassy can confirm you as a missing person. Sometimes families need documents proving a death, which we can provide."

Bobby became my protector as well as co-conspirator and guide, and when the preparations were sufficiently under way to know they would soon be completed we drove to the port to purchase tickets. The harbor bustled with people. A barge had arrived from upriver; its goods were being unloaded. The quay was a slab of concrete that suddenly fell away, with no fence or protection. And across the water, in the distance, were towers and wide buildings: the city of Brazzaville. In another Congo, and a quieter world.

Men plied our quay talking loudly and like ants they ran up and down a loose plank of wood leading to the barge. They rubbed shoulders and pushed past one another, as if in a race, and the boxes on their heads seemed in a perpetual state of falling. Meanwhile our barge was being loaded: its long platform was being piled with wooden boxes. I walked the vessel's length. The sheet metal was beaten like the surface of a golf ball. Muddy water lapped against its sides. Rivets had rusted in their cavities. But the barge floated, looking peaceful. "There are better," Bobby said, but boats were irregular, and as I had learned with food at Jose and Nana's, it was generally advisable to seize opportunities as they came. The barge was simple, without rooms for the passengers. A cage of iron rods stood at one end, with a cabin making a shelter over the captain's quarters and the steering room, and a few huts in a cluster. A hole in the platform led to the hull, where more cargo—netted sacks carrying sheet metal and building materials and bicycles—was carried by the workers. The port once used to assist the loaders with cranes and motors. These now sat silently on the edge of the port. A giant hook hung above us in brown and green iron. I stepped aside.

We entered the port's one-story office complex. It smelled of whitewash and rice. The rooms were used as a depot for confiscated items, the barge captain said, from merchants who owed taxes or who had been caught shipping contraband. The Congolese Office for Control monitored the port. And new on its list was chicken—it was testing samples for bird flu. The captain smoked a pipe through broken red teeth. He wore old whites and his pants were an inch too short. He sat in a tall office chair wearing a pair of binoculars around his neck.

"We are leaving in two days then?" Bobby asked.

The captain chewed on his pipe. "Depends on when we finish loading. It could take a week."

"Oh no," said Bobby, leaning over the captain's desk. "In a week your barge will be too heavy to cross the sandbars. Don't give me this nonsense. In two days we leave." The captain huffed. Smoke rose from his pipe in black streams. And he absentmindedly started to play with a glass paperweight in the shape of a hippo.

With so little time until the departure the excitement rapidly built. And I felt a sort of release from the house and the city. In town I found a missionary library of old books and spent a full afternoon studying maps. I no longer skimmed over the names of obscure towns: I looked these up in the encyclopedia, imagining the colonial boats docking at these places, bringing gifts and threats of war. The library had detailed nineteenth-century reports in geography journals, of the conferences that carved up Africa between European states, and of King Leopold's lucrative and genocidal rubber trade. I came home with notes tucked under my arm and visions of a primitive landscape. I felt a precipitous thrill while packing my bags. And I finally informed Nana of my departure, giving her a tin of milk powder bought at the Indian shop, saying it should last until my return.

The house was changing as well: I first noticed it in the food. Every evening Nana pounded chili, adding extra spice to shield us from the soporific heat. She banged at the pestle, looking worn and unhappy. Bébé Rhéma's nose was still running— the clinic visits had not completed the cure. Among the other changes, Corinthian had taken over the running of the boutique business, but he was faring no better. The clients still promised to pay their debts as soon as they "touched some money." And Jose had briefly stopped watching the news, preferring wrestling, which the Congolese called *catch*. He would sit, engrossed, intently watching Texas beat Spiderman; he would lean forward and sideways with the men on-screen. He never appeared as unemployed as in those moments. One day I said, "You know it's fake."

He looked taken aback. "*Fake?* This is a serious sport."

Texas slammed Spiderman. "Didn't you see? Texas didn't actually hit him. It's made-up."

He grunted. "If you're so smart, do you know who's going to win then?"

I sat a few moments to watch with him. We talked about the news: Jose agreed there had been nothing worthwhile of late. After the conference the reports had slowed to a trickle. Even Richard Bentley's byline had disappeared from the papers. I had heard he was in England, on holiday. I wondered who might be living at his place, enjoying his five-star bed and shower; then, in my room, I noticed the smell. It first came as the briefest of whiffs. Suddenly it was strong. But the corridor had only its usual dampness—the smell of the mold inside the walls. The rug felt clean. Under the bed I found feathery dirt. I ruffled Jose's old books, raising the dust. It was too dark to see outside, but the knocks from Nana's pestle were steady.

"What is it?" she called back.

She arrived with her hands dripping and a pepper seed on her cheek. "A smell? It must be your clothes." She looked unfazed, not moving, and straight at me; I detected a touch of sadness in her expression; I thought perhaps she had again fought with Jose. The smell was steady now. It grew faint when I moved to the corners of the room. The source seemed near the wardrobe. I followed the trail, sniffing at the air, higher and higher and climbing the bookshelf's metal frame. Leaning precariously, I pulled at an old bedcover bundled on the wardrobe's top—a hole had been carved through its middle. Shreds of cotton puffed up and settled, revealing a decomposing rat with gelatinous worms running through its body. The fur had been eaten.

12

I received a message from Goldman Sachs. It came from New York, from a mathematician I had interviewed with several months before leaving for Congo. The markets were doing well, he said. The bank still wanted to hire. I had forgotten about this job. It reminded me of some of the other messages I had received from America—mostly from friends—that I had skimmed over, filed away and forgotten. My curiosity now piqued, I looked them up; and I began to read with care—noting the dates, and how they had been written, and if I had written before, what I had said. Some were simple keep-in-touch exercises, carrying the tone of Christmas wishes. A friend had been in Bangkok, and seen the bar girls do tricks with their vaginas; someone had sent a mass e-mail from St. Tropez. But most messages were more serious. Sam had gotten a new job at a trading firm. James was moving to Chicago to be closer to his girlfriend. Sarah had bought an apartment at an exceptionally low interest rate. People were taking professional exams, making investments, saving for the future, falling in love. It was the eve of my departure. Was I nervous? Of course. But I imagined the story I would find in Équateur.

"What's that?" Stella asked, looking at my screen.

"Some job."

"In New York? Do you think they would take me?"

I grimaced.

"Today you leave me double the usual," he said, tapping the table with his fingers.

A terrible stink followed me out of the house. I was glad to leave. Before the sun had risen I made my way down Victoire with a large bag on my back, looking like a camel burdened by its hump. I took a last look at Victoire, and felt there was nothing I would miss: not my room in the house or the street with its moving crowd; I would not miss those broken pavements with protruding iron rods. If it hadn't been for that robbery, I thought, I would have long ago been gone. But I felt sad for the family. I told Nana before leaving that as soon as I earned something I would make a wire transfer to the family. If I was successful on my trip, I said to her, we would no longer have to worry about money.

I also spared a thought for Mossi, though I found it difficult to dwell on him. The moment in his room still seemed too close. I remembered his helpless gestures, the pity he had evoked.

As I waited for the taxi Anderson sauntered up, arms swinging. "Monsieur Journaliste, you're leaving? Without telling us?" A Renault stopped at the curb. "Too bad," Anderson said, smiling. "We will miss you at the riots." He opened the sedan's door and showed me to my seat, as a valet might. It felt odd that he was the only person who came to see me off; he touched my shoulder, and I was moved by the gesture. He slammed the door, saluting me. "Safe journey." The driver scolded Anderson for not being gentle with the car, and then asked me to pay double price. "Your bag is using an extra seat."

"Normally we would put the bag on top."

"But there is no top."

I can see. "Why should I pay extra because you're missing a top? Why don't you have a top, *chauffeur*?"

The Maghrebis had burned the hood in Paris. Thankfully too, the driver added cheerfully, for he had gotten the car at half price. Containers full of these burned vehicles were coming to Congo from France, the driver said, and there was big demand. It felt a bit like riding in a convertible.

The port was busy. It was a day of departure, and moving was always a busy affair—the various and superfluous levels of bureaucracy were present: to check papers, apply stamps, extort money. Bobby had been keeping a watch on the loading of the barge and he called out just as it was being finished. I bought a piece of coconut from a vendor carrying a plate over her head. I sucked at the white flesh. At the gates a group of men were slumped in wheelchairs. As soon as they saw passengers arrive they started to propel themselves forward, whipping the wheels with powerful arms. Handicaps with legs pushed the others, running. The band moved in a howl, talking quickly to each other. The attendant at the gate took his time to inspect my ticket but wheeled the metal door open in time. The handicaps eyed me from the road; some of them laughed and they talked with the attendant in a friendly manner. To either side stalls sold CDs, travel adapters, umbrellas for the rainy season, and colored ton tiles and tobacco from Brazzaville. I was later informed that the handicaps monopolized imports from and exports to our neighbor city; by a colonial law they still paid discounted rates on the boats, and the city both loathed them and relied on their service.

Our departure was surprisingly quick. The crew hauled in the ropes, twisting them around the post. The barge floated freely. At the port, a plastic wind vane in the shape of a bird circled its mast rapidly. People stood under the silent cranes and hooks, watching us with concern, holding checkered handkerchiefs, swatting away the flies and mosquitoes. I didn't have anyone to wave to. I saw the building on the Boulevard where I had tried to interview a minister; it stood tall among the row of crumbling high rises. At that moment, leaning beside Bobby at a railing on the rear end of the barge, my back toward our direction of motion, I felt an attachment to the city; and I began to fear our unknown passage. The water swiftly slipped beneath me, dark and yielding. Small waves rose and chuckled. Bobby wiped his face, stroking his cheeks. The engine choked and came alive with a firm rumble. The captain blew his whistle, signaling the early departure. Kinshasa drew distance. The barge slowly shifted, like a mass of land separating from the earth.

PART II

HALF EMERGENCES

13

A sequence of wooden kiosks had been erected on the barge. Most were stuffed with supplies. A few were empty. The kiosks were near the center of the deck, where in a long pile running the barge's length, goods were covered in thick nets. Around this pile were groups of people: passengers tending to their affairs. Some had come with food, others with rings of rope that tied together plastic canisters, called *bidons*. Boxes of imported whiskey were guarded by vigilant agents wearing distribution company logos on their shirts. The goods traveled to be exchanged for rural produce: palm oil, roots, meat, banana wine and beer. A narrow corridor on the deck was not covered by cargo, and on this stretch of planks we walked. The wood was painted white and led at the back to lavatories and quarters for the crew: huts that seemed little larger than pig cages. Sacks that crew members stepped over littered the doorways, and toothbrushes in metal cups lined windowsills. Between the cabins were strung clotheslines from which identical overalls, torn in the same places—along the arms, over the chest, at the groin—flapped like pennants, dripping water in a pool that grew sideways with the gentle sway of the barge. Bobby and I were among the more privileged travelers: our quarters lay in a wooden kiosk. Its splintered planks gave us a roof but on the sides it was open to the world, and at night, the dark. Under this Bobby had set up our tent.

The barge's pipes were dry. Carrying my toothbrush I scoured the boat, trying the taps at the stern, near the crew quarters and even in the captain's office. But they only squeaked. Eventually I moved to a side, where the barge sloped slightly, and I scooped from the river with a mug. The water was translucent; twigs and winged insects floated. Everything in the water looked old. Brushing my teeth, I stood at the barge's rear end, watching the river, as a remarkable scene unfolded over the water and along its edge.

We were quite far from the city already, and the houses onshore had thinned, giving way to green and brown bamboo and patches of red earth. Along the water villagers soaped their bodies and scrubbed clothes. The trees moved by slowly. And from ahead of the barge rows of pirogues set off with heavy loads and strong-armed rowers pushing against the riverbank with oars. The long, black pirogues were carried downriver and alongside our vessel; and the men frantically rowed, now coming at us from all sides, from the far horizon of the river and along its length, shooting out of the jungle like arrows. The barge was soon surrounded and the crew gathered at the bow, watching anxiously. All at once the rowers flung thick black ropes, like snakes, from their pirogues. A bell was rung fiercely near the captain's quarters and the crew members poured out of their rooms. Ropes flew through the air in high arcs and lashed at the barge, wriggling on the deck, slipping away, falling into the water; they were flung again with more fury. The crewmen thrust forward, pulling the ropes with venous arms; they screamed at the rowers. The pirogues fought the flow of the river, approaching and falling away. Our motor's pitch heightened. The canoes were laden with heaps; they bobbed and rolled in the river, threatening to capsize in the swirling currents. The men heaved their oars and restored balance, rowing faster and more desperately until the pirogues drew closer, rose on a wave and dipped, and moved within our wake. Here the river was calmer. The crew tied the ropes to posts and the pirogues flowed steadily, without effort. The rowers drew their oars, dripping, out of the water; they breathed heavily. And by evening we tugged a collection of crafts like balloons wanting to drift away on the river.

At once the pirogues unloaded. And there was even less space. In the morning Bobby and I climbed out of the tent and found our faces against bags of dried fish. It had been a night of noise and movement. The paths on the deck had narrowed. We squeezed between the crates and reached the rear end of the barge, the designated bathroom area, where we pissed off the edge. It didn't feel awkward, or public—the barge was almost an exclusively male environment, and this permitted a level of both immodesty and squalor.

The pirogues were commercial vessels from the villages; and I realized that the scene I had witnessed was the attaching of the city with the jungle. The two quickly integrated. Men walked to and from the pirogues, over the ropes, carrying bottles, nets and livestock. They became for us a source of fresh food, and they relieved the traders of their city stocks. Negotiations sometimes lasted until the morning.

Most pirogues concluded their commerce and left by afternoon. I saw them detach from the barge and drift downriver toward their settlements. In the evening the traders, having few customers left, relaxed by their stalls to reggae and rumba. A pair of drums was used intermittently. The night ambience on the barge was of charcoal-stove fires and radio sets. What beer was available was shared, and when I was feeling social I would buy a couple of bottles, and drink a half.

There was no repose on the barge. Traders lay about the deck, limbs spread over their wares—one had to navigate them. A few stood out, attracting crowds. One sold coiled springs, toys that slunk from hand to hand. A man in a fishnet vest, for a little money, imitated animal sounds—hoopoes, chimps, forest buffalo.

The traders, I noticed, were poor city men. It showed in the way they ate cassava dough from their palms; their shirts were soiled from wiping their mouths and faces; their slippers were broken. They drank from filthy mugs. The pirogue men, although poorer, appeared less neglected, less outcast. So, it seemed that, like on sixteenth-century ships with their crews of slaves and prisoners, Kinshasa had sent on our barge its lowest elements as emissaries to the provinces.

The barge advanced northward, making a breeze against the rolling humidity. And soon even villages were rare: I was startled at how quickly we had left all signs of human development. Passing us was a constant level of jungle, without variation in the kind of tree—buttressed, stout, covered in woody creepers—or in the deep shade of green, the cauliflower-like crowns. The sound of the barge was a steady drone. All this created a distinct tension.

And it was Bobby who, briskly humming the tune to *Kuch kuch hota hai*, addressed this unease.

Flies covered the crates in clusters, unnaturally still, and rising as a slow cloud; fellow passengers, seeking shelter from the sun behind the cargo, were taken by surprise, exposed as Bobby moved the crates; their hands claimed the bags he shifted. But Bobby made new stacks with the cargo and the flies returned, followed by the shade-seeking crouching men. Room was made around one crate. Two others became chairs. And to pass the time on the slow-moving barge Bobby suggested we play checkers. He had brought a board and counters.

We took our seats. Bobby was clearly in form: from the start his counters flew across the red and black squares. But it had been years since I had played. I took long pauses. Bobby picked impatiently at the splinters on the crate. "You're not in the game of the century, man. Don't worry so much about losing."

By the second or third day word had spread and people gathered around us to watch. *Dames* had been one of Mobutu's favorite games, Bobby told me. The market invaded our cramped space: men smoked over us; monkeys hung from wooden crucifixes; blocks of hippo fat and meat lay on straw mats, heated by the sun, attracting insects. Chickens ran loose, flustered by sniffing pigs, flapping their wings above their heads and clambering, half flying, over men's feet. Cages were pushed out of the way; the pigs panicked, shoving their noses at the ground and chasing the fowl for the length of their leashes. But Bobby and I played on, immersed, and this was how we spent the time until one morning when we heard a shot.

There was the jolt, and the fright, but the emotions seemed somehow unsurprising—one couldn't help but feel that we had been waiting for something to happen; that there could not have been more eventless days. The strain had begun to feel unnatural, too full.

A ragged soldier was at fault. His uniform was typical, scavenged from enemies: the shirt came from Kabila's guard, his hat from an invading Angolan army and his pants, a darker green, belonged to eastern rebels; the pants were folded up at the bottom, revealing a hairless shin. I had seen him prancing about the deck in rubber flip-flops, inseparable from his Kalashnikov—tied to his arm with rope so no one could steal it. For the entire previous day he had walked about the deck like this, swinging his arm, the weapon unusable and its bayonet oscillating dangerously. This was the gun that had been fired.

In the clearing where the crowd had separated we saw him at the barge edge. Beside him was the captain—still in short white pants, and looking through binoculars. The barge had drifted relatively close to the land, and the captain seemed to point at the monkeys clambering over the branches. But the soldier shot uselessly. The fire from his Kalashnikov raised spikes of dirt on the riverbank, and the branches showed no movement. The animals were gone. The captain cursed openly. The soldier puckered his lips and made an obscene sucking noise.

Calm returned to the deck, but in a heightened way. The barge had been unsettled and made alert by the shooting. The soldier stayed on the deck with his gun. And people withdrew: some slunk into the hull; a few crawled along the ropes to the pirogues. Bobby carefully moved our board to the kiosk, where it was quieter, and we continued where we had broken off: with my counters frenziedly fleeing. He joked about how fast I was running, but his voice had hardened, and he looked over his shoulder. The stress seemed to find expression in his movements. The forest was unbroken, a stretch of drifting green. Soon my pieces were cornered. I was three strokes from annihilation when I played a lively combination, breaking a portion of his defense and stalling his conquest. "You're just delaying the end," he said.

"I'm playing to win."

Bobby got up from his seat, as if taken by an urge. He told me to wait and made for the back of the barge. The evening was coming to a close. The sun hung over the water, which glistened red and gold. Migratory birds skimmed the river surface, on their last legs before nightfall. Monkeys screeched across the water, their calls echoing. I could have waited half an hour; it felt too long.

Then, over the crates, I saw Bobby with the captain. They were sharing a smoke. I was about to call out when Bobby looked over and waved, as though nothing had happened. At first I was perplexed. Then I felt cheated. I tipped over one end of the board. The act was involuntary—I was surprised that I had done it; but already on this journey I had begun to feel outside myself. In this strange landscape, with its strange people, the monotony had begun to make me feel detached, distant, and it was as though by that act I had for a moment removed years of manners and teaching, obeying a destructive instinct. It somehow satisfied me to see the counters scattered over the deck.

The AP informed me that I was missing a number of stories in Kinshasa. The government had begun to make election announcements. Bentley had returned to Kinshasa and was reporting in a rush. The editors called to ask where I was— though they had known about my expedition. The line was crackly. They were annoyed. They asked how long I intended to travel. I realized that I had also missed the earnings from those reports. I thought of the family in Kinshasa. And I felt a creeping doubt—if I had not erred by coming to the jungle. The pressure on me grew—the fear of coming out of this empty-handed.

Bobby became unfriendly to me. I would see him walk through the market, alone, to buy grilled fish. He carried them on hooks and ate in the tent, from the newspaper. In the evenings he would lean over the railings looking over the water, and the foam. When we met it was awkward, and I felt embarrassed—I feared he would bring up the game, though I felt it was he who should apologize for his rude behavior. As the days passed it became clear that neither he nor I would express regret. An impasse formed between us. And during this time the fever on the barge grew: the market, its goods and livestock and kiosks. As more and more city produce was exchanged for animals, the squawks and noises woke me even earlier in the morning. I felt stressed, on edge—and this stress was irreconcilable with the heat, which wanted to draw one into a stupor.

Looking out on the river, often alert, as if searching for something, I one day became conscious of the disappearance of the beaches. The river was walled by jungle. And watching this green continuum, I felt lonely. It was not from a lack of company. I was constantly meeting people in Congo—and also leaving them behind. I came to new people, negotiated with them. I tried to move forward. But there was no continuity in this.

I thought of Mossi. His support had been strange. Yet it had seemed to come from genuine concern and good-heartedness. Despite his precarious condition he had made himself my mentor. I felt I could not return what he had given me—the encouragement and confidence when I needed it most. And now I was moving on. The constant movement was grinding, fatiguing.

The solitude swelled within me, creating a sense of abandonment and also an aggression. I somehow felt joined with my surroundings. I feared meeting one of the annoying poor men on the barge. I thought the anger and violence might come out if I were provoked.

One of Mobutu's many palaces appeared on the riverbank. Set on a mud cliff, it was a decrepit colonial-style construction: with pillars, a triangular roof, whitewash, paved verandas. The dictator's palaces were legendary. Jose had told me that they were walled with jade, that the doorknobs were jeweled, and that he decorated them with Picassos and Fabergé eggs: unthinkingly spending wealth that belonged to the people.

Though Mobutu had died nearly a decade earlier, one still felt his influence everywhere. Particularly here, in the jungle—an ancient part of Congo, and of the world. People here were remote, disconnected. The coming elections were meaningless; everyone of this area would vote for Mobutu's clan. I was coming into an old place, with deep-rooted mentalities from Mobutu's thirty-two-year rule of Congo. By the end he had made himself the Founding Father (le Père Fondateur), the Builder (le Bâtisseur), the Marshal of Zaïre (le Maréchal du Zaïre), and a demigod who in videos materialized in the sky, among the clouds.

But the man of these grand titles and visions had simple origins. Joseph Désiré Mobutu was raised by a single mother. Unlike many African dictators he was not the son of a chief or notable. He had been a troublesome child. He joined the army at a low rank. Footage from his years as a journalist shows him to be a scrawny young man, uncertain and deferential in the presence of Belgians.

This was the same man who took it upon himself to restore—even create, for Congo hadn't existed until the colonials—a national identity. Like most colonial nations the newly independent Congo was stuck in imitations: of European materialism, tastes, culture. The country as a whole aspired to be *évolué*. But Mobutu revolted against such dependency: with increasing force he transformed Congo, to the extent that over the years it became difficult to distinguish his willful design from whim and neurosis.

Mobutu's delusion was to create a certain "authenticity." He changed Congo's name to the older Zaire. The river and the currency were now also Zaire. He banned European dress. The official costume was now a half-sleeve suit called the *abacost*. He banned Christian names, even his own, Joseph Désiré. Henceforth the president was to be known as Mobutu Sese Seko Kuku Ngbendu wa za Banga· the all-powerful warrior who, because of his endurance and inflexible will to win, will go from conquest to conquest leaving fire in his wake.

Gradually everything became "Africanized"—or Mobutized: all authenticity was his creation. He began to address the nation like a tribal chief from Équateur: *"Nye Nye."* (Can you be silent?). The crowd would reply: *"Nye"* (We are silent). *"Na loba"* (Can I speak?). *"Loba"* (Speak). *"Na sopa"* (Can I speak frankly?). *"Sopa"* (Speak frankly). *"Na panza"* (Can I speak openly?). *"Panza"* (Speak openly). The jungle was where Mobutu came from. This was the authenticity he knew. And he sought in many ways, through his policies, to return Congo to this bush. He didn't build roads—ostensibly to protect himself from coups—but it had the effect of isolating the people and restricting their development. The population became stalled in his fabrications. So when Mobutu told the people that they loved him, it seemed that they did.

There could have been something, in all this, of an attempt to rewrite a horrific past, to deal with the ignominy of history. For the province of Équateur, Mobutu's inspiration for a return to African ways, was also the site of the Belgians' worst massacres: of genocidal killings; of hands cut off for harvesting insufficient rubber. This jungle, along the river, was where Conrad placed his Mr. Kurtz.

But Mobutu was no visionary: that was Lumumba, whose achievement had been to unite Congo and claim independence for all its people. He had created a genuine nationalism. And Mobutu's ideas were from their conception absurd. "Authenticity" turned out to be just the replacement of one imitation with another: his name for the country, Zaire, was a Portuguese distortion of *Nzadi*, a tribal word for river. He "invented" the *abacost* after a trip to Mao's China. The chieftain's cane he carried—reputed to be a source of his powers—was said to contain fetish from India, obtained during his visit to Indira Gandhi. Mobutu, having nothing to lean on, became a mimic; he created a disconnected people, and a confused and conflicted Congolese identity—if one could call it that.

The colossal Mobutu creation eventually crumbled. His palaces were pillaged. People turned his airplanes, homes and limousines into camp-like family dwellings. The exotic animals in his garden-zoos—tigers, orangutans, birds of paradise—were eaten. And sympathizers of Mobutu's regime—like Annie, the bank teller in America, and her husband—became exiled. The dictator himself died in Morocco, a guest of the king. The revolution supplanted Mobutu's whimsical order: figures of the new regime replaced his monuments. The country was renamed, along with the currency and the river. There were new *fondateurs* now, new fathers. So history was again destroyed and manipulated; memories were allowed to fade. The palace drifted past; it had begun to be buried by the jungle. A vendor pointed out that Mobutu had once lived there.

I had seen the vendor before. He wore a black T-shirt and dark glasses. I had seen him behind a vendor who had covered his chest with fish, hanging on hooks, open-mouthed, like a coat of mail armor. Now the vendor squatted beside me and I saw his leg was limp; he had to half drag it along the deck. He held out his hand, as if to ask for money. "Go away," I said, waving my hands frantically. But he didn't want charity. "I have gold."

It began the harassment. The vendor would appear before me, by surprise, several times daily, flashing sand-like grains and yellow chips in his palm; he said his wife was in the hospital and he needed the money; he explained it was urgent to extract a bullet from his leg; he showed me a grotesque lump at his knee. I started to turn away from him. And for two full days I successfully avoided the vendor. But one afternoon I was peering into the captain's control room, curious to see if the dials and speedometers on the rusty dashboard worked, and the vendor's reflection appeared in the window. He climbed down a container with his arms, pullling himself closer, and from the inside of his pants he unraveled a crumpled sheet of carbon paper. He spoke with gravity. "I got it, you worried about customs people. Put the gold inside paper and X-rays can't see." And without waiting for my refusal he added, "I give you good price. I know you want better quality. In a big nugget, not small like this. I know, I know. You are my most difficult client!" and he dragged himself away, making a pitiful sight, to find these new objects he thought I wanted. I felt all worked up with an unbearable annoyance, a desire to be left alone. Meanwhile the captain had returned to the helm and he ordered the barge to speed up to avoid inclement weather; apparently the rains had come early. Once again the pitch of the engine rose, and I felt the barge momentarily surge.

It had become more difficult to sleep. The tent had begun to smell of sweat and humidity, and we lay wrapped in our sleeping bags, with Bobby occupying most of the space. He refused to budge, even when I pushed him with my elbow. And his attitude to food was also changing. When I asked for sardines from our provisions he said we should save the cans. I began to suspect he was hoarding the supplies, or had perhaps sold a few. My nose itched from the dust, and I sniveled.

"Stop that," Bobby said.

You stop smelling first, I thought. And then I found myself unable to sleep. I listened to the motor, the insects, the traders moving about at night. Each set of steps that approached I thought would stop at our kiosk. But these inconveniences, and my angst, disappeared once we arrived at port.

It took only half a day for the traders to wrap up their wares. The stalls came crashing down. The noise made me tense. I stood against the railing. Lights on the pier made a glow that reflected in the water, giving it a dark shine. The jetty was not deep enough for the barge to dock so we moored at some distance. And a group of pirogues came from the village. They were loaded by the traders working in groups: sacks and crates passed from hand to hand and down into the boats. Progress was quick. But the moving machine of people suddenly stopped. Agents at the port were calling out to the rowers. That there were sanitary inspectors seemed itself remarkable, and now these inspectors were saying they had instructions for bird flu, and that our barge was teeming with live birds.

The traders decided to cull half the livestock. Chickens were chosen for their plumpness. They tried to fly away, squawking, but were gripped forcefully by their wings. The few roosters were let be, and they watched, standing still, as off the edge of the barge the chickens' throats were slit with old knives and the birds gurgled. Blood fell into the river in a spurt, then in drops. The dead birds were flung into piles, wrapped in fiber by the women and sent away on the pirogues. The birds still alive were marked with paint by their owners, separated by species, and quarantined in mud sheds onshore for seventy-two hours.

The killing dramatically reduced the level of noise—the cages of flurried activity had become piles of dead meat, and the men and women at work did so efficiently and in silence. Passengers were not allowed off the boat until the inspectors gave a signal. So we waited several hours to disembark. Bobby, in a relaxed moment, pointed to a man in a tight suit jacket and horn-rimmed spectacles and said, "He has the Look Baudouin," referring to the Belgian king. Apparently Bobby could tell the man didn't need glasses. It was a fashion that had become popular in the 1980s. And he began, of his own accord, to tell me about his past. He had inherited his shop from a cousin, he said—before that he had worked in Kuwait, and before that on a ship. The idea of running an electrical shop had never appealed to him: it was why he had invested in real estate. "Everybody told me not to do it—Africa this, Africa that. But I got a chance to buy this property and look at what happened. If I get even 20 percent of its worth I'll be rich."

I asked what he planned to do with the money.

"Retire, of course. And pay for my daughter's marriage. She lost her mother, poor thing."

The captain announced we would stay the night in the village-town. It was called Irebu, and its residents were hospitable. Most passengers found places in villagers' homes. Bobby negotiated a mattress for us in a storeroom that belonged to a man who seemed important, because he had a large yard. But when we lay down to sleep I saw the ceiling covered in bats all the way to the eaves and I convinced Bobby to move to the courtyard. Again we were in the tent. It felt unusual that the floor didn't rumble. I wanted to return to the barge. Outside, familiar night insects clicked and chirped, each playing its part in the forest cacophony.

In the morning we met the yard owner, a burly man called l'Américain (the name was a compliment in Congo, meaning innovator, and nonconformist). Within a few minutes of our meeting he urged me to have children; and he asked if I might possibly marry a Congolese. That afternoon l'Américain took us to the river. A funeral was taking place. Canoes studded the water, and slender girls with powdered-white cheeks sang beside long-oared fishermen. The girls resembled eerie dolls, and their singing sounded like moans. Bobby and I decided to leave. We looked around.

The town of Irebu was organized like in the textbooks: around a market, with the fields at the periphery and houses in between. In places the houses blended with the forest, making it difficult to find a boundary. Passing through the market we inquired about prices; and we huffed indignantly when vendors tried to fleece us. Bobby and I seemed unconscious of our animosity.

Near the river, at the far end of the market, I found some food being cooked (everything else was either raw or unclean). A woman stirred a metal casserole lodged in a mangled dead tree. The casserole contained a bath of leaves and chili, but its vegetarian aroma was polluted by the vendor next door who hung thighs of forest buffalo from iron beams.

The market apparently contained crocodiles as well—they had been found by our captain. And the hides were now displayed prominently on the barge. The beasts had been emptied of flesh and their rutted skins, pale white on the inside, had been cut open and clipped to the clothesline, stretched to more than twice their normal width.

The news came soon after: a routine inspection by the crew found a malfunction with the engine cooling system. The captain said he had known all along that something was wrong; he had sensed the engine's strain. He ordered an investigation and after a few hours announced we would have to take apart the engine. The town sent its mechanic and together with the technicians among the crew they tried to fabricate a solution. They spent all day inside the hull, which became like a secret cavern. Boys were sent to the village to fetch tools and to bring platters of soft drinks and food. All of us waited, our plans on hold.

The engineers said they could fix it in a day, that the problem was not serious. They worked for two days, then four. And we began to wonder if they were intentionally delaying. The captain eventually delivered the outcome: the repairs had revealed a different problem, with the piping. We would have to wait for a barge to bring us spare parts. The town became downcast. The market stayed open later that evening; traders discussed alternatives. A barge could be weeks away. Our journey had run aground.

For supper l'Américain's wife gave us bowls of hot manioc and sugary tea. The night was humid and warm; I left the tent. The sky was covered in puffs and the moon danced behind the clouds, its light dimming and swelling like a strobe. Bats flew out of the attic, moving in wide circles and flapping among the trees. The village no longer seemed charming; the water lapped continuously against the mud, and I could only think of the dark depth of the river, which seemed impassable, and of our disabled boat.

A small festival started on the barge. The doors to the hull were wide open and people swarmed the deck, dancing to music from the large speakers. Villagers joined. At the back, under his crocodiles, the captain emitted misty fumes from his pipe. The scene, and the music, seemed foreboding: our predicament would not be soon resolved.

I felt the urgency of needing to move forward. I had staked too much on this journey. My irritation grew. During those days Bobby and I ate at a single restaurant (we called it "the shack") because of a promotion running for barge passengers. The establishment seemed dubious, thrown together at the last minute, and one had the impression it would shut the day we departed. Lunch was advertised as a buffet, but the staff served meager portions. It was a murky place. The odd shaft of light shot through holes in the wall and roof, and a lamp without oil stood in the corner. The restaurant also appeared to never stock food—it possessed no refrigerator, and as soon as we ordered the owner would issue instructions and a boy would run out the back, returning with bags from the market. Even though our time was now worthless, perhaps because we were reduced to waiting for the barge I became annoyed at this slowness.

The owner of the shack became excessively friendly with us— and one day we discovered why. It was the day the gold seller pounced on us while we waited for dinner; he said he was the owner's cousin. *Mon frère, mon frère*—anyone in Congo could be your brother. He decisively pulled himself onto a chair and announced he had found a nugget. When I told him I didn't want it his face darkened, and I thought he was going to be angry and leave; but his smile returned. "I know. Your friend want nugget." Bobby stamped his feet, dislodging the bench, and the gold seller was about to say something, but Bobby stamped again and the gold seller was dragging his leg away. He appeared at our tent. Bobby threatened to beat him. But the man would not be dissuaded. Finally, tired of the evasion and realizing its futility, we agreed to meet the duo at the back of the restaurant. It was our intention to make clear that this would be our last discussion. But that would not be: it was the gold seller and his cousin who offered us the most viable exit.

They tried to sell us anything: promises of gold turned into promises of diamonds, into truffles and truckfuls of timber, into maps of hidden treasures left behind by Belgians. When the cousin learned Bobby traded with India he chattered with the gold seller, who drew a plastic wrapper from inside his pants. It contained a map, heavily stained and covered with what seemed to be the rectilinear shapes of buildings. "I need a metal detector," he said gravely. Bobby asked to see the map but the cousin smiled knowingly. He said we could have it for a hundred thousand dollars. He tried to sell us a diesel generator—for light and cooking in our tent—and Bulgarian-manufactured Kalashnikovs; he said there must be something he had that we wanted; he asked where we had been going before the barge stalled. And he offered to take us by boat. The clamor rose outside our shed.

Boats were easily available. The cousin said we should have at least two engines. Canisters of gasoline were purchased, foraged from various houses and businessmen. Bobby was initially hesitant but the duo moved forward with such speed and conviction and when they spoke it seemed so utterly sincere—they asked for an advance of only half the money—that already it felt too late to refuse. We became accustomed to the idea, even optimistic. Bobby said if we were lucky enough to find good motors we could make the journey in two days.

I began to enjoy the port in my way. I bathed in the river, near the rocks, where the villagers said crocodiles didn't swim. The water was cold and stagnant. I gave it iridescent patches of soap. Once my toe slipped on a slimy smooth object and I nearly fell. I waded out of the water, jumping, making big splashes. Later in a dark room packed with townsmen I watched *Sholay*, a Hindi movie from the 1970s—probably gotten from a trader—on a fifteen-inch television. The movie had no subtitles. The villagers clapped during the dances.

A strange event occurred one night when I was reading by a flashlight in the tent. Bobby and I were camped in the yard. A family of three arrived. The visitors were poorly dressed and without slippers. The skin on their feet was so cracked that it looked like dried clay. The father was the only one who spoke. He seemed simple enough, until he asked me to make his girl speak. She had been mute from birth, and he had heard of Indian magic. I shook my head helplessly. The father grew annoyed. He said he knew I could cure his girl. This was the reputation the Indians had in the country. The family sat by the gate for many hours, and left sometime in the night. The next day I told some

villagers about the incident—the supernatural was daily conversation at the port. They said I had done right. It could have been
a ruse. Those people were from the bush, and the village was at a
delicate time. There had been a vampire visit some months earlier; it was said to have arrived with a terrific sound, terrorizing
the people for weeks until it was slain by the shaman. Villagers
shared their stories of misfortune: the vampire ate livestock; it
caused a roof to implode; it emptied the fishermen's nets of river
fish; it infected their lungs. A fisherman's boy told me he had
found the dead beast. He wanted to show me. It was just outside
the village, he said, near the fields. I tugged at his shirt as he
climbed with agility over fallen trunks. We passed old dwellings
without tops, shielded by tall grass, and we entered a clearing in
the jungle where covered with creepers and leaves was the frame
of an aircraft. The fuselage gaped open, half sunk into the floor.
The boy, standing behind a tree, thought it could be worth a lot
for its strangeness, that he could sell it at the port. I looked up—
but the forest was impenetrable and I couldn't make out the path
by which the plane had come.

We left the carcass as we had found it. And on the walk back
I learned the boy—whose name was Bahati—was a refugee from
Rwanda. His family had been killed by the Rwandan army. A
villager had adopted him. He said he liked international news, so
before my departure, at his request, I bought him a small radio.

At the last minute I worried something would go wrong. Even
Bobby sensed the precariousness. Over and over he inspected
the boat—his marine experience showing as he scrupulously
checked the hull, the engine and the safety equipment. We ran
through our provisions and checked the maps, with Xs at land-
marks so we wouldn't get lost among the islands striping the
river. We checked with l'Américain that the gold seller and his
cousin were trustworthy. Everything seemed in order, and I felt
vaguely satisfied.

The sky was overcast on our last night in Irebu. Only a strip of stars remained, in the northeast. It looked like the Big Dipper, but I fancied I could make a Big Dipper out of any seven stars. I felt heady, on the brink of new discovery: I had worried that our journey might end with us stranded in the village. Suddenly the starry strip made a huge circle and melted into the black. "Are you all right?" Bobby held my arm. I had fallen, tripped on a root. "Help me up."

I was still uneasy the next morning when our party of three— the cousin came along but the gold seller did not—set off. The craft rocked less once we started moving. My nausea eased. It was a relief to see the forest pass with speed. The boat angled upward, and I sat at the bow to give myself a view from a little height. The shore grew distant and the river bloated. There were the familiar islands of reeds, called floating islands. We passed an area where the water was so wide that it extended to the horizon; we could see no land, and the river seemed an ocean. The cousin navigated our canoe through the marshes. Perspiration dotted our faces. The wind made waves on the water. And the rains arrived.

They first appeared as a white mist wrapped around distant trees. It made a beautiful sight: the water hit the earth and rose as pale fumes among the green. The trees were empty of monkeys, and eagles circled above, expecting invertebrate meals. A hush broke the silence. It sounded like rustling leaves; but too steady. The rain approached and grew louder and louder. Our envelope of water, from above and below, became complete. A howling wind rode the river and slammed into our boat. The motor whirred noisily, raised in the air, and plunged into the water. We pressed our legs against the boat's sides. The rain had become a deluge that hit us like stones; the boat rolled; water climbed its sides and seeped into the hull; the river began to threaten. I was newly aware that we could drown. With a mug I scooped out the water, but it felt futile.

Night came more quickly because of the clouds. We moored

the boat. The wetness made me cold and clammy. We were not alone: I saw figures flit among the trees. There was a glow: a torch carried its canopy of light into the jungle. And it occurred to me that we could have been followed. But by whom?

I had become dirty, and I had begun to itch uncomfortably on my legs and back. The constant rain gave no respite, and it was dangerous to sleep nude, but I was worried I could catch pneumonia. I wrapped myself in a damp towel and fell asleep, shivering on a raised plank of the boat. For as long as it rained we wouldn't have to worry about the mosquitoes.

The next day we moved ahead, along eroded cliffs of black mud and between marshes and riverine reeds. Branches arched over the water, along with colonnades of green bamboo. Roots protruded from the cliffs of dissolving laterite, which made the river muddy. The rain poured, then slowed to a drizzle. Bobby passed around fruit; the bananas were mashed, and I scooped up the paste with my tongue. The cousin set up the tent like an awning over the boat's rear; it was hardly effective because the rain came in from the sides. Our progress that day was meager. And at night for a long time I watched the blackness pass; shapes emerged, black on black; I seemed able to discern different shades; perhaps the forest gave the blackness new dimensions, new degrees, I thought. A mosquito came into the weak beam of my torchlight. It settled on my knee, stretched taut; the insect, brilliant in the light, spread its legs and probed. I smacked it. Poor mosquito, I thought, what a delirious death. I scratched my knee. We passed a house on the cliff. It had lights and seemed a bungalow. Yellow filled the doorway and window, and there was a form. Against the light we saw the silhouette of a person looking at us.

I tried to sleep but the motor roared all night. We were trying to outrun the weather. Some hours before dawn I was woken by a heavy thud. I sat up. The cousin cut the wailing engine. The boat was stuck. Bobby thought it was a sandbar. The water was too opaque to see. Leaning over, the cousin reached with his hands into the propeller blades and pulled out some knotted weeds. He pushed us out of the swamp with an oar. The boat budged by inch; the cousin slipped and fell. It had been two full days and we had not made a third of the distance. Sometime that night I asked if we should turn back.

Bobby thought we still had a chance. The cousin rubbed his bruise as though it weren't his decision. The boat labored. The engine choked and we turned it off. Just before dawn the rain grew furious again. The currents swirled and the boat twisted. Visibility diminished. We became stuck in more weeds. The river turned violet. We stopped and passed the morning on a bank, eating bananas and canned sardines; there seemed no point in saving our stocks. Twigs and felled trees floated by, still alive, bearing green leaves. And in the torrential downpour we pushed the hull into the water; it made a splash. Bobby now held the rudder. And the boat moved more quickly, now aided by the current.

Only on our return did I notice how the rain forest bloomed. Everything seemed calmer. Lightning arced through the sky, but without thunder. The animal cries were muted by the sounds of rain. And the forest gained definition: details became visible against the green. Creatures leaped from the trees with out-stretched arms. The throats of bullfrogs expanded into bottles. Monkeys hung by their tails and playfully touched the river. Areas of the shore were covered in white mushrooms. Lichen-colored tree barks glowed orange. Cicadas called at 6:00 p.m.

At the village a monkey had been imprisoned in a bamboo cage. L'Américain kept it as a pet, feeding it passion fruit. He was sitting in an open-walled hut. Half a trunk of wood had been lit and smothered, and smoke from the orange-glowing log rose through a hole in the thatched roof. L'Américain rested in the shade. His wife brought us a buffet of pineapple. The monkey licked its fingers. I ate so quickly I wasn't aware when my hunger was extinguished, and I finished the meal moving slowly and giddily, like a bee that had feasted on honey.

The barge was still stranded, and the only sign of life on it was the clutter around the crew quarters. Another barge had passed in the interim and embarked most of the beached passengers, but it hadn't had the requisite equipment to repair our barge. L'Américain proposed we borrow his motorbike. He offered to arrange a party on foot: local boys would serve as guides. If we waited a week it might be possible to rent a 4x4. But they seemed ideas of folly. The cousin backed out. We would soon reach the peak of inundation, he said, and any journey would be too risky.

Bobby rashly promised that we would return in a few months. The cousin said once the rains slowed he would be glad to join.

Bobby had contracted a cold. Solemnly, sniveling, he made for the bat room.

I sat on the riverbank for a long time. I felt exhausted. Our journey had clearly failed. I had made a mistake by taking such a risk. And I had now gone several weeks without writing a story. The money I had given the family would have been finished. I thought I would have to pick myself up and return to the old routine in Kinshasa. It would be a struggle.

But something happened that afternoon to change the course of my time in Congo. I heard a noise behind me, in the bush. It was Bahati, the Rwandan boy, who came to the water. He had brought his radio, and together we listened to the international news. I told him about our misadventure upriver. He had heard. And after we turned off the radio he said we could perhaps go cycling together. Two Pygmy settlements were located not far away, he said. If I was interested. I was not particularly hopeful— but it seemed a last possibility. So the next day we borrowed two bicycles from l'Américain and set out.

It was raining so the ride was difficult. The high elephant grass made it hard to see. We reached the village after half a day. It was a semicivilized settlement. A Pygmy chief with a brown civet-cat skin over his shoulder came to greet us. He held a slender shield, the wood carved with motifs.

From a pathway into the forest we saw some children return. They were not particularly short, as one might have expected from popular myths about Pygmies. Armed with bows and arrows, and with catapults hanging around their necks, the children had caught some small birds that they carried in bags of woven leaves. A woman appeared, her face bright red, colored with a pigment obtained from tree bark; in a wooden bowl she carried some nuts and leaves.

The chief said his ancestors had once worked on a colonial plantation. When the plantation closed the workers had nowhere to go, and they had become habituated to the settled life. Most crucially they no longer received the plantation company's food shipments. The village was now destitute: like an urban slum set in the jungle. The wooden dwellings smelled of decomposition; food lay open on the ground, which was wet in places. The fields had long been reclaimed by the jungle. Some men emerged from their houses in ornamental headgear, thinking I was an important visitor, from the logging companies.

The Pygmies had lately been rediscovered by the companies. New Congolese forest laws—meant to conserve the ecology and their habitats—had given these tribes authority over traditional lands. The Pygmy chief had sold his rights to the loggers. He had given away a vast swath of land, and all he had asked from the loggers was some soap and bags of salt. It was painful to hear of his naive trade. I asked the chief why he needed salt. He said his ancestors had once known how to extract the mineral from plants, but his people from years of plantation work had forgotten how. The need for soap was evident, from the dirty children gathered before us. And the chief was certain the loggers could never wipe out the forest—"Just look," he said, "it goes on forever."

There was an odd moment when I asked if his ancestors might have allowed the woods to be given away. He seemed to become troubled. "I will tell the spirit of the forest that his trees must be cut down," the chief said to me. "It is so his people can survive."

I wrote a story for the AP about this extortionate logging. It was a story written with some passion—for the Pygmy chief showed me something about the world, and its crisis.

I had come to Congo with natural sympathy for humans living in the forests, stemming from a belief that these people practiced traditions that were thousands of years old, and that they had over the ages learned to exist in equilibrium with the animals.

But the Pygmy chief showed me that the tribes were no longer living in primitive ways. Globalization had reached even these villages—in the form of sneakers, guns and cigarettes, and most violently as demand for raw materials: wood, food, meat. Severed from the forest, the world consumed it rapaciously. The Pygmies were being encroached upon by this global need. These tribes lived in the forest, but they were no longer purely of the forest. They would not survive the change.

On the periphery of that village area I met a woman with a child on her back. Bending over, she was tilling someone else's field. She said she worked from 6:00 a.m. until 8:00 p.m.—a fourteen-hour workday. But she earned only enough to eat the leaves of beans. Her hut was tiny and dark. A white rabbit cowered in the corner. She squatted inside, waiting for the leaves to boil.

This woman struck me as something new in the world. She did not fall into any obvious category of African destitution: she was not a refugee or diseased or the victim of rape or violence. She was willing to work. It seemed to me that by any system of distribution of wealth—communist, socialist, capitalist—she had no reason to be poor.

When the leaves had finished boiling, the woman started to

mash them into a paste. I asked the last of my questions. She replied listlessly, seeming too tired to listen or to tell me to leave.

In the hut the baby had begun to cry. The woman squatted up to him and put a sliver of raw sweet potato in his palm. He made a fist. And like that, holding this morsel of hardly edible food, he fell asleep.

This story about the forest, which in my excitement I called my editor at once to relay, struck a chord in him—and made the rounds within the agency. Months later it won a prize. My editor told me something personal for the first time since we had begun to work together: he too had begun his career in Congo. He had also struck out on his own to find his first stories. In this way we formed a small bond. I got the sense that he wanted to help me. It was the first success of the journey.

14

The excursion with Bahati had made me more comfortable in the area, and with traveling on my own. Previously I had assumed that I would leave on the next barge with Bobby, but now I became curious about the city on the equator to our north, called Mbandaka. It was the capital of Équateur province, founded in the nineteenth century by the famous explorer Henry Morton Stanley. I decided to discuss going there with l'Américain.

I reclined beside him in the hut without walls, before the log that warmed our feet. To the fire he held a bamboo tube with herbs stuck inside; it smoked; he sucked on it. When the downpour lulled crickets started to chirp, and the birds, the monkeys and the trees came alive. An armored caterpillar crawled with its hundred feet, trying to reach a puddle. The town was dark. The land in its immediate vicinity had been cleared for agriculture, and beyond that there was only forest. I told l'Américain about the Pygmy village. He said the logging was worse near Mbandaka, and that he should take the Pygmy chief to see. I asked how many hours it was to Mbandaka, by motorbike. He grimaced, as if strained by the thinking. "Between eight and twelve," he said, twisting his hand. It depended on the condition of the roads. "Have you heard of red mercury?" I said. *Mercure rouge*.

His face showed no recognition.

"Mercure."

"Mercure."

"Rouge."

"Rouge."

"Mercure rouge."

It didn't register. L'Américain stared and then said, "Wendji Secret."

"Secret?"

"Wendji Secret," he said definitively. It was an area the government had cordoned off. There used to be soldiers there, but people claimed to have recently visited it. No one would say what they had found—perhaps it was a mine, he thought, known only to the locals. It was worth a look, and it lay on our route.

Not long after, I strolled out of the hut. L'Américain appeared to have fallen asleep with the bamboo in his mouth. Muddy rivers ran around my shoes. I was quickly drenched. I returned to the tent and lay with damp hair against the sleeping bag. The blackness weighed on me like a cushion. Bobby slept shirtless. His rolls of fat glinted. *Rut-rut*, a night bird hammered against the wood of l'Américain's house.

Our failure had so far been masked beneath the nostalgia of the end of our journey. And it was as if we were saying good-bye without actually uttering the words when we stayed out late each night, for no reason, and the conversation turned ludic. There was some reminiscing about the journey itself: how many miles, days, mosquitoes. Bobby grumbled about his land. He told us about the 1970s, when Congo flourished and "the ferryboats from Kinshasa went all the way up the river." There had been working railways, public works, tourist agencies, and enterprises from India, Greece, Portugal. Mobutu, Bobby said, had restored a sense of pride in being Congolese. He had seemed to have all the right ideas, before everything suddenly came apart. L'Américain concurred. He told us about the day he brought the first VCR to the district—and the sense of magic as he pushed in the cassette and the images appeared. "One thousand, two thousand, ten thousand," he said. The wealthiest men in the province had tried to buy him off. The cousin said he too had possessed a valuable once that he would not sell: a bonobo. "She was like my child," he said. The bonobo would use his toilet and eat at their table. She even had a bed with blanket and pillow. For five years he had lived with the ape, taking her with him whenever he moved. But one day, during the war, he was forced to flee. He thought the bonobo was probably dead. "Those were the good days. When will we enjoy like that? Maybe in fifty years Congo could be stable."

Bobby said, "Remember the Rumble in the Jungle?" The cousin spread his arms above his head to make himself large: "The Greatest." It was an unforgettable moment in the history of Zaire—even the cousin, who had only been a boy, remembered how in 1974 Muhammad Ali had brought down George Foreman by inventing the rope-a-dope. The bout had made Kinshasa known to the world. Bobby remembered the subsequent craze for passion-fruit juice. Ali had been spotted with a glass. And for a while, Bobby said, it was all the ladies would drink.

L'Américain's log crackled.

It was our last night together. It ended in an ambience of remorse. We smoked the pipe and shook hands before turning in, and in the morning, as I stepped out of the room quietly so as not to wake Bobby up, I turned back to look at him; we would not meet again, though he would call once to offer me a one-carat diamond for five hundred dollars. I didn't wait long before l'Américain skidded into the yard on a red Yamaha that roared and spewed black smoke. The pounding of pestles paused; women stood and marveled. They had made us a bowl of hot chicken. The meat was spotted red: blood clots or lean muscle, I thought. L'Américain gobbled the bird with its skin, sucking at the bone like a vacuum cleaner. And the Yamaha rumbled again, but now the vastness of the jungle belittled its roar.

The journey was laden with holes and puddles. Makeshift bridges had collapsed over waist-deep lakes and we waded through the water, walking on the shallower banks and pushing the Yamaha through the middles; sometimes the bike drowned. In the worst places we had to hoist it between us; we slipped, fell, got mud over our backs. We rode past men pushing wooden carts piled higher than their heads with green bananas. Women carried masses of honeycombs in bamboo baskets. Boys held out packets of green peas. Sacks of potatoes lined the road. And villagers shouted out to us as we passed: "L'Américain! L'Américain!" He waved at them.

Those who had heard of Wendji Secret said it was only a few miles farther. We drove through the dirt, our shoes and shins covered in splatters of mud. And finally we reached a paved road. The Yamaha screamed ahead. "Chinese make this road!" L'Américain yelled, as we passed a convoy of trucks loaded with enormous logo. A lot of Congo's wood went to Europe, to be fashioned into tables and bookshelves and sold all over the world, even back in Congo, at exorbitant prices. IKEA got wood from here. The forest grew smaller. The paved road diverted to a jungle port for logs; again we hit the dirt. L'Américain drove us straight through a puddle of water and I lifted my legs, but it wasn't a puddle. A cloud of butterflies rose, turning the forest effervescent: blue skimmed the grass, crept up tree trunks and flitted above; blue mixed with yellow—other butterflies. At the next village they said Wendji Secret was an hour behind us.

But we had been too careful to let it pass.

I came into Mbandaka with a feeling of sadness. The city was desolate. There wasn't a stray cat to be seen, or even a beggar. And for two days I went hungry. The restaurants were bare and food needed to be ordered in advance; the locals drank beer for lunch and dinner. Drink was cheap. Heineken operated a brewery on the city outskirts.

For the United Nations Mbandaka was mainly a military outpost, and its garrison-like building was at the center of town, surrounded by barbed wire. Inside, at the end of a dim corridor and past a thin wooden door sat a heavyset Frenchwoman—the information officer. Her skin was sunburned, and her wide-open cotton shirt showed her red chest. I asked if the UN could help me get home.

She made a grumbling noise and asked, irritably, for what reason. I explained, in brief, my journey. "So your base is Kinshasa?" she said.

At the end of our discussion she told me to write a letter with the subject "Return to Base." I was to write it outside her office.

A janitor was working his way down the hall. His wooden broom knocked against the cement.

The woman filed away the letter. She had me sign a contract stating the UN was not liable for my injury or death. My writing was jagged. She had verified on the internet that I was a journalist, and she asked what I was working on. I told her about the Pygmies, the trees, the loggers.

And just before leaving I thought to ask about Wendji Secret.

"Wendji Secret?" she repeated.

I told her I had tried to find it.

"It's a *fosse commune*."

I didn't know the phrase.

"A mass grave," she said. "Mass grave."

Her voice had become hard again. She said that Wendji Secret was one of a series of mass graves—with names like Tingi-Tingi, Wanie Rukula and Boende—that had been refugee camps, sheltering thousands of people. The boy Bahati had lived in one of these, I realized. But in 1997 the armies of the father Kabila and

Paul Kagame, the Rwandan president, had decimated the refu-
gees. The villagers, still afraid, had intentionally misled us.

It brought me head-on with the war. Here, in a remote part of
the forest, almost a thousand miles from Rwanda and the center of the conflict, I had stumbled upon one arm of a network,
stretching eastward, of mass graves. It was to feel the power and
reach of Congo's war.

The AP editor called me with news: the bureau was prepared
to fund my travel to a limited degree. I would have to obtain
permission for each journey, but they were willing to give it a
test. They had been pleased with the Pygmy story, which I finally
wrote up and filed from a derelict internet café in Mbandaka. I
didn't feel ready to return to Kinshasa. The mere thought was
depressing. I told the editor I would like to go east. He agreed—
as long as I closely followed the preparations for the elections,
which were gaining pace. My gamble had paid off unexpectedly.
This journey had earned me my chance.

I sent the family in Kinshasa some of the money I had earned.
Nana started to list the problems at the house. I promised her
more.

It took several days to find a UN aircraft, with an empty seat,
going to the war. I had begun, over the days, to feel apprehensive
about the conflict. Now on the verge of leaving, I was less sure
of my readiness to confront it. The knowledge of the graves had
also awakened this apprehension. I passed the time wandering
in the city, and got an elderly cobbler to stitch together the split
soles of my shoes. I tested his repairs, pulling at the stitches and
jumping before his stall. The shoes felt like new.

15

B unia, a small city in Congo's far northeast, on a mountainous plateau near Uganda and Sudan, is one of Africa's most mythical places. To its east is Lake Albert, a haven for smugglers, and a source of the Nile. And to its north, in a national park, is the only place in the world to see the northern white rhinoceros. But lately the animals have needed to be airlifted out: the militias have nearly killed them all, and not for the horns, but to eat.

I felt I was continuing Mossi's work, in a way. While in Kinshasa we had discussed his investigative reports at length: about the pollution on the coast, and rebels trading weapons to fuel the conflict. But now I did not believe Mossi's tales of adventure. He had been fantasizing, I thought. Still, he was gifted with a keen sense for the news. I felt I was covering the stories he was unable to, and carrying out some part of the undertaking he felt was necessary.

I did not come to Bunia directly. News suddenly broke: I was sent to write about an earthquake in the east that had killed some people. Then I followed Kofi Annan on a brief tour of Congo. Everywhere people seemed eager to tell stories of killing from the war; and these excursions only built a sense of anticipation for when I could travel on my own again.

I had been assigned a flight to Bunia transporting a military platoon. It was a Russian propeller craft, white and emblazoned with "UN" in black tape on both wings. The interiors were plain, cream colored. I felt I was in a bus. The soldier beside me was sleeping. No food was served; no film was screened; the only drink available was water. I spent the journey looking out the porthole, as we passed the thick of the rain forest, and the silver snaking river.

Bunia, to those familiar with this war, is best known for two UN officers who were killed three years before, grilled on metal barrels and eaten. The cannibalism is unverifiable: it allegedly happened at a remote gold mine, and the ragged man imprisoned for it does not remember the eating. He cannot be blamed: the miners were mostly drugged, and the war was then at its height. Bunia had been invaded. The Ugandan army had planted its flag in the city, lined gutters with corpses and blocked the main roads using human intestines.

Such wars are familiar to the continent. Indeed, in descriptions, from the reports in newspapers, this war can seem a repeat of others. But the crisis here is vaster: in deadliness and brutality—five and a half million dead, by the most commonly cited count. More than in any war since Hitler. And yet the daily carnage passes hardly noticed—in part because it is so singularly unspectacular, so primitive.

Fought in isolated jungles and hidden from the world, this war has only relics—machetes, knives and guns designed in 1947—for weapons. So the killing proceeds slowly, and without much noise.

Another familiarity: the war is African, but it is sustained by the world. Neighboring powers—notably Uganda and Rwanda, whose armies are trained and equipped by Western nations—feed the ambitions of Congolese warlords and sell them weapons.

The warlords need the arms to control territory and valuable mines. They pay for the arms with the mines' produce—gold, coltan, tin and other minerals—which Uganda and Rwanda export to the world, for use in computers and jewelry.

And so Congo's war, isolated though it may seem, ebbs and flows with global consumption. The war is in fact deeply relevant to the world's economy—if it ended today it would probably incite a panic in markets. Commodity prices would spike. Supply chains would be disrupted. The production of many electronics would likely stutter, possibly cease.

A blond Ukrainian woman came into the aisle of the aircraft. "Ve vill be landing shortly."

The soldiers, South African, seemed to become anxious. The plane veered, and a utilitarian wheel, its shaft encased in metal, unfolded from the wing.

We came at Bunia from the south, flying over the green-capped hills of the famous Blue Mountains. Fires burned in single points, like cigarettes the hills smoked. The land was lush where cavities had not eaten into it: mines lay abandoned, as wounds in the earth. It is Africa's El Dorado: the land around Bunia is so rich with gold that the Congolese call it *moto*, hot. In the distance was a green thicket, but it was encroached upon by fields; in places one could see where a forest had been felled. The wind and rain had caused erosion. Hill upon hill had been shaved of its stomach.

The runway drew closer; the approach produced a feeling of suffocation. The city lay in a long valley, a cluster of metal roofs. It was an arrival laden with expectancy, and a certain anxiety: the stories of the war had, in the mind, built up the place; and one felt the burden of experience needing to confirm the myth. The aircraft's wheel skidded on the tarmac, then rolled. The UN airport was a structure of stacked container boxes. The few workers there looked miserable.

Arriving in such a state, without specific destination, with

only an idea, one found oneself relentlessly looking: the mind
was like an antenna that probed, that latched onto small emotions. And on the uncomfortable motorcycle ride into town, fifteen minutes long, I acquired the idea that people here needed
proximity. The road, rising and falling, was bounded on both
sides by tin houses that, like the airport workers, were huddled
in groups. Now a large white tent in a field—the UN. Again the
cramped tin constructions. The driver seemed to skirt the main
city, taking a string of back roads to the convent guesthouse.

An attendant with a beatific face ushered me in. The convent
had only one kind of room, he said—simple, square, and with
a narrow bed. A netted window faced the inner garden quad-
rangle, in which grew some red tulips, long-stemmed. The floor
and ceiling were of gray cement, so one didn't want to look up or
down. Outside, a large metal awning blocked the view of the sky.
It felt like a bunker.

Just fifty yards from my room was the UN base, lit by halogen lights and guarded by tense soldiers behind sandbags, their
rifles always fixed on me when I would approach. The area was
secured by convoys of white Hummers that patrolled ceaselessly.
All day and night they broke the silence with the abrupt static of
their shortwave radios.

But my first understanding of the war would come at some
distance from such instruments of violence. That weekend I was
visited, at the convent, by a curious-looking Congolese couple.

Their politeness was disarming. The man, small, wore a hat,
brown with a brown ribbon. The woman, taller than he and
much younger, was lipsticked and in a bright-green dress. They
seemed too well dressed to be living in a war. Unknown to me,
I had been watched as I arrived in Bunia. This couple knew my
name, and that I was a journalist. They wanted publicity for a
company they were running. The man said they were entrepreneurs, and inquired if I might have time to make a small tour. I
felt it was an odd request.

The wife left us, saying we would meet later, while the man and I took Bunia's main thoroughfare, the Boulevard de la Libération, flanked on both sides by rosebush-like barbed-wire hedges. We walked gingerly—I was wary of moving in the open. The dust in the air created a slight haze. And prominent on the side of the street were a row of old gas pumps. Defunct, their hoses in coils, they seemed to have been replaced by humans: men squatted together—the proximity again—holding shiny brown bottles and funnels. They watched us pass. At the boulevard's end we descended a mud slope into Bunia's poor quarter.

Only it did not seem so poor: the alleys were narrow and the houses close together, of lightweight tin, but absent was the shantytown clamor that automatically suggested poverty. The couple's company collected garbage, it seemed. We were met by their sole employee, a dirty ex-militiaman who pushed the garbage barrow. Such men were capable of great violence. I took another look at the entrepreneur, his fine clothes. He smiled, said I should not worry.

Even the most silent homes were peopled. Sometimes I caught glimpses inside and saw, in the soft light from small, high windows, people squatting on the mud floor, still. A woman would emerge from the house with a sack of garbage and make a little conversation before returning, shutting the door on us. Lives here were interior; little noise escaped the thin walls. A few hens strutted about some of the yards, rasping.

The streets showed scant sign of the dense habitation. A few food wrappers, used condoms outside doorways—these the barrow pusher, large, docile, removed, bending over slowly when the man instructed. Sometimes, between the houses, one found areas of openness that were unused and seemed to lead nowhere. Inexplicably empty of both man and animal, it was as if the land had been contaminated; or as though someone had lived there and been removed, house and all traces.

I asked the man about the silence. He explained that Bunia

was a city in flux. Most residents had been displaced from their homes and took refuge here. Some, like him, had stayed for years, but few had made this their home; people came and went, shifted by the war. Then he began to talk about how his company was good for the community.

His calm tone seemed to suggest that people had become accustomed to certain ideas—violent displacements, the war, the silence.

We had come to the man's house. It was in the same neighborhood, but of a slightly better adobe construction. Their little daughter joined us. His wife had prepared a special dish for me: oily macaroni. The presence of the girl put me at ease. I considered asking to stay as a guest, but when I was shown the house after the meal, I saw that it had only a single bedroom.

Polite until the end, the man accompanied me to the convent. For much of the distance we walked alone. The sunset curfew had been lifted in Bunia some months earlier, he said, but people still preferred to remain inside. "The refugee mentality makes it difficult. They think only of leaving, not of making a life." And then, unexpectedly, we passed a bar. Youths crowded the entrance, pressing against each other. They surged inside. The pressure built. And like bottled fizz they spilled out. The man lit a cigarette. That was when Bunia's quiet fear struck. The sudden gayness, the flashing lights, I found them corrupt, unsettling.

16

I felt spit out. On this sparse, bleached terrain, I felt exposed— not, as in Kinshasa, by the profusion of people and things, but by the alarming paucity. And the city, not at a lake or river or mine or port, without an obvious reason for existence, seemed spit out on this land as much as I felt spit out on it.

And what indolence. The people in the shantytowns seemed stagnant within their houses; a construction crew in front of the convent worked languorously, in an extremely restrained way.

As I walked around the city, looking for stories, searching in the broad spaces, my eye became fatigued, finding nothing to rest on, and always hesitating. The news that came over the radio was constant and straining. Some militias had become active, and every other day a village—of twenty or fifty people—was attacked.

The AP took these stories, which were painful to write; the war had come closer, and one somehow felt one knew the villages— they had become imaginable. I often became tired. And then one afternoon I was woken. It was the telephone. I reached for the counter; the room spun, blending. Outside, the convent workers sang loudly, tending to the flowers.

"Where are you? I've been calling all morning."

"Sorry, what's the matter?"

"You haven't heard?"

"About what?"

"Man, how can you lose when you're there? Twenty dead in a militia attack outside Bunia. Bentley reported it two hours ago."

I felt the enervation, and fell back on the mattress. The ceiling was matted by the cobwebs of long-legged spiders, crawling, moving ungainly as though on stilts. Watching them I fell asleep. When I woke it was late afternoon; I left the house berating myself. The UN spokesperson would not answer her phone. I climbed the slope to the base, but the guards said she was busy. So I hurried down the boulevard to Ali's shop.

Ali was a mysterious man. He was one of Bunia's important traders, from Pakistan. I had met him the week before, while looking in his shop for Indian tidbits. His main commerce seemed of face-whitening cream: bottles colored shocking pink stacked along the walls in pyramids like a Near Eastern monument. Chest-high shelves divided the shop into aisles of cigarettes, food. He stocked some higher-margin goods: a teddy bear with a forged Harrods tag, a Chinese video game. Two suits wrapped in plastic were pegged high on a wall, and hung without shape. The shop belied Ali's reputation. He was known as a loner, who had appeared in Bunia sometime during the war, and who received nightly convoys. Yet he seemed open with me—to talk freely. He seemed to know this part of Congo intimately. And so I wanted to make friends with him.

I rapped on his counter, rattling the glass. Ali came in hunched, a rag towel in one hand. "Was it you making that noise?"

"Did you hear about the attack?"

"Of course. I had to divert my supplies."

He seemed pleased to see me. He was a small, wiry man. Coming to sit on his stool he drew a comb from his trousers and tapped it on the counter, discharging a black and white powder over the glass. "I was wondering about you, actually. Do you want some roast chicken?"

I shook my head.

He laughed, but with hostility. "What's the problem? You're missing out. Roast chicken from Kampala is what the militiamen eat . . . the amount of chicken they have looted from me."

"The UN doesn't secure your convoys? Or the roads?"

"They don't even buy my cream."

The shop comforted, though my head felt heavy. The row of leather sandals on the ground seemed expected, familiar. A layer of dust over the toys and video games was now brilliant in the angled evening light. A client, a man in a soiled tunic, bought a tin of condensed milk. Ali packed this in a page from an old women's magazine.

It seemed his obsession—he wiped the countertop with the soiled rag. My mind returned to the news failure. But the feeling of urgency was gone. The tiredness had returned.

Perhaps Ali sensed my mood. "So you missed the story today."

I thought he was trying to provoke me.

"You're sure you don't want roast chicken?"

I shook my head again.

"You want to meet the militias?"

It was my turn to be surprised.

"I can arrange a meeting. I don't want any commission." He said this in a puritanical way—as though he would never think to take a commission—and also, I felt, with some reproach: as though I had given the impression of distrusting him.

"Where are these militias?"

"Fataki." It was a northern town. "Powerful group."

"You just want to help me?"

"You'll also find out a few things."

I frowned.

"You know the problem here is the UN. The soldiers are all in illegal business. They take gold from the militias and send to Karachi." Much of the UN's force around Bunia was from Pakistan. "You'll see for yourself at the helicopter bases there are no X-ray machines. If I go around, even to supply milk powder, everyone will know. They don't want any competition. They are even selling their water, man. They are selling their rations to the militias."

I said there might be a story in that.

"I am not lying to you. Even in Bunia you can buy the UN water. Where is it coming from?"

I passed among the aisles to look for some batteries for my radio. A noise came from outside: teenagers, arms interlaced and reaching inside each other's back pockets. I rolled together the batteries in my palm, making a heavy metallic sound. On the counter was a box of chocolates.

"You don't have Fruit & Nut?" I said.

But Ali had stopped listening, and was contemplating his pink bottles. "I hear there is a cream for whites," he said. "It makes them orange even without the sun. You know it?"

"Who would buy that here?" I was again thinking of his proposition—Fataki, the name was itself explosive. And there was the excitement of discovering a different part of Bunia's war-hit territory.

"Man, just saying!"

"I think I'm getting a fever."

He held his hand against my forehead.

"Only a little."

He went on, "You know Miss Ituri is going to come to Bunia. The beauty contest. We will go together and have some fun. Nice girls there, good music. I think you will like it."

And he said he was going to close the shop for a few minutes; it was time for the evening *namaaz*. He yelled at a sentry outside to lock the grill.

17

The officers at the UN said it would be no problem to go to Fataki. There was a regular helicopter, and my papers were in order. They made me sign a new liability waiver. Ali gave me the necessary details, told me where to go. And on the evening before, I was all packed and ready.

But that same night I received a call—civilians were being prohibited from Fataki. The violence had escalated. It was the militias. But the timing of the announcement seemed suspect. And I felt too much on edge now to stay in Bunia. I confronted the UN logistics man, who seemed genuinely apologetic. He offered me a trip to Mongbwalu, the town made famous by the cannibalism story. The helicopter was due to leave the same morning—and a special UN patrol, he said, would take me on a tour. I was promised it would be worth my time.

I was the only civilian in the helicopter, among a dozen bearded soldiers with shaved upper lips. I squeezed between them into the oval compartment, our backs to the porthole windows. Yellow earmuff-like headsets were passed around. A high-pitched noise above our heads grew until it was deafening. The rotors began to shift. With the noise it was impossible to make conversation, and we spent the journey alert, looking at one other.

Mongbwalu's base commander, a clean-shaven Pakistani, was a gregarious type. Before we could go anywhere, and though we had only a few hours, he insisted that we have tea. "One cup won't delay us." The porcelain was brought out. We were seated in a gazebo. The commander talked with bravado, as Mongbwalu's overseer, about military strategy and politics. He asked who I was, why I had come. And quickly he seemed to decide that I was not of any use to him. He began to brood; the offer of tea seemed regretted; the invitation had been personal, too anticipated.

So the tour began with a bad feeling. The commander changed his mind and did not join; and this seemed to demoralize the troops. We quickly descended the hill, in our convoy of twelve jeeps loaded with troops and weapons, to face the pathetic and undernourished villagers. They stood outside their shacks, watching us. The Pakistanis hardly spoke to me. They showed me nothing. The tour seemed already spoiled; my presence, I felt, was resented.

And I was startled when we left town. The drive became long and wearying. The Pakistanis seemed only to be carrying out some duty by taking me on this drive, without slowing or stopping. From the backseat I looked at the hills—there was a wide, black gash in one; we seemed to head for it. The convoy suddenly stopped. But the soldiers hesitated. Half in a daze, I got out.

It was there, unexpected, among the tall grass, beside a mud hut—a charred white jeep. I cautiously moved toward it, attracted, and with half a mind that the convoy could leave without me.

So this was the jeep of the ill-fated UN officers. It had reportedly been their last refuge during that final attack. Their corpses were later found with the stomachs ripped open, and missing their livers and hearts. One of the bodies, according to news reports, was lacking its brain—it led one to imagine some kind of cannibalistic ritual.

The jeep was being used as a clothes hanger. Its wheels were gone, and grass and plants grew from under its axles. A rear door had the precise holes of bullets, around which in circles the paint had come off to reveal gray metal. The upholstery had been ripped out, with the seats, the engine, the piping and wiring. A heap of metal lay within. So the car was now a shell, with shirts and shawls and scarves of abstract flower motifs carefully laid out over its chassis. On the roof was a basin of washing soap and clothes clips.

In another country I might have expected this jeep—symbol of the historic moment of the UN's first military intervention in Congo's war—to lie in a museum. Like Mobutu's palaces, the jeep might have been preserved for viewing and memory. But the fates of both had been the same: pillage, decay and slow infestation by the jungle.

We returned to Mongbwalu, and again the emaciated people came out—their faces now seemed pocked, the scars seemed to run deeper; and I felt bitten by the air. I could not stare at them for long. I was returned to the field where the helicopter waited, its chopping noise audible, the grass set at a steep tilt. Children stood in a large enclosing ring—though the helicopter had been a weekly event in Mongbwalu for years. They seemed like the townspeople, never tiring of the convoy. I turned to look out as we were raised into the air. The children were now running onto the field, among the soldiers. Their small shirts blown back by the gust from the rotors, they frantically made signs at us.

Those children somehow softened the memory I would keep of that journey, and of the place.

I was glad when Bunia's shiny roofs appeared.

The town seemed still, oppressive. I decided to cool off with a beer at the Hotel Ituri—the place I had passed with the garbage company man. The lobby, also a bar, was like in a cinema: vast, and dark. In a corner, under a bulb, glowed the green felt of a pool table. The walls were sparsely decorated with posters of beer. The tables were wooden and the tablecloths solid red; to one side was a shelf of drinks; the bartender wore spectacles but still poured outside the cups. Girls sat on high stools, sipping from straws; prostitutes seemed to stick to the walls and hover around anyone who looked as if he had a little money. Cracks and holes—seemingly from bullets—pockmarked the building. The toilet had been defaced by ballpoint pen with love and hate messages.

The man on the high stool next to me was a masculine sight, with a hairy face and thick eyebrows. His jeans hung low, on a wide belt, and his CAT sneakers had been washed. He fidgeted, shaking his leg. And it was he who struck up conversation: "I have met Angelina."

"Who?"

He nodded knowingly.

He asked if I didn't believe him. "I have proof." Without provocation he pulled out his phone—with half-closed eyes, taking his time and pretending to be careless, he pressed some buttons. The trembling instrument was thrust to my face. "Naro, you are so sweet. Xo. Angelina." He let me hold the phone. But when I tried to scroll down he raised his arms—and I became nervous when he stood and stepped closer, talking fast. "Are you jealous, man? Trying to delete the message?"

His temper lasted all night. The bar grew more lively. The rumba became loud. A projector screened dancing girls on the wall. He announced us as bar partners. The bartender immediately refilled our beers. Naro was showing someone else his phone—but this man said he didn't believe it was Angelina Jolie. They got into a shouting argument. "Congolese are so stupid," Naro said to me. The bartender said Naro was a Lebanese freight agent, that he exported gold to the Middle East. Naro again turned—"Tell me, do you think I am a liar? Do you?" I tried to draw him away from the argument but he would not listen. The Congolese was now pointing at his face. Naro twisted his hand. The bartender raised his voice. The mood had become too intense. I rushed out.

The evening had instead amplified the anxieties of the morning's excursion—I felt burned, that over the day I had slowly been used.

Mossi called that evening to ask for help. He had become involved in a business venture with a politician—in an attempt to escape his poverty. The politician was suing him. He was being menaced. I called a lawyer I knew in Kinshasa, who promised to get on Mossi's case. By making the call I was committing to paying the lawyer. But I was glad Mossi had called me, I felt grateful to be able to help. I worried for him.

18

I have it!" I yelled.

"Have you got it?" she yelled back, from the window.

The Italian nuns who ran the convent guesthouse were partially deaf. They were a pair, Mariana and Luigiana, who wore Mother Teresa blue-and-white tunics and lived in an apartment near the front gate, at the top of a staircase. It was Mariana who now came hobbling down. I had intended only to pay my bill (I had just picked up some money from the Western Union, discovering, on the way, Bunia's gold-industry apparatus—shacks that were purchasing and purifying counters, open-air truck garages, government offices that sold fifty-thousand-dollar permits), but it turned out Mariana had been looking for me. A guest was to arrive, a regular client from the UN who preferred the room that I had mistakenly been given. So the rooms were not all identical. I resisted, but Mariana was firm. "You must move." And when I became silent she softened. "I tell you," she muttered, "business is not my charisma." I watched her slowly return to her apartment, pushing her hand on her thigh to climb each step.

The only vacant rooms were on the other side of the convent, near enough, I learned, to the toilets to receive their smell. And as I packed my clothes and folded my sleeping bag—whether because I did not want to move, or because of the dust—I began to sneeze; the sneezes turned into coughs, and into a wheeze. My eyes teared, my cheeks puffed up, and my nose began to run; the reaction was asthmatic, and of a violence I had not experienced in years.

I spent the morning outside with a kerchief tied around my nose, to protect myself from the pollen. Then Naro arrived. I had forgotten—it was Sunday, and he had said he would bring lunch. In his bowl was couscous, some in a salad, and the rest in red sauce. He said we should eat while it was still hot.

At first I had thought Naro talkative, perhaps a little rash—not unusual for a man who spent his every evening at the bar. But I found it strange that he would choose to befriend me, an itinerant journalist. And the big smile on his face, the enthusiasm with which he had come—it made him seem lonely and bored.

We ate in the convent dining hall, beneath a wooden sculpture of a crucified Jesus. The tender, hot couscous did me good—it soothed the soreness in my throat. We tried to eat slowly, and repeatedly offered, out of politeness, to serve each other. Each eyed the couscous, hesitating to help himself. Soon the spoon rattled in the bowl. We slouched in our chairs.

Another attack was reported on the radio—even on Sunday, I thought, these militias have no pity. I did not see it at the time, but the recurrent attacks had already begun to follow a pattern that pointed to a serious threat to Bunia.

On the way out Naro and I stopped by my room. It was dark.

"What is this place, man?" he said. "It looks like a dungeon."

"The other room is going to be much worse."

"Man, Hotel Ituri is not so bad."

"Their cheapest room is fifty dollars. That's a bit expensive for me."

"Then stay at my house, no? It's small, but we can put a mattress in the front room."

I picked up my bag, feeling buoyant, and locked the room. I would come back for the other things later. But halfway to his place Naro stopped at the Hotel Ituri—he had realized that he needed to inform his landlord. I took a seat outside at a white plastic table, waiting.

There was a crackle and flicker above me—a blue tube. An insect, mothlike, had been burned by electrocution.

On the street was a typical evening scene: palm oil vendors with yellow canisters on their bicycles; motorcycle-taxi drivers, mostly ex-militiamen, chattering in corners. Menial laborers walked by, having finished their odd-job shifts at the shops, restaurants and markets.

And the foreigners: UN personnel, civilian and military, in jeeps; aid workers from Belgium, Italy, America. There were also the entrepreneurs. A group of Indians passed, all nearly identical, in shirts and pants and oily hairstyles. I felt a sudden closeness, and was about to call out, but they seemed focused on themselves.

It had been less obvious in Kinshasa, because of the politicians and the corruption. Here Congolese society was plainly limp, poor; and every aspect of life was organized around the foreigner. And among the foreign employers the Indian had a special place: known as the most exploitative, rarely paying more than the "market wage"—meaning the minimum acceptable to the poor laborers, who were not in a position to negotiate.

The Congolese would complain and complain about the Indian, but they would accept that only one race treated them worse: the Congolese (the African, more generally). In this was a double compatibility: the African seemed to accept and imitate his ruthless masters by an extension of his colonial ideas; and the Indian naturally admitted the black man at the bottom of the castes.

But the Indian-Congolese relationship was more ambiguous than this, and also more intimate.

It was the difference between the two kinds of Indians one met in Africa: there were those who had been brought generations earlier by the British; and there were the new immigrants. The two bore little connection. While the former had built an India within Africa, with strict rules of marriage and gastronomy (it was they who had given Africa the samosa and chapati, now the poor man's staples), the latter lived as a hedonist, producing the *métis*, the half-caste.

This aspect of the Indians was considered a benediction by women, who knew that their *métis* children would have a status above the Congolese. Kabila's government was filled with *métis*. *Métisse* girls, with paler skin, were considered most desirable. And though the Indian *métis* fell below that of the European, he was still more likely to avoid the life of a laborer. He was more likely to survive.

The new immigrants surrounded themselves with Congolese. They were strangers in Africa, without friends or relations, invited by no one. They had been sent, as emissaries of the great immigrant-business communities: the Shiite Muslims, the Punjabis and Sindhis; the Chinese, Lebanese and Israelis. A senior community member, usually a wealthy individual, would hear of Bunia's profits, and front the capital to send a young agent.

Among people thrust into Congo in this way there could be little camaraderie. Naro and Ali knew each other but rarely met. The Independence Day celebrations in Kinshasa had been muted for the same reason. The traders' affairs demanded no collaboration; each created his own world. These were not individuals doing business—what mattered more was the intangible, foreign tribe of which one was an extension. Here, at the extremity of global commerce, each exile was made outcast in the other's society.

I felt a presence behind.

It was Naro standing at the hotel portico, with pursed lips. "I'm really sorry," he said. "The landlord is not agreeing. It's noth- ing to do with you." The meeting had apparently turned hostile: Naro had been bringing home too many girls, and the landlord wanted to charge for electricity, for water, for the unauthorized use of the house. It would be too precarious to have me stay. "I'm really sorry," Naro repeated.

I don't know why, but that got me down quite badly.

And I was feeling cold—the fever was acting up. A breeze had begun to blow; the sun was setting. I asked Naro for some pills— Panadol, Tylenol, whatever he had. He ran inside to get me some. I returned to the convent with his medicine.

But in the morning I could not move. I awoke feeling giddy. The grill over the window faded and came into focus. My slippers, in the corner of the room, seemed far. I stayed in bed, watching my toes wiggle. There were other signs: my ears seemed blocked. I called out, and suddenly they popped; sounds were exception- ally clear; even the silence seemed present, as a bass static. And my sleep had of late become disturbed. The dreams had grown more vivid.

I gave an account of these symptoms to a doctor who ran a clinic on the boulevard. I remembered his place for its large red cross on the signboard, and because the adjacent buildings, Italian and American aid operations, were guarded and locked. But when I swung open the clinic's gate the yard was deserted. The doctor was on his second-floor balcony smoking a cigarette.

The office was a spacious hall furnished with a glass-topped desk and a long metal table, cold to lie on. Above me oscillated a halogen lamp. In the corner was a pair of repaired crutches, and next to those, in a tall wooden cupboard, bandages, ointment and little bottles of medical supplies.

The doctor listened patiently. He pulled at my cheek and shone a light in my ear. He asked how the fever had felt. A stethoscope was coiled over his chest, and his white gloves stretched up to his elbows. His eyes, behind chunky lenses, were larger than normal. They looked me up and down with interest. "Do you have your own syringe?" he asked, almost hopefully.

"Don't you?"

"Sometimes foreigners like to bring their own," he said, drawing a needle from his cupboard. It was new—he unwrapped its packaging—but its tip looked enormous. "Don't be alarmed," he said, "it won't hurt."

He pricked my finger and took blood on a swab. The diagnosis didn't take long: "I think you have malaria."

I nearly sprang off the table. "Call a friend to take you home," the doctor advised. But whom to call? He told me to use the malaria pills I had brought from America, still untouched in their box. "And try to take rest for a few days."

But inaction was forced on me. That night, at the convent, as had happened all week, the electricity went out. I came to the front of the convent and yanked on a rusted metal bell; its vacant trill invaded the yard. The beatific boy attendant appeared, his face brilliant, as though covered in oil.

"There's no electricity," I said.

"I am sorry, monsieur. It will surely return."

"Why don't we have a generator? The other hotels all have one."

"Monsieur can ask the sisters tomorrow. Jean-Paul is only a simple employee."

We looked at each other, and I dropped my eyes. Jean-Paul still had his chin up. "Don't worry, Monsieur Anjan, after the elections we will have electricity. We will be like America and France. We will have democracy."

It was an extraordinary declaration. But a fever had begun to affect the country. The vote, which would pit Kabila against the vice president and former warlord Jean-Pierre Bemba, was drawing closer and gaining proportion in people's minds—no longer was it simply an idea or a foreign-imposed aspiration. There was a sense of mobilization in society, a feeling of ownership. And now, only weeks from the polls, the expectations seemed to have become limitless.

It was bound to be a unique moment for the news. The world rarely turned to Congo unless the war flared up; and now, during the elections, for once Congo would be important. I felt I had to profit. I decided to start preparing. But just as I started to feel the excitement I came to face the bureau's power politics.

The AP called to inform me that senior correspondents were being flown in from London, Cairo and Johannesburg. Without warning I was given a list of stories that I wasn't to touch, stories that were fantastic: trips to the volcanoes, to see the gorillas; to the diamond mines in the heart of the country; to remote reserves that were home to the okapi, a rare cousin of the giraffe found only in Congo; and to the giant copper mines of the south.

The editor wanted me to team up with the correspondents. "As what?" I asked. He said I should continue working as I had planned to—I should know where to look for the news, I had been living in Congo. And the chief Africa correspondent wanted to chat before she arrived, "to pick your brain, share ideas." It sounded as if she wanted to steal my stories. The head of African reporting was in a sense my boss, but before that day I'd never heard of her. Now suddenly I was important.

I had come to see the editor as a friend—and I wanted to be frank. So I told him the plan sounded suspect. He owned up. "I'm only trying to protect you," he said. Once the correspondents arrived the AP would buy fewer stories from me. "I know it sounds unfair but we pay them a salary, so we have to prioritize their work. Anything we spend on you we have to justify. If you collaborate at least it'll guarantee you some wordage."

So that's how it was—Congo was becoming world news, and during this time I was surplus. The call felt like a stab.

I had not anticipated my own camp would become an obstacle. I had counted on the elections for extra money, to live better and for travel. The list rankled more—I had worked hard to earn my place with the AP in Congo; and now, in a stroke, a dozen stories were being taken from me. The correspondents had claimed the country for themselves. The big stories picked off, I foresaw battles with the editor, requests turned down. Areas of Congo, it seemed, would all but close.

There was also a feeling of loneliness. I had come to depend on the bureau. The editor was my most sustained link to the world—we spoke or wrote to each other almost every day. We had never met; he had only seen a copy of my passport; our link was imaginary. But we had, I felt, formed a trust—because the editor had once been a stringer in Congo. Moving about the country alone, I tended to share my impressions, what I marveled at, the emotions of the moment and the banal; often they went to him, for few people understood these places. He had seen and felt the jungle. With my family I had to make them imagine entirely, and often I abandoned my attempts, able to leave them only with half-formed ideas. The editor's sympathy therefore provided little consolation. I felt he had betrayed our alliance.

I became disturbed—more deeply than I immediately realized. I lost morale. There was a sort of mental paralysis. I fell asleep during the day, the bedsheet pulled up to my chin. I awoke, restless. The room seemed friendly; I feared losing it. A paranoia developed. The nuns threatened: another source of authority. Had the UN man arrived? I hid from footsteps, pretending to be asleep. People passed my door without stopping. I felt unknown, secreted. I kept my radio beside me. My alarm was set to repeat at the hours of the bulletins. In this way I spent my energy, feeling futile, alone with my noises. But I could never relax: in the rustling of the trees outside my window, in the dormancy of the red tulips, and in the voices on the street, there seemed a quiet vigilance, a sense of suspended anticipation.

For the first time we received evidence that the militias were indeed moving—that the proximity of recent attacks had been no coincidence. The radio announced that General Mathieu Ngudjolo, leader of the Congolese Revolutionary Movement, a militia of about ten thousand fighters, heavily armed, was approaching some key electoral sites in Bunia's sector. Of course, this alone did not make world news. We had to wait for something to happen.

It was the day I began to take the malaria tablets. I hadn't trusted the doctor's diagnosis, because I felt my condition had not been growing worse. Then on the weekend I felt ill again, and I decided to take the pills as a precaution. They couldn't do harm. Four pills, taken all at once, for three days in succession. I lay under the blanket and clutched my pillow, feeling the atmosphere infuse with darkness. A sharp banging disturbed me. Naro had stormed into the room; I hadn't heard him knock. He wore a broad smile and was dressed to go out. "I have arranged the evening," he said. "We will meet some of your people."

"I'm not feeling great."

"You'll feel fine after a drink."

"The doctor told me to take rest. I'm on medication."

"For what?"

"Malaria."

"You don't look like you have malaria. Come, come. The doctors here call everything malaria, and the next day I'm always hale and hearty."

"I don't know. You go ahead without me."

"But I already told them you were coming. Listen to me, they are representing big businesspeople, good contacts to have in Bunia. They are also from your part of India. Maybe they will help you."

Naro didn't let up. He waited by my bed and then outside the door while I changed. His intrusion put me in a bad mood; and in retrospect I should have told him off. Once I had gotten out of bed, though, I moved more easily. "Hurry up or we'll be late."

"Shut up, man, I have malaria."

Was I tired or just dejected? Stepping out could be pleasant, I thought. But as soon as we reached the bar I felt I should have stayed at the convent.

They were three Tamil brothers—boys, really—gaunt and mustache. Their shirts were collared, in checks and stripes. Their jeans were light blue, and seemed of thick cotton. Originally from Pondicherry, the Tamils had learned to trade in Uganda, and had crossed over to Bunia less than a year earlier. They were unruly from the start: slapping backs, calling to the girls, loudly jeering. Naro raised his volume, easily keeping up. He summoned a garçon to our table. The Tamils ordered double and triple shots. It was announced that no one should drink beer. I asked for water. The conversation went low; I saw the exchange of glances. Naro ended the awkwardness with a lewd comment. The Tamils laughed. For the next hour I sat in Naro's shadow, content to be silent. The boys stared at the bar girls, some of whom had appeared at the counter, strutting around, flattered by the attention; they made doe eyes and batted eyelashes; some were draped over chairs. A girl rose, wearing a black cocktail dress that exposed petite shoulder blades and was backless down to the tail of her spine. She looked savage, *brut*—she was perhaps here for the beauty pageant. Men in cravats and ties loitered, eyeing her. When the garçon returned with our second round of drinks one of the Tamils was leaning back in his chair, bending its legs. The chair buckled, and the garçon spilled some gin on him. The others laughed; the garçon looked terrified. The Tamil, who was wiping his shirt, cursed. The garçon asked if he was all right. The Tamil lost his calm. "What? You're back-talking to me?" And suddenly he started to fling his arms. The boy cowered and held up his hands.

Naro grabbed the Tamil. "Enough, man!"

I started to feel drowsy. The temperature had dropped. As I stood the plastic end of my chair scraped against gravel.

"What, man, you're going?" one of the Tamils said. "Where is he going?" The Tamil was clearly drunk. "Arre. Come on yaar. At least have a drink with us. Get him a whiskey on the rocks," he told Naro. I indicated with a finger that he shouldn't place the order. The Tamil clicked his tongue. "What is this? *Who* do you think you are?"

Naro touched his shoulder. "Chill, okay? Chill."

"Don't talk to me like that," the Tamil said impatiently, pushing Naro. "*I* can't accept this. It's just not done."

"Come on," Naro said to me, "order something."

"I'm not feeling well. I told you."

Naro leaned over to me. "Man, one more drink is not going to kill you."

"You have a cold?" the Tamil across the table yelled. He was standing and holding his glass to his nose.

"Malaria," I said softly, looking at my bottle.

"Rubbish," Naro countered. "He doesn't have malaria."

I eyed Naro. The Tamil seemed pleased. "Gin and tonic, double shot!" he instructed the garçon. "And make sure the tonic has quinine."

"Quinine!" the other Tamil shouted. "Don't you know that? It's what they give to malaria patients." The Tamils put their arms over each other's shoulders and started to chant. "*Qui-nine! Qui-*

nine!" The garçon left my drink on the table. I rolled it in my hands and took a sip. Bitterness filled my mouth; I pulled away. The Tamil beside me watched with wide eyes. "Come on! Cheers."

I felt the first shiver. "I should go," I whispered to Naro. "I'm in bad shape."

The young Tamil blocked my path. "You can't waste alcohol!" He nodded to the others around the table, gaining their approval. "You have to finish the drink."

"Drink," the group chanted. "Finish the drink."

I looked at Naro pleadingly. He set his glass on the table and tilted his head, meaning we should go. "He doesn't like us," I heard someone say behind me.

"Thinks too much of himself."

"Let him go, the bastard."

Naro held my arm because I was feeling limp. At the convent I swallowed a Panadol and crashed into the blankets, smelling medicine in my mouth. I was utterly exhausted. I rubbed a palmful of Vicks over my neck and put on a buttoned-up rain jacket and scarf. Over my feet I pulled thick white socks up to the shins. Naro had left the door unlocked; it swung back and forth, letting in a draft.

My last hours in the convent were suffocating, dazed. My legs felt numb; the air seemed saturated with dust. I felt the urge to urinate. My eyes would not open; the sun shone as a uniform orange. The imagination brought fleeting relief: I dreamed of walking out my door and past a basin. Everything was a sparkling-clean white. I felt a warmth start at my loins and radiate over my body. The pungency. I called Naro. He said he would find someone who could help. Who else do you know in Bunia, he asked. "Try with Ali," I said.

"What happened?"

Ali was hunched over the bedside table, chewing tobacco. I

remembered the alarm of being moved, the sense of helpless-
ness as my feet slid over the rocks and as the clothes were pulled
off my body. My joints hurt. I was under a soft quilt in a back
room without windows.

"Relax," he said, his smelly face close to mine. "You need to
rest. Don't ask too many questions for once."

19

I took the medication for two more days, which passed in bouts of sleep and semiconsciousness. To this day I don't know if I had malaria—I believe it could have been that those pills had decimated my immunity.

But the illness, I felt, had protected me from some terrible fate: the room, the toilets, and then the troubles with the AP and Naro—the misfortunes had all seemed enchained, as though from a single cause, and somehow bound to my residence. I was relieved to be out of the convent and its austerity, so isolating.

Ali made sure I was cared for. The domestic, a village girl who seemed about my age, and wore faded rags, made me baby-food porridge each morning. In the afternoons I had ginger tea; before bed the tea was of lemongrass. She followed me, as a precaution, a few paces behind, when I walked slowly down the house's main corridor, bounded on one side by a wide mosquito net from the height of one's waist to the ceiling; so one could look into the yard and upon its mango tree.

The attention, excessive and relentless, soon made me uncomfortable. It made me feel a settler in the house, parasitic; I worried about overstaying. My room, clearly for guests, with only a bed, a cupboard of bedsheets and a shin-high table, provided some peace; but the slightest noise in the corridor would disturb me. I carried a fear of intrusion. On waking I would wait by the door, listen for movement, step out only if there was silence. And the recovery hardly gave respite: once fully cured, I felt intolerably ill at ease.

Ali said the UN was trying to hide its illicit dealings in Fataki—it had not reinstated the right of civilians to fly. He did not bring it up again.

And sometimes it was he who seemed to reach out to me, uneasily; like when he relayed a piece of gossip about the domestic's sister, whose husband had stolen a quantity of money.

One evening, when it was quiet and the shop had shut early, he suggested we have dinner together. He was excited—a new satellite dish had arrived, making the Indian selection of channels accessible. We watched *Antakshari*, a musical game show in Hindi that my parents used to follow. Ali hummed the tunes. The sofas on which we sat were of liver-brown upholstery.

"Listen," he said, chewing. "You should stay as long as you want. There is no problem. You are very quiet. And the house is very big."

I swallowed the insufficiently chewed food, quickly taking water, and thanked him, adding that I might not need to stay. But I was grateful for his offer.

He pushed the bowl of meat toward me with the back of his hand. "Whatever. The room is there if you want."

"Are you making accounts these days?" I tried not to sound too cheerful. But already I felt obliged, that I should be nice to him.

Ali had lately been writing for long hours, in the shop.

"They are so boring," he said, "I find them very boring, four times a year. Why don't you do them for me?"

"Sure." Again, my chirpiness. It was a tone I despised. I could hear my voice become shrill.

"You will mess the whole thing."

He licked two fingers and wiped them dry, staining the napkin in orange lines. The napkin, crumpled, fell next to his plate. "But maybe you can bring me a white girl." He gave it some thought. "A young girl maybe. Sometimes I worry about AIDS . . . Do they have AIDS?"

The TV lit up, making a brightness in the room.

"Usually they are careful," I said, uncertainly.

"That is good. I like the UN girls, or journalists." He sat up. "I want to do it without the condom. I never get the chance. These black girls," he sucked on a finger, "they have infections. And they are always wearing strings. You know the line that goes between their asses? I hate to think of that string."

He ate a little, then chuckled to himself. "You know they use a powder, up and down. 'Clean, clean,' they tell me." He laughed. "You know how they apply it? With a toothbrush. I tell them not to put it, but they say it is antiseptic or anti-fungus . . . It becomes white everywhere. I always make them wash, first thing. Otherwise you don't feel like touching it." He spoke almost with pity.

The *Antakshari* contestants now sang an uplifting music. Their clothes were of embroidered silk; but the creases were too sharp, and one could see the dress had come straight from the shop—had been purchased specially for this appearance; then the singers seemed less splendid.

Ali bit on the tip of a green chili.

"White girls," he said, "I don't really know, except from the porn. They make a lot of porn. They like sex." There was a pause. He looked at me.

I hummed.

"In Congo you can make a nice porn business. The girls are very simple that way. If you get angry they only think they did something wrong." Ali seemed to become excited by this. "I like to make them scared. They look at you. You can make them do anything. I think they also like it."

And I felt, by his talk, that he must often converse in this way.

"You have never taken a black girl," he said.

It was evident.

"Why not? They are waiting for the young men. In Bunia you know, it is banana, the secret. Feed your girl banana fry every day. In two weeks she will become heavy, and big"—he tensed his oily, stained hand, showing how he would grab the breast, as though to hurt the girl. Then again he was calm.

The domestic came in to take our plates, and as though oblivious she leaned over the table, her shirt falling so one could see, against her black chest, her white brassiere. And I could not help but, in my mind, to undress her, to see her breasts under the lace, their largeness, their points, and then see her face anxious, desiring.

But Ali was looking over her form. The girl, silent and still bending, glanced at him, then at me. Without looking up again she collected all the plates and, the plastic rattling in her arms, left the room. I watched her behind, the quick movements of her bare feet. And I now felt that she had not been innocent, that she had deliberately dropped her shirt before my face.

"She thinks after one night you will marry her." Ali ran his arm under his shirt and scratched his chest. "She was married, in the village. Her husband ran away."

He was still staring at the television.

"Don't look again, even if she shows you."

The *Antakshari* hosts introduced a young couple who were to sing a 1970s song. The orchestra began again. But the people on-screen seemed unintelligent; the hosts' low-cut dresses led the eye only to areas one did not want to imagine; the bodies seemed of loose flesh.

"These TV shows are becoming too commercial," Ali said. "Half of it is *tamasha*. Advertisements, talking. People sing for

only twenty minutes, and they are more interested in looking like film stars. Look at their teeth. All *tamasha*." Needless
excitement.

After a while he sighed, leaned back and looked at the ceiling.
"So boring, nothing to do." And that made all the talk, the tension, the descriptions of aggressive sex, seem like restless chatter
about hobbies, like gardening or collecting stamps; they were
ways to keep oneself occupied, to pass the time.

The girl had however desired an end. The way in which she
had offered herself: there was the realization of how the Congolese must feel they were seen. Her gesture had been unambigu-
ous, coarse; she had applied the mood on me; she had seen me
with vulgarity.

I recalled Fannie and Frida, the girls Nana had thrown at me.
The desire with which they had seen me, the ugliness of their
approach—it became apparent.

I wondered why Natalie came to mind. Was it because of the
domestic? The feeling of frustrated desire, of a promise somehow
corrupted. It seemed so. The aggression of this scene seemed to
transfer easily to her memory. I had only crossed the boulevard,
from one side to the other, but the people seemed so defiled.
And somehow I felt infused with Ali's energy—his excitement
in seeking. I had moved far from the purity and charisma of the
convent, with its beatific boy attendant.

I would keep the room, freeing myself from the worry of needing to find a place and pay rent. But mindful of Ali's reputation,
I made adjustments—such as using the back door to leave the
house. This alley was quiet, without traffic. I didn't want people
to think we were associates.

From the gate I walked left, briskly over the mud, to the first
left turn, which opened to a wider road, sloping up. Here was a
corner café. Its picnic chairs were full. Customers ate chickens—
Bunia's food of choice, with the more expensive tilapia—with
twisted legs, as though the birds had been cooked live and

had tried to shrink away from the flame. I ordered fermented milk, which came in a beer glass. And I took a seat that became available.

Across the road was a row of colonial-style houses, of the sort I now lived in with Ali, with narrow pillars on the red-oxide porches. Bunia had only these constructions; nothing had been built in ten years, perhaps twenty. Called *dukkas*, after the Indian word for shop, they had at the front a commercial space, and the owner lived either inside or on top. And today, even on this side street, the *dukkas* had a buzz about them. People emerged from one in special dress. During the days of illness I felt I had lost my bearings; I could not easily tell what was new and what was normal.

But on walking farther I realized I had missed a transformation in the city: people thronged the boulevard. Cars were parked in long rows. A new wooden stage had been erected and strewn with banners. The vice president, Kabila's main rival for the presidency, was due to fly in. His name was Jean-Pierre Bemba, and his chubby face was all over the crowd, plastered on white cotton T shirts and blue flags.

I pushed my way into the crowd, past the men, women and families, past the circle of women doing a bend-over forward dance. The gathering swelled as the hour of arrival approached, until people occupied the full width of the street, from near Ali's shop to the cafés. The money changers and the *kaddafis*, the men holding bottles of gasoline, were gone, but vendors were having a heyday selling lollies: mixtures of frozen milk and sugar wilting on wooden trays.

The music, the beating of the drums and the dancing grew louder, reaching a crescendo. We looked up. But Bemba was not there. The noise diminished. This constant rising and falling put everyone on edge. People tussled for space. We were parched. And it was clear that the abnormally long wait, the surges of emotion, had been deliberately orchestrated.

The crowd required agitation; Kabila was ahead in the polls; Bemba needed to create momentum: it was plausible. But the campaigns, the speeches, the T-shirts and the promises: it seemed too abstract and intellectual a contest for former war-lords, who only a few years earlier had pledged to kill each other.

But in these elections Kabila seemed the man of peace—to end their feud he had named Bemba his vice president. Kabila seemed willing to bring calm to Congo, though it was unclear how much of the country he would control. A victory for Bemba, on the other hand, seemed certain to plunge Congo into new chaos. Born into a wealthy family, he was willing to take great risks to win power. During Congo's conflict he had left his man-sions and servants for the forests, where he had made himself into a powerful warlord.

As one of the milk lolly vendors said to me: "Power falls from the sky in Africa only once every twenty or thirty years. Each man becomes a dictator. He will do everything in his means not to lose his chance at the presidency."

Finally Bemba's large form moved across the platform. "Wel-come, welcome," he boomed into a microphone, grimacing. Women cheered. The waving flags caught sunlight like glitter. Bemba seemed put at ease. He began to laugh at the crowd at his feet. "I will clean up your problems in six months." Now there was clapping. "Who do you trust? Me or that liar?" But the clap-ping had been too quiet—and for a moment I felt that the people had come for the free handouts, the T-shirts, money and ban-ners of cloth.

Then the crowd gave a roar. Bemba was saying that he would prolong the war. "If I don't win the elections I will return to the bush!" he yelled, his eyes filled with rage. "We will make a new army." Arms in the crowd rose in the air, trembling, fin-gers spread out. Women quickened their circle dance, hooting through their hands. Bemba scanned the frenzied people. Slowly, he smiled. I could feel the violence in the atmosphere. The vice president had the power to incite this in the poor.

The city was continually tense after Bemba's appearance. The attacks diminished, then stopped. There was no news about the militias' movements. I became suspicious. The wait was first strange, then intolerable. One felt something was being prepared. I fell into a strange depression—again I was eating a lot. Even Ali's offer of having prostitutes over in the afternoons suddenly began to seem interesting. In an attempt to satisfy my agitations, and to avoid succumbing to Ali's degeneracy, I decided to find a way to get out of the city.

I planned a trip with an intrepid American, a middle-aged Massachusetts man whose office, next to the doctor's clinic, I had walked into one day out of curiosity. He worked for a small NGO, and seemed as eager as I was to see what was happening in the countryside. He arranged a journey on the pretext of a field inspection, and had me join. We left Bunia four days before the elections.

It was a quiet morning.

From the outset we seemed alone, the only moving object in the landscape.

Our first stop was about twenty miles from Bunia, in a field with goats. A few men stood around, under the occasional stooping acacia. These were former fighters who, under a special program, were being convinced to return to life as civilians. But the program was failing: many of them were returning to the militias they had previously deserted.

They looked wary, if fatigued, and very black from working outdoors. The American left me to talk to a different group—but we constantly kept an eye on each other; one never knew whose side these men were on.

And now they approached me. First they made clear that they wanted never to use a gun again. It was a line, I felt. I was then eagerly given a story, like a piece of village gossip, about the recruitment of two herders some days before. A plain-looking outsider, a Congolese, had come to the village and discreetly sought out the men. A few days later the men had snuck out, at night, abandoning their families.

So the militias had passed through this area. There was no sign of them now. I don't know what I had expected to see: a garrison-like encampment, perhaps, or some evidence of the military.

The men said they could barely afford to eat from their herding. "It is not a life." No doubt they had lived better by their weapons, plundering. But their main complaint was that the UN could give them more useful things to do: they wanted computer training. They asked if I could give them the internet.

For lunch we stopped at a town called Iga Barrière. A short street was its marketplace, where vendors sold meat. As I had everyone else I met that day, I asked our vendor, while chewing on a brochette, if he had seen militias of late. He had not. But he said that the skewers from which I ate goat had carried human meat during the war. And he burst into laughter.

Only a few miles away there was unease: at Kilo-Moto, a productive gold mine, the men hardly engaged me. They allowed me to watch from the edge of their holes, in which they stood, knee-deep in stagnant water; the blood fluke, which swelled one's liver until the veins burst, was common here. Shovels scraped against rock.

Above the pits men chatted and shook the golden clay through sieves. On their way out of these mines they would be strip-searched by the South African company that had hired them as day workers. And in the morning they would again be inspected; only the healthy would be handed permits. In this way the company was assured its gold.

The mines were exploitative, but the villagers were grateful—few other jobs paid two or three hundred dollars a month. They told me that they usually spent their earnings by sunrise, on alcohol and women. They called it "having a wife for one night."

We drove past fields, and over winding paths on hillsides. The light fell in shafts between clouds.

Among the herders that day I had sensed not anger or resentment but boredom. Their asking for the internet in that field, where they did not have access to electricity and clean water—showed their desire for a life on the edge. I said, "You can get the internet easily in Bunia." They felt I had misunderstood. "We want to have it here."

The extravagant, almost whimsical nature of Congolese demands—it was something striking about the people. It led to frustrations. And it perhaps, in part, had to do with the unreasonable expectations of life that Mobutu had created. His destruction had been exhilarating. For a while, in the Zairianization of the 1970s, Congo roared. That was a time of unbelievable wealth—a great carnival. Ordinary people accessed great sums without work. It was felt that Congo's famed riches were, at last, in the hands of its people, and that because this was their destiny, their right, the carnival would not end. The labour of four or five decades was consumed in those few years. And the country was left exhausted. The carnival, however, is still remembered, and beloved. It is part of the nostalgia—perhaps society's great nostalgia, proof of the Congolese achievement.

And now the ex-fighters were being given fishing nets, reeds to weave baskets with and goats to herd. It was an offer of homogeneity, of the individual adventure without the individuality or the adventure. One fished, wove, farmed one's plot. There could be no defiance in this, no drama, no impression of direction or conviction. The men, emerging from the bush, wanted lives; they were being offered jobs. They wanted a way to express themselves.

They found it in the war. In it they marked the world, with

pickax and machete. Victims were boiled in barrels, crushed by pestle, raped until hollowed out and made to carve themselves until they collapsed; there was "autocannibalism"; and the "shortcut death," which misleadingly required more effort. One sensed an inventiveness, a kind of glee perhaps, at work—something greater than the desire to cause terror—and that this was not killing by machines but by men progressing through the world with acute awareness, in the way that they knew—making their acts extreme, seeking the spectacle, and allowing for no generalities: each victim was made personal.

We entered Bunia.

The heaviness, one felt it at once.

There seemed more people than usual on the street. The American dropped me off at Ali's place, and I sat outside the house waiting—for what, I did not know.

On a whim I called the garbage company couple. They said they were doing well; more people were subscribing to their service. But otherwise they had heard the same, unbelievable rumors.

I went on a walk—past the UN base, the soldier's rifle as always fixed on me, and along the route of the Hummer patrol, and under the UN's halogen lamps, where dogs chased cats chased rodents across the beams, throwing long shadows, and between the children who sat under the lights to do their homework. I gave a last look around myself and decided to return to the house.

And now I noticed some people standing about, staring at the hills. Their murmurs were tense.

At last the wait was over.

20

Ali had predicted it a week before, over a TV dinner. But he had seemed in one of his moods, to exaggerate. And I had ignored him. The preparations, however, had kept growing. The patrols had been made longer and more numerous; soldiers had been added to the UN watchtowers. Helicopters were circling overhead and tanks had been deployed. And I knew that the rumor, which had seemed absurd, was in fact true. I became half-dazed. General Mathieu's army was only a few miles away, and moving upon Bunia.

The legends were swiftly exhumed: the bloodbath here three years before had been the pinnacle of his career: General Mathieu's drugged army had come out in pink wigs and ladies' robes. They had danced to street music. Corpses had decomposed in the gutters; the city had taken weeks to clean. One story had it that red flowers soaked up blood, and this was why the little red gardens had been planted in the convent and at the airport. The nuns said they were not surprised. Bunia had always been like this. They spoke breathlessly, using broken French, English and Italian, and in alternation, like the heads of Siamese twins. A hundred years earlier, I gathered, a militia had knocked on the convent door. The missionary had recorded it in his journal, now kept in the Vatican. Hundreds had been killed with clubs and machetes. "For a stupid thing called gold." Those people had died for man's "lust" for shiny metal. So little had changed in Bunia, and in the world. "But we Italians are not like Congolese," Luigiana said.

"Killing is not our charisma," added Mariana, wrapped in a white robe and watering the tulips from among the plants, so she seemed to rise like a floret.

The election work seemed already undone; no one would come out to vote with the general threatening.

As the UN prepared, traffic on the boulevard became gradually dominated by military trucks, green and white—the white trucks were for the UN. And because a Security Council resolution had decreed that as a foreign army the UN could not fight alone, the national army—green trucks full of morose red-eyed men wearing chains of bullets as necklaces—was being mobilized.

Neither gave assurance—General Mathieu in recent months had reversed nearly a year's worth of territorial losses to the UN, which was reeling from scandals and seemed distracted, adrift. It was incredible that the general had been allowed to reach Bunia, the UN's regional headquarters. And the Congolese soldiers' glumness was not to be trusted; under supervision, they were behaving. Their faces were oily, their heads matte black. One occasionally saw a soldier digging with his tongue into his teeth: they were being fed. But these were special combat provisions. The soldiers were otherwise paid only ten dollars a month, and often met basic needs—food, money, sex—by looting anyone they found unprotected.

Ali, as much as he had been excited before, now seemed less sure of himself. He was often outside, and at home he had turned quiet—almost timid. I felt he too was overwhelmed, surprised by something.

I was aware of the threat and the danger we were in. But my feelings, in this place, seemed displaced—it seemed almost unnatural, and painful, to feel emotions. And as time went on there grew a sense of distrust in me.

It was a distrust that stemmed from the conflicted responses the general produced in society—responses I recognized, and found alarming. "Mathieu will save us," I heard more and more. Though the Congolese knew the gravity of his crimes the general had many sympathizers—not only in Bunia, but even in those villages most severely affected by the war. The contradiction was the same as with the women who had danced at Bemba's speech: Why had they hooted? Did they believe that Bemba would protect them? But wouldn't Bemba's troops terrorize other women? Where was the solidarity?

It was there, but perversely misplaced. A family that could hardly afford to feed itself would borrow to buy a relative a gift of honor. It was almost impossible, engineers said, to build a road—inevitably someone would steal the building materials. Electrical cables were ripped off and sold by communities that would have used them. And women who should have united to demand an end to rapes instead each supported her own rapist. So at times it seemed as though the Congolese willed their own demise: they seemed too ready to flee and protect themselves and, once the danger had passed, too willing to repent and reconcile.

A day passed without news. There was a rumor that the government was trying to negotiate with Mathieu. And it was while I waited at a café for more concrete developments—I felt safer outside—that a vendor came up to me, an old man selling balancing figures made of wire. He told me to give one a little push—the wire structure, balanced on a cone, almost fell off, but stopped at the last minute and swung back to equilibrium. The trick was a counterweight at the bottom. The vendor chuckled, saying he had made it himself. And he moved on. Only later, much later, did it occur to me that he was perhaps the first vendor I had met who appeared to want to spread, more than his wares, the amusement that they created.

The city also showed its stranger sides. I came across a gold seller in one of the boulevard's wooden cabins. Before him was a plastic bag, the size of his fist, heavy with mercury; the metal was used as an attractant, to purify gold. He put his hand inside the bag. I told him the mercury was poisonous. He put his other hand inside. And then, as if for show, he dipped his hands faster and faster. "See, there's no problem." He laughed. I looked away. There were such signs of recklessness.

At the back of Ali's house, on one side of the yard, was a nondescript shed. The tall doors opened, creaking. In an iron-grill cage were three rows of crates, covered in tarp. Over the floor were arcs in the dust, where the crates had been dragged into position and stacked. The ceiling was high. The smell was musty, of animal and nest. It felt remote; I heard sounds from the street, of people calling, of feet, of birds and dogs. I understood none of the communication, and I couldn't help but feel the city was being emptied, that I was in it alone. I came out of the warehouse, and as soon as I shut its doors I heard a flurry of movement inside, as though the animals had come out of hiding.

Daylight receded. The shadows became longer and longer, until they were all at once gone. I shone a torch at the road and illuminated the glass, dust, salt. Headlamps from passing trucks flooded my beam. A light persisted; not far away a pickup had stopped. In the back were two long benches where four soldiers sat back-to-back, weapons pointing up. I withdrew into the shadows. "Hello?" one of them yelled. I said nothing. The soldier made a grimace. The pickup drove off. A moth fluttered over me.

Feeling cramped, distrustful of my environment, of the forces protecting me, and of the people, I decided to go out and meet the danger. A number had been circulating that supposedly belonged to General Mathieu. A Congolese reporter had given it to me. So far it had not worked. But I began to call the number repeatedly—and that evening someone picked up. The man on the line confirmed himself as the general: *"C'est bien lui."* "It is he." I asked if he was going to invade Bunia; he did not answer. I said I wanted to meet him. And surprisingly, he agreed. He told me to come to his hill.

I had not imagined this would be possible. And now, the invitation secured, the danger in the journey became apparent. General Mathieu had given me his word, but could he be trusted? In Bunia there was at least the UN—here the law still had meaning. On the hill, militia territory now, I would be completely at his mercy.

I approached Ali.

But he seemed hit by a kind of neurosis. He became feverish, explosive, angry at me—he said I had done a foolish and thoughtless thing. What made me think I could call General Mathieu on my own? Shouldn't I have consulted him first? "This is dangerous, dangerous," he said. But he insisted that we go. "I will have to come with you." I wondered if we should go at all. "No, no, we should go." He was now calmer. "There is no problem, I know these people. I know how they work. What the hell, man, I used to have six bodyguards to piss in the bush." He smirked. "*Six*, just to *piss!*" So he had worked for the militias. It explained his conceit. Ali said that if he came with me nothing could happen. "We take zero risk. If I get even a small feeling of trouble, straightaway we come back." He spoke in an intense, committed way—it was reassuring. As was the manner in which he conducted preparations—methodical, compact, wasting no energy. In the morning he was in the jeep, his hair wet and pulled back tightly, before the allotted time—I was even thankful to have a driver of his experience.

When the bureau learned I was going they told me to take along a photographer. His name was Riccardo, and he was an Italian freelancer who happened to be in town. We had met before, while covering the earthquake at Lake Tanganyika. As it happened, I was glad to have a third person in the vehicle—since we had started to move, Ali had begun to show signs of strangeness. And though Riccardo was not known for being discreet—he had come to Africa seeking adventure, of all kinds; he had traveled down the continent by motorbike and up its rivers by barge; he was a hit with the African girls—this was also his first meeting with a warlord of such standing, and the gravity of this, perhaps, made him quiet. He lay in the backseat, as though asleep. The only sign of life he gave was the glowing tip of his cigarette.

Everything else about the journey was noisy: the engine rumbled; boxes shifted and cracked in the boot; the wheels smacked when we landed in depressions—the road was pitted, it seemed, with tunnels. And most of all, Ali came into boisterous spirit. He rolled down his windows and had the speakers blast Nusrat Fateh Ali Khan. Everyone we passed turned to look. The engine revved. Bouncing in our compartment, we roared across the countryside, throwing up a cloud of dust. Ali hummed to the *qawwali* and looked in the mirror, turning sideways to appraise himself. He seemed emboldened, to reach for our destination, and to find expression in our journey; he made the adventure feel large. We turned off the regular road and onto a dirt trail. Ali drew his compass. "We're right on course." The altimeter on the dashboard wobbled, indicating we had started to climb.

I often found myself looking outside. Where there was a plant or tree, it seemed wild, reduced, with thick bark; the savanna vegetation grew in spurts; and around the trees the land, golden brown, was covered in dusty shrubs.

Ali's violent driving eventually did us in. We were on the slope, not three miles from the general's camp, when the engine started to grow hot. Ali did not heed my warning; he continued to drive; and the swelling gauge hit red. The hood began to steam. He drove sluggishly to a depression in the road, at the bottom of which lay a puddle. The radiator cap spluttered open and discharged a fountain of vapor. Ali poured in some muddy water. This was also coughed up.

"It needs rest," he said, staring at the radiator. At last he was sober. He turned the Nusrat off; the party atmosphere was gone.

When we restarted the climb our progress was slowed by check posts—slim logs set on small piles of stones at each end— every hundred yards. The militiamen who manned them grew progressively older and less drunk. One of them came to our window and peered inside. Ali screwed down the window and he jumped back. Near the top of the hill we came to an isolated hut. On the porch was a boy, aged about fifteen, eating a pack of glucose biscuits. He wore the fatigues and green beret of the Mobutu army. As though suddenly aware he had a job, he started when he saw us. *"Qui? Quoi?"*

"General! Where's your general?" Ali shot back.

Ali, Riccardo and I drifted about the hut's bamboo-rattan furnishing: three chairs and a couch were arranged around a low table decorated with a square of yellow lace. But the place reeked of falseness; one felt uncertain; the homely ambience was not achieved.

While we waited, the boy, who had finished his biscuits, became engrossed in Riccardo's camera, which was being explained while held up to his face. The boy frowned, and then, his forehead still wrinkled, smiled—but suddenly he bolted for the door. There had been a noise; we went to see. To one side of the summit, over the hill's edge, had appeared a large procession. The boy adjusted his beret.

It was like the entrance of a king of old: a group of scouts led, skipping left and right, jumping high, turning with their guns. They looked more like dancers in a parade; but it was their way of vigilance. When they reached the hut they felt us up and down, and every object—belt, pen, telephone—was inspected, opened, tested.

The general wore a crisp yellow shirt and brown trousers, which he picked up at the pleats to sit. On his feet were bronze-buckled sandals. And if one looked at him alone, omitting the entourage, one would see no sign of the militia. He had dressed to match his new message. The conflict, he declared, was to end. "We want to rebuild the country. Isn't that what we've been fighting for all along?"

He leaned forward. "People have grossly misunderstood my work." "Work," *travail*, the term seemed important to him. "I have been constantly protecting the people," he said. "It is the government that has always changed. But if the elections are sincere, we can collaborate."

"Collaborate with whom? In Kinshasa and abroad they are accusing you of war crimes."

He smiled. "My friend, didn't they tell you? In all wars the first victim is truth."

He had quoted Aeschylus, the father of Greek tragedy.

The discourse, the strategy: to the last detail they had been engineered. The ten thousand fighters of the Congolese Revolutionary Movement were to quit the bush and fight instead for the government. In exchange the general would be installed as a colonel in the army. He had also arranged for a lesser militiaman called Cobra Matata to join in his plan. Both men would receive amnesty. But the general was concerned the amnesty would be seen as an admission of guilt—it now mattered to him what people thought. "You have been in the army? . . . No?" He frowned, as though I might then not understand. "War is an extraordinary situation, isn't it?" I agreed. "There is a lot of disorder, you will agree, even without experience." I showed I was willing to accept that. "Decisions are difficult. Sometimes you don't have the full information. Different things seem acceptable, because of the context. But what is the justification during peace? Peace crimes are actually more serious—we should punish them more heavily."

He sought to convince; I accepted. "That's an interesting perspective."

He leaned back. "I know." *"Je sais."*

He was too smug.

"I don't know what the courts will think."

"Which courts?" He waved at my face dismissively. But it surprised me now that the general was willing to go so far in his trust of the government. I asked, "What if they break their promise?"

There was silence; sensing weakness, I pressured. "Aren't you worried?"

He searched my face. "Do you know something?"

It was perhaps the only real moment between us.

"No."

But I became uneasy; I asked him a few questions about the disarmament plan; and I wanted to know about his time as a nurse—for he had once worked for the Red Cross. It was when his wife and daughters were killed by a militia raid on their home, he said, that he took up arms, "so no one would have to suffer like I did." He almost seemed a martyr.

The government would acquiesce to nearly all the general's demands. He was appointed colonel in the army, the state arranged a banquet in his honor and his ranking officers were accommodated as promised. The colonel offered the army his expertise, helping to plan raids on his old allies among the militias. He was commended by senior officers; a promotion seemed coming. Some months later the president summoned Colonel Mathieu to Kinshasa, lodging him at the Grand Hotel. The colonel ate and drank while waiting for his audience. He was collected one day and taken to prison. He was stripped of his rank. The pardon was rescinded, and Mathieu—now only Mathieu— was deported to face war crimes charges at the International Criminal Court in The Hague.

Stalked by the scouts, I took a walk. Some of the fighters wore

leopard skins over their chests. Others had gray ash on their foreheads in crosses. A group played a game with stones, for want
of marbles, catapulting the pebbles with their forefingers. Some
held up tall bundles of hay and banana leaves: procession paraphernalia. The crop stood beside them, looking almost human.
Ali looked as if he was trying to approach the general, who was
posing for Riccardo, standing tall and pointing at Bunia. The
meeting had left me agitated, because of Mathieu. I had tried to
relate those atrocity stories to his face: I had pushed, and pierced,
and where I had expected strength I had felt fragility. Mathieu's
talk of peace crimes—it seemed a kind of realization of what he
had done, and half a plea of insanity, for comprehension of his
condition. I walked more quickly. And I spoke in sharp tones,
approaching one of the boys. His name was Olivier. He was
smoking a hand-rolled cigarette. But he said it wasn't a joint. He
drew a clump of marijuana from his pocket; smoking off duty
was against the battalion's rules, he said. The weed was rationed
for combat. We stared at each other. I gestured to Ali. *"Chalo,"*
he mouthed. "Let's go."

The scouts had placed heavy rocks under our tires, in case
we had tried to escape in a hurry. Now they were leading the
procession up the hill. We dragged out the rocks ourselves. The
sky was overcast. Heavy drops began to fall on our windshield.
The wiper squealed. In places of mud the wheels slipped as we
descended. The fighters at the check posts demanded cigarettes.
Some jeeps passed us, going uphill: they slowed to stare into our
car, and at us. They seemed anxious, to be looking for someone. We were silent on the drive. The rain seemed to open the
savanna, making it wide. The jeep felt intimate.

I typed up my dispatch at an internet café that I had specially
arranged to be open late. The editor worked in a frenzy. That
Mathieu's militia was disarming would be front-page news; he
wanted to beat the other agencies. We did. This was to be the big
story I had tried for so long to obtain. But the thrill was mod-

erate. And the editor too seemed spent, his intensity as though from an addiction, producing in him, once it was finished, a deep enervation. My feet crunched over the sand. Normally the noise, on the open street, would have made me self-conscious; but the people were turned away, seeming absorbed in their own affairs. I came into the house. The lights were off. The tap trickled, slowly filling my cup. I felt quiet. Before stepping into bed, by compulsion, I listened for sounds—expecting, as on most nights, to hear an unusual movement, a furtive scrape. On this night there was no alertness to wrestle with. I discovered the mosquito net had developed a hole, and I covered myself completely with the hairy blanket.

In Équateur, the environment, the world, had seemed old, unshifting. But here the war and mining had, for a century, shifted the people and the land. So this was a stasis in continual movement: the ways of thinking had become frozen, so that each change seemed unexpected, and severed from the previous change. There could never be a whole understanding; there was only reaction.

I dreamed that night about the family—that something unhappy had happened. The house's gate had almost come off, and there was a terrible ambience in the house, Nana walking in circles, talking desperately. The next day I called them. Jose picked up and said they were fine. I felt my dream was even more real.

21

C ongo's borders were closed. The government statement was solemnly read out on all the radios, despite its insignificance: the country was vast, and its frontiers highly porous. Anyone could have walked or driven in without detection, even on the day of the vote.

I arrived at the polls at 5:30 a.m., a half hour before they would open; voters were already in line. They were mainly the elderly, perhaps hoping to be home before the sun grew hot. A few younger citizens courteously let them pass; there was, after all, no reason to rush. We waited for the hour. The people were solemn. They twitched, squirmed. When I moved to the front they turned to stare: it was normal. I asked them to show their cards; they lifted the orange plastic in unison. Generally I had found the Congolese shy to be photographed, particularly in the provinces. But here the people edged sideways and out of the queue, eager to squeeze into my frame; it was disconcerting. I began to feel that the abnormal obedience and the shuffling of feet were the acting out of a part. It seemed merely another reaction, this performance of democracy. And when voters turned to journalists that day I sensed they were seeking something from the world—a reward, perhaps, that they believed they had been promised.

The vote was fragile. Including those for seats in the provincial parliaments, twenty thousand candidates were listed on the ballots. *Twenty thousand.* The organizers had wanted to include all Congolese, to shun no one; but the proportions had become bloated, unmanageable, almost comic. Voters juggled with newspaper-sized ballot sheets, each page a three-foot square. A single ballot sometimes counted six pages. And millions of bales of such pages, with 300,000 electoral agents, had to be delivered to the country's interiors, to the fifty thousand polling stations to open that morning. Congo's roads—only a couple of hundred paved miles in a country half the size of Europe—were insufficient, so the UN had to activate Africa's largest air operation: special planes and helicopters that supplied innumerable cars, motorbikes, bicycles and pirogues. The smallest necessity was imported from abroad and conveyed through this network— kerosene lamps, generators, uniforms, pens, notepads, paper clips, chalk, cases of money for salaries, and food rations. The complexity caused delays. And here the fragility showed. Agents went unpaid for weeks. There were allegations that salaries had been "eaten" by superiors. Election workers went on strike. Some torched their precious polling equipment. The tension mounted; small dramas played out. At a base near Bunia a soldier shot dead an agent who had told him to travel a hundred miles to vote. The agent had made the error—the law had confused him. The soldier's lawyer pleaded insanity. It might have worked if the world had not been watching: the military tribunal, seeming keen to prove its commitment to the vote, ordered the soldier executed.

From across the country came stories of villagers who had walked for days, supplies on their heads, families in tow, to reach a polling station. Most could not explain the vote, or why they showed such determination, but they seemed to bear a deep faith that what they were doing was right, and that it would somehow help them. And here also society showed its symmetry: turn-out was higher than 80 percent in many districts worst hit by the war. The contradictions I witnessed on that day reflected, in fact, other confusions—of history; and in some way, of Mobutu's conflicted relationship with his idol and father figure Patrice Lumumba.

On June 30, 1960, not a month after assuming power, Lumumba forced an abrupt independence from Belgium. Already before the proclamation there had been killings. The implosion was now immediate: within days the army mutinied against its Belgian officers. Nearly all the Europeans fled the country, leaving behind only a few *évolués* with any administrative skills. People were recklessly promoted: among them Lumumba's personal secretary, a scrawny twenty-nine-year-old Joseph Mobutu, was given charge of the army. And Belgium, spurned, tried to exploit the turmoil. Hoping to retain control of the copper mines it split the nascent country by supporting the province of Katanga's secession. Belgian soldiers were deployed against the Congolese army. Lumumba appealed to the UN. Peacekeepers were sent, but they were unable, sometimes unwilling, to remove the Belgians. The violence did not abate. The secession still threatened. A desperate Lumumba appealed to the Soviet Union.

And the dictator raised his head. In a classic Cold War move the CIA cultivated the malleable and ruthless Mobutu. Lumumba seemed unable to suspect the protégé he had handpicked and mentored; his trust was sweepingly betrayed. The first arrest he escaped. Mobutu then sent him to Katanga. Shortly before his death Lumumba showed sympathy for his former secretary, saying the young man did not know what he was doing—the relationship to him still held meaning; he showed that confusion. Congo's hero of independence, it is said, was caught and cut to pieces by his enemies and scattered across the jungle from an airplane—the body was so dismantled out of a fear that otherwise his spirit would reassemble and return to haunt its killers.

Mobutu appeared liberated: now freed from Lumumba's fiery politics and wholly backed by the UN and the West, Mobutu gradually marshaled the force to crush Katanga's secession. In a second coup in 1965 he disbanded the government. He then instated himself president. Upcoming elections were canceled, allegedly in the interest of national security. Peace was reestablished. The Europeans returned. The Americans as well, for business. The economy was restored. Mobutu was praised. In 1970 he was received by Nixon for a twelve-day official visit—one of only a handful of leaders so honored. So Lumumba's death seemed already ignored, and forgotten by the world. But in Congo, strangely, Mobutu resurrected his former idol, declaring him a national hero and building him a monument. He also promised to salvage Lumumba's vision. With the blessings of his Western allies, in 1970 he organized elections.

Congolese were obliged to vote; the ballot showed a single candidate; the police and army went from door to door, harassing people. It was a further treachery.

Mobutu's methods—assassination, dictatorship, repression—had ample precedent in African history; he did not invent these. But in characteristic fashion Mobutu transformed the destruction, and made it extreme. It was Mobutu's trap to introduce two ballots, so that people had to choose between a green ballot for "unity" and a red ballot for "disorder." He said it was difficult for his people even to understand this, the need for two ballots—how to explain all of democracy? But his ridicule of the Congolese (and of Lumumba's work) was allowed to stand: the country was too rich, and the dictator was needed as an ally. For the majority of Mobutu's dictatorship the CIA used Kinshasa as a base to quash communism in Africa, and in return America, France and Belgium helped to militarily suppress Mobutu's opposition. The foreign patronage proved crucial to cementing Mobutu as dictator, and to restricting, stunting and eventually arresting the emergence of his people.

It explained the unpreparedness and ignorance in Congo; in the society I found, the decades of damage had become rooted. A man asked me before the vote, "Is Constitution a man or a woman?" At the polls I met a woman who tried to vote with beans. She did not know how to use a pencil, the officially prescribed tool with which to mark ballots, so she had brought carefully counted beans that corresponded to her candidate's number. There were efforts to educate: a tireless Congolese nun had set up a series of literacy camps. She taught the X as the motion of a woman's hands when grinding leaves, and the check symbol as the shape of a mortar. But the camps were few and held only in the cities, and on the day of the vote many villagers arrived at the polls after long journeys holding pebbles and peas. The literate had their own difficulties: election officials would later say they found scribbled beside candidates' names notes like "I love you!" and "God's child."

Those ballots were disqualified.

I had become acquainted with an American official sent by his embassy to monitor the vote. We had breakfasted together at the Hotel Ituri. The American was young and he spoke quickly, in a flurry of ideas. He had come to Congo from Venezuela, and before the Foreign Service had worked in a prominent corporation. On Election Day we met for lunch, as we had planned, to share our observations. I listed some of the irregularities I had seen: ballot boxes improperly shut, officials marking ballots for people. "But does it matter?" the American said, suddenly pulling us out of the conversation.

"Meaning?"

"I don't think anyone really cares about Congo"—it was not an uncommon opinion, but the American official said it with a certain pride, as though he had reached that conclusion independently.

I asked why the West was spending a billion dollars on the elections. "That's not small money."

"It *is*. Elections are nice, but it's not why we're here"—his voice trailed off.

"Phelps Dodge?" The firm had a large mining operation in Katanga.

He shrugged.

I learned that Kabila, despite publicly proclaiming mining reforms, was quietly according lucrative concessions to foreign companies. He was under pressure: the companies benefiting were from the countries funding the vote and, as the American indicated, aided in negotiations by their embassies.

It seemed a dangerous hypocrisy: to raise a people's aspirations with the intent to betray.

While waiting in line at one polling station I found myself beside an elderly woman. She was shy, and wouldn't talk easily. When I brought up Lumumba she clicked her tongue and looked away. But her neighbor, a girl, had overheard; and she began to prod the old woman, to tease her in Swahili. "Tell us, tell us." A man before us also turned. The woman finally looked up at us all. "I hope this time the winner has more luck," she said, smiling wryly. "Our country has had enough martyrs."

At the end of the day, once the last voters had left and the polls had closed, I stayed behind in a classroom to watch the officials count. The room felt like a cave. We were illuminated only by dim kerosene lanterns, which gave the official orange tunics a rich glow. It was 2:00 a.m. when the last box was snipped open with scissors. And the large, white ballots were spread over the table, around which were seated nine Congolese officials. The single man standing unfolded a ballot. "Kabila," he called, holding it open at his chest. The others leaned forward to inspect it. There was a round of nods. With a piece of chalk a tally mark was drawn on the blackboard. The sheet was placed at the top of a pile. More Kabilas were called. Then a Bemba. More nods and a tally. This ballot was also placed on the pile.

22

It had become logical to leave Bunia. The story of the elections would continue in other places. There was also a feeling that more violence was to come, and I was drawn to this.

Kinshasa had erupted during the vote. Anderson and his fellows had cleverly calculated: their riots on the Boulevard had been forcefully repressed. Photographs had emerged of police lashing fallen men with metal chains. In a single day nearly a dozen demonstrators had been killed; the government's force had been plainly disproportionate. Something seemed to build.

Ali stood at the doorway as I left his house. He was resentful. He seemed to think that I was abandoning him—and he hardly said good-bye. Our journey he felt had been the beginning of our friendship, trust, and he had imagined we could have other adventures. That we might form a partnership. I too felt the sense of solitude, the pain of having built another relationship only to let it go. Even if Ali was an odd character, an unlikely friend. I didn't stay long in front of his house—as soon as the motorcycle taxi arrived I mounted it.

I looked forward to seeing the family again, though I worried about their state. The dream still felt vivid. Mossi might be wretched. Kinshasa would not be easy to return to.

Outside Bunia's airport, by the entrance, a group of vendors hawked Gouda from the backseats of their bicycles. The cheeses were wrapped in plastic, ready for transport. I purchased two pies, and sent these over the conveyor belt, through the X-ray machine, at the airport entrance.

The check-in counter was a blue wooden desk that soldiers carrying heavy haversacks were streaming past—a Hercules aircraft had just landed, and from the aircraft's belly, over a hatch descended like a tongue, a single file of African soldiers marched onto the desolate yellow field. Hup!

PART III

MATTERS OF BELIEF

23

The mystery of the capital was gone. Coming from the countryside, I was able now to see it for what it was—a severed and self-contained chaos. The roads leaving Kinshasa, I knew, ended abruptly in the jungle. The people were receding, more and more isolated. The capital's importance was self-proclaimed.

I arrived with the impression of having been waited upon. An army major greeted me on the tarmac, introducing himself as a friend of the family and escorting me to the parking lot. I did not need to board the UN Japanese-made minibus, crammed with expatriates and going to town. Jose had skipped work to pick me up in a borrowed sedan. He received me with a warm hug, almost fell over me.

I sat in the car, my bag on my lap, wrapped in my arms. It was evening, and we drove down the long road that led from the airport, on one side bounded by a low wall, and on the other by fields dark like the sea.

We passed the lamp-lit markets, and a succession of burned cars stranded on the sidewalk. One felt the disturbance. We came to Massina. Jose did not mention his job. He had been asking enthusiastically about Équateur and Bunia. But now he became distracted and I found myself trailing off to ask him if something was the matter. "It's going a little," he said, pulling at the steering wheel with both hands to turn the car around a corner. I stopped talking, and he did not break the silence.

Bozene was expecting me. I was slapped on the back and shaken by the arm (my hands were holding the bags). Children followed me in a herd, football in hand and tripping over themselves. At our gate I was introduced to Jose's brother, Marcel, who had moved into a house on a parallel street; it was Marcel's son, a hefty boy with big feet, who carried my bags into the house. Nana was there. Frida as well. I felt I was coming into familiarities.

My room had not been cleaned. Nana asked for money to buy supplies. And in the house there was of course nothing to eat.

The hospitality had been reserved for morning. The girl from next door was sent to fetch eggs and bread, which Nana insisted on making for me. I waited at the table. Everything in the house seemed as I had left it. Jose sat on his sofa, showing nothing of the previous day's apprehension. I could discern no sign of crisis. A drumming noise came from outside: a bucket was being filled with water.

Then from the kitchen Nana gave a shriek. Jose ran in, and it was he who made the grim announcement: my toast had been burned. I said it wasn't a problem. But Nana looked distressed as she set down the plate with a clatter. I saw that she had scraped off the burns with a knife, leaving the bread pale, uneven.

On her way back she stopped at the corridor and turned to face Jose. "Can't you see I'm stressed?" It sounded like a plea.

Jose smacked his lips, without turning.

"You've done nothing all day. The clothes I ironed are still on the bed. You haven't even stepped out of the house."

Jose stood upright. "Stop talking like you're solving world

problems. All women work the same and I don't hear them complaining."

"Their husbands have jobs. Why do I have to go to the neighbors to borrow for our meals?" Nana lost control. She began to yell. "I should unplug the television and gramophone. What a man! Shameless!" That last word was spit off her tongue, as though she had been unable to say it calmly. She herself seemed stunned. And now she looked as though she would cry.

Jose, who had so far seemed embarrassed by my presence, ran up to my plate, overly skittish, and emitted a hiss through clenched teeth, as though appraising the toast and feeling sorry for my breakfast. "She didn't mean it badly," he said. Nana stared with a puzzled and then disgusted face. She became hard. She turned her back to him. The confrontation was ended. Nana occupied the kitchen and Jose resumed his place on the sofa. They wouldn't so much as look up when they passed each other.

Silence, and again one became conscious of the wider space. I ate in this stillness, in the muffled light, smelling a mustiness, observing, absentmindedly, the darkened grains on the wood furniture, and then Bébé Rhéma, in her diaper of torn-up plastic bags, sleeping peacefully on the floor. Her limbs were spread in all directions. Occasionally, she quivered her yellow-mucus crusted nostrils. She had appeared undisturbed by the argument, but now she made a growl. Jose stood. A deep grating noise followed. The baby rolled over and opened her eyes. Nana came running, but she appeared just as Bébé Rhéma turned quiet. Still in the vomiting posture, her mouth open, the baby breathed heavily. She closed her eyes. Her limbs relaxed. She returned to her erstwhile state of sleeping.

"Tired," Jose remarked, looking over her.

"We need to take her to the hospital," Nana said.

Jose shifted his tone. "She has been like this for one week."

Nana glanced my way, looking weary.

"You will come, no?"

And it was clear that we would not otherwise be going.

Jose's brother had taken his car on an errand. His wife didn't know when he would return. Before the evening, she offered. But by then the day-duty doctors would have left. Jose said he could ask the man down the street—he had often helped the family— but that this man had lately begun to talk about his own dif- ficulties. It was a way of requesting relief, or of complaining that too many were asking favors. "Does my family have to do every- thing in this house?" Nana said, to no one in particular.

We prepared with speed and in silence. Jose called out once to ask if Nana had the keys. Rudely she hushed him. Cupboards were opened, clothes and papers were scattered. Nana pulled a dress over Bébé Rhéma and packed a large handbag with two bananas, a feeding bottle, some towels and a few spare diapers. Bébé Rhéma wailed when lifted by Nana. Jose emerged from the bedroom in bloated pleated pants and with a ballpoint pen in his shirt pocket. We waited, sitting, as Nana lulled the baby back to sleep. Eventually Corinthian's battered red car came around the corner. It rocked over Bozene's bumpy surface and stopped at our gate. We trooped through the neighbor's new restaurant; the lunch crowd was just leaving. I found the car's front seat broken, and I shifted over the wires of its inner frame to find a comfortable position. Jose sat behind with Nana. Bébé Rhéma, fully awake now, was securely wrapped in a bleached cloth. I was beginning to feel nervous about my role in this journey.

"Bé-bé!" Nana cooed.

As we departed the house, over the sand path leading to Vic- toire, our car was forced to plow through a stagnant pool stretch- ing across the road. The fender pushed against the frothing turbid water. I worried that we would get stuck midway. Farther along our route, on the *ville*'s wide roads, the pools were larger and more numerous, and the dull-gleaming expanses seemed to smother the city from below, reflecting the continuum of cloud and draining color. One's eye became accustomed to the sudden contrasts. The concrete buildings were dark with moisture and vertically streaked bright green. The river—we caught a glimpse of it, busy with barges—glowed.

Soldiers patrolled the roads. Corinthian stiffened. Jose urged him to speed on. Nana tried to hide the baby between her legs; but the bundle was too large, and she fumbled. The roads around the hospital were congested; we found no convenient parking. Corinthian used a space marked for doctors. The family sat still a moment before emerging from the car. Jose and Corinthian straightened their shirts. Nana was weighed down by the bag and the baby. The family, exposed in the parking lot, looked exhausted and out of place in the *ville*. And here they began a conversation—as though making a plan. But the talk became casual. I began to feel impatient, that they were delaying.

I had my own discomfort about the hospital, from a previous visit. This was some months earlier when, seeking a story for World AIDS Day, I came to write about the "hospital of death." The idea was not original, but it was the kind of simplicity—half-obvious, half-exaggerated—that I had seen sell in the papers. The doctors obliged, took me within. Thirty minutes later I terminated my visit, abandoning the hospital. The setting I was shown—women with flaccid breasts, tunics falling off, reaching out for me from their beds in a delirium; the doctors asked if I hadn't brought a camera—had felt deceitful, deliberate, obscene.

A nurse came to assess the baby. But suddenly she was summoned away. We stood with some uncertainty in the middle of the ward. Staff passed by without paying attention. Nana became agitated. She stroked Bébé Rhéma, as though it were she who needed comforting. The ward was large, like a dormitory, with two rows of metal beds around which, on the floor, sat patients' families with bags of green bananas on stems, tins of manioc and bunches of serrated medicinal leaves. Some empty beds were sheetless, gray. I stood near the ward's door and looked out onto one of the gardens. A sign read, "Internal Medicine." Another said, "AIDS"—the ward I had been to. Families lounged on the grass as though on a picnic.

Nana urgently called me in. The doctor had arrived. I stood behind the family as he tapped Bébé Rhéma's chest and listened with a stethoscope. Nana pushed me to the front; the doctor understood and led me to the accounting office. Jose followed. The costs were explained in French; Jose asked questions, in Lingala. After I had paid, the doctor returned to the family and announced that Bébé Rhéma would be hospitalized for fluid in the lungs. The nurse took over. The doctor continued on his rounds. The family moved on. Jose stayed behind; he was staring at a whitewashed wall, seemingly bemused. Nana called. He turned, and one saw from his face that in fact he was suffering.

It came as a grim satisfaction—there were so many waiting infirm in the hall—but I was relieved to see the doctor take charge of the baby with such assurance. And the family was now merrier. The drive home was fast, easy. Jose, as if reclaiming his authority, said he would ensure the baby was checked on every day—Corinthian and he discussed which relative might be called upon. Nana stared out the window, her cheek against the glass. At one point, when I had turned away, she gently touched my hand. I looked up, and she smiled briefly.

Jose had Marcel over that evening: the election broadcast was due, and there were rumors of news; but more than this, Marcel's family livened up the house. Nana, moving restlessly between the rooms, had already lamented the emptiness. She cut into the block of Gouda, whose thick creamy slices we ate with hot beignets. The girls chased one another in the corridor, almost asking to be admonished by the women. Nana pleaded with the youngest girl to be allowed to do her tresses; that diminished the noise. The men were on the sofas, drinking beer, shouting; the anxieties of the day had found new release.

I felt on edge. I needed company, and leaving the house I half skipped down the street to Anderson's kiosk. His chair, set back, was empty. I turned in to the plot that was just behind the chair. Anderson had once told me he rented a storeroom here. On the exterior of the large house was a blue door, partly open.

The man was inside, on a stool, shirtless. His legs were apart. Slightly out of breath, I said, "Anderson." On the floor, between the dirt and the dust that had come off the wall, were pipes and hand tools; he threaded a plastic tube through the pipes, which he held end to end, and applied a bolt to keep them together. I felt he had remarked the enthusiasm in my greeting, and that he was trying to be sullen, to maintain his unpleasant persona. He finished with a set of tubes. "Monsieur Journaliste, it took you so long to say hello to your friends. What is that you are carrying?"

"A gift," I said, offering the Gouda. He dropped his spanner to receive it with both his hands. He stared at the pie, which measured the size of his stomach—and I felt his surprise was above all sensory, that he could at once be holding so much cheese.

"It is good." His tone was offhand. But, again at his tubes, his hands and toes moved briskly.

I said it was nearly time for the election bulletin. He looked at his watch and shook his head in disbelief. He set down his tools and dusted his hands. I waited at the door. The evening was humid. He came carrying the Gouda, which he set on the kiosk—he said he would give it to a friend who owned a refrigerator.

Anderson set our radio to the correct station. Down the road other radios were set up, at other kiosks, by young men. The dials were turned in unison, raising the volume. The broadcast was thus forced on passersby. The act was aggressive. But it seemed without effect: people still ambled, chatting amicably, making their usual commerce; their insensitivity, too callous, made them seem familiar with and in a way participant, in communion with the anger; and from that moment on even the quiet on the street, I felt, concealed a menace. Anderson continually toweled his face. And I now felt his serenity, the dullness I had taken to be for me, was his way of preparation for a nearing upheaval.

"The riots were a success," I said.

He turned.

His face was shining from sweat.

"Monsieur"—he hesitated—"we were *magnifique*. Magnificent. More than ten thousand demonstrators in front of the presidential palace. Imagine." He held his palm open before us, as though to show the palace's immensity, and that the crowd could confront it. "We proved our force."

"Maybe you should have raided the palace, like Versailles, and finished it right there. Maybe that was your moment, Anderson."

"Oh, Monsieur Journaliste, you shouldn't be talking like that. Wasn't Versailles raided for democracy? We will wait for the official results—if there is no fraud we will surely win."

"Kabila is getting many votes in the east."

He slammed his hand on the kiosk. "Are you taking money from them? To say such a thing." But he had become agitated; his movements were tight. He pointed to a house on the row facing us. "See how he has raised his walls." It was true—the enclosure was so high one could not even see the roof. "That Papa works for Kabila. I already told him, move out of this area. Please." And at once I felt the fear that Anderson could so easily incite.

"That Papa should move," I said.

But he was looking up and down the street, and making a guttural music to himself—it was my punishment—he was not letting me speak. From the kiosk I took the Gouda and felt the crosshatches on its crust. Its label, worn, was illegible.

I held it out. Again he extended both hands to receive it. "Anderson," I said, as though mulling the sound of the word.

"Monsieur Journaliste—you should not betray us. In such times we are counting on our friends. Think about that Papa."

Some people passed, hurrying.

Anderson opened his eyes wide.

The radio brought news: two cities had completed counting. And though the sample was too small to draw a trend from, there was such an air of expectancy in the country that the first results were bound to make a deep impression. The newscaster held his breath: Bemba had won both cities, by solid margins. Anderson stood up and raised his arms. He turned around like a boxer in a ring, pushing his chair away and shouting across the street to the other houses. "Bemba! Bemba!"

The cry spread down the main road and the avenue. Taxibuses honked madly. I heard feet running in the alleyways. The Opposition Debout rallied people from house to house, urging them to step out and celebrate. A gunshot. Then another. Anderson couldn't keep still. "I told you," he said, vigorously shaking my shoulder and holding the back of my head. "I told you Congo is coming back to its people."

24

There was fraudulence—as there perhaps is at the center of any belief. Two weeks later when Anderson defected to Kabila's party the street expressed shock but gave no punishment: he continued to operate his kiosk, at which the same friends gathered to banter every evening. Perhaps Anderson, and the others, had never believed in the cause; if I had known this at the time I would have understood my own apprehensions differently.

The feeling was of being in a kind of madness. Bemba, and his apparent success, seemed incidental to it; the communion grew, religion-like—out of an internal need. I felt that purity in the aggression, that deeper angst.

And it was this fraudulence that made anything seem possible, that made everyone seem to have secrets to which I was not privy.

From my room I heard the youths approach, their shrieks gradually decomposing into the constituent boys' voices. They passed the house. Again they became distant. Jose said it was the Kata-Kata, exploiting the unrest. Already some dwellings and shops had been damaged. Jose hung clothes over all our windows and over the grill door, and we began to pass the better part of our days in these dark, familiar patterns, in the suffocating smells of the body and detergent.

Mossi stormed in one day. His place was no longer safe—his gate had been breached and the yard was now exposed to the riots. He wanted to sleep with us, even on the floor of the living room. But Nana threw him out without even hearing him out. I pleaded with her—telling her the man had nowhere to go. But she was hard. I felt myself shorn, as if something close to me had been lost. The scene was wretched, and reminded me of the time Nana almost threw me out—when her niece Frida had stolen my money. I watched Mossi leave, pulling his hat over his head, his long legs taking big steps over the dark earth.

I told Mossi to meet me in the city, at a center for counting and storing ballots. I thought the tension here might be acute. The gated compound was guarded by two policemen. Inside was a long row of rooms that resembled one of Bunia's *dukkas*, surrounded by a dusty yard, over which lay ballots stacked like bales of hay. Loose papers blew at my feet. Officials hurried between the rooms. Outside, at the compound's gate, people loitered: a policeman, unusually alert, tried to clear them off, swinging his baton. But the people scattered and returned, and merely their presence, it seemed, annoyed the policeman.

Mossi did not come. He told me over the phone that he had sought shelter on the city outskirts. I felt I had lost the man who had lived in my mind for so long in Congo. I tried to get Mossi a job, but the old journalist seemed to have gone off the deep end. The editor told me he filed strange stories—and was constantly talking about his personal problems.

Outside the center I was stopped and asked why I was walking alone. It was the Republican Guard, Kabila's personal army. I offered money; they took it, and made me wait on the side of the road. They seemed to have no plan for me. I stood beside the soldiers, and people passing would give me uneasy glances. An hour passed, then another. I began to panic. But when the others left a soldier casually asked for a cigarette. I had none. He said I could go; I hesitated, and walked away uncertainly. I turned back to look at him; he waved me off with his gun. I broke into a run. Then I had a thought that he wanted to shoot me, so I ran faster, thoughtlessly. It became more and more difficult after that to leave the neighborhood: everywhere one saw the army deploying.

The election results came every couple of days, unpredictably, district by district—as long lists of numbers that took hours to sort through. And the Kata-Kata became my preoccupation. They visited now every night, moving more slowly, lingering. On hearing their cries I would move to the window and push apart the clothes. I got an oblique view of the youths, jumping against our gate, shaking the metal, jeering at us, taunting. They did not approach. And it was their sound, a fugue-like cacophony of similar phrases which could have been confused with the play of children, that was most disturbing.

I had in a way come full circle with the street children. I had seen Corinthian strike fear into the boy who had eaten Nana's hair cream. I had an idea of how the children were expelled. And I had experienced the abandon of the 25th Quarter, the cemetery. But only now, confined by the youths, and watching them— howling, in the safety of their numbers—from our grill window, did I think of the riot as a way for the children to return and confront the violence against them.

An opportunity to leave the neighborhood came at last when the electoral commission summoned the journalists. The results were ready. The street reacted as though it had already won— Anderson and his men raised their bravado, rounding up people, working them up. A large crowd had gathered at Victoire to chant for Bemba. *Mwana mboka*. The son of the country.

The family assigned Jose's nephew Serge as my escort for

the evening. Serge arrived at the house dressed in a suit and crocodile-skin shoes, a plastic pen in his pocket. We took longer than usual to find transport—fewer buses seemed to be running. From the start Serge adopted a grave face, fixed on the road.

The bus's slowness, dipping into puddles, made in me a kind of tightness in the chest. I tried to forget the tension, the street, and Victoire. I tried to observe the scenes passing. But in no person's expression could I find calm. And those pedestrians who seemed to show joy or to laugh I felt incapable of trusting.

Then, on the road near the stadium, some Chinese came into view; they seemed sedate, servile. They were repairing the road—it was the worst season to be doing so—and in some places tinkering with the wiring for streetlights. I thought: the elections are hardly over and already the foreigners are here. A supervisor moved along the workers, arms crossed behind his back, and I saw that it was a fashion in China to have one's sunglasses, when off the eyes, not raised over the forehead but lowered on the mouth.

Mercenary workers: China, like the West, was hungry for minerals, growth—instead of democracy, China offered construction. And the effect of those abject workers was clearly visible. Roads, stadiums, bridges—cement structures were creeping over Kinshasa, seeming to renew the city, to offer a way forward, as had, at various moments, the constructions of the Belgians, Mobutu and Kabila, and the ugly imitations of the *nouveaux riches*. Congo, still an outpost of progress, still with something to offer the powers seeking supremacy, had grown accustomed to such renewal by foreign structures (foreign, even when built by Africans); to this society, in fact, such renewal had become vital.

It was an attitude I had noticed at a party in Kinshasa. A wealthy Congolese journalist had invited me—the party was at his cousin's house, a Belgian garden villa, on whose large balcony the people mingled. The scene, of young men and women, in Western clothes, drinking beer and martinis—it was without vitality. The youths seemed arrested. Merely to occupy that space, the clothes, the paraphernalia—this seemed the achievement. Inside the house, old, resilient, rain had seeped into the walls. The paint was coming off. The corridor smelled of fungus. The toilet did not flush; a barrel of water was provided, with a handleless rusted tin for a mug.

One could tell those youths were non-*évolué*: there was that lack of pride, that consumptive wrecking of the structure. It took my mind to photographs I had seen from just after Mobutu's fall, of Congolese with their livestock squatting in his palaces. And I felt I now understood something of Annie's fear—that her family, on coming to America, would turn her house into a "camp."

The pillage—momentary, chaotic, exciting, growing horizontally by razing, leaving nothing material—was also ambience. So were the riots. It was part of the postmodernism, the Congolese excitement that needed to be appeased; and it could hold people in such heightened states. Ambience held together the street children's existences. It was in the wigged prostitutes at the bars. And it was in the self-flagellation at the churches, where the Congolese listened with rapt attention to the scolding, sweating priests.

One was surrounded, in Kinshasa, by darker ambiences. One did not have to seek them; rather, one could hardly find escape. The ambience could seem an escape, a refuge; but it was itself something to be escaped from—and it seemed as though while the individual pillaged the material, the ambience pillaged him.

Marcel had recently leveled his yard. He wanted to build himself an office cabin. But he was never allowed to: as soon as he bought cement requests came in from the neighborhood—for a wall, a toilet, a broken roof, a sick child. The requests were deemed more urgent than his outhouse office. Marcel lent out his cement. I was at his house when some of the ragged men hauled out his sacks. Marcel was not paid. He did not expect to be: the implicit agreement was that when he needed help (that is, when he became poor like the ragged men) he could ask them to return the favor.

Clementine's restaurant, next door to our house on Bozene, was frequented by half a dozen men who ate every day for free. She did nothing: the men were of our community, some even of our street. It was their small way of hurting her, she said, so that she did not become "too independent," "too capable."

And I had always wondered if Nana's clothes business had been deliberately, even unconsciously, sabotaged by Frida. But surely Nana must have known that Frida would not repay.

It was the internal menace. Nana, Clementine and Marcel were docile in their misfortune; when I asked why he had given away his cement, Marcel said, "It is our custom." *Coutume*: a powerful word. I got the impression that to succumb to custom was in a way to return to the simplicity, the safety of the old ideas: of man as weak, of survival in groups. Jose, perhaps because he was *évolué*, had the courage to try subversion. He had a little metal box, kept in the master bedroom, that I had seen him take out irregularly and call the "emergency fund" (I had only seen it near empty; still he indicated that I should tell no one). The fund was for Bébé Rhéma's hospital visits. Even this had to be saved in secret. Marcel later said, in a more reflective mood: "Our customs are without pity."

Those who built large escaped custom—and existed in isolation. The *nouveaux riches* who raised mansions on the hills were said to have "eaten alone," and they spent colossal sums to protect themselves from the societies they had abandoned. It was the price of independence. And besides the historical ideas, for this reason—of becoming menaced by one's own society, like the wretched on the street, who could die in their dwellings—it seemed also out of a fear of his own rise that the Congolese was pointlessly creative. He turned bottle caps into imaginative, anonymous art; he played endlessly with words, inventing vocabularies; he pillaged; he made sexual art. He squandered his talents on such emotions. His creative activities, stunted, were without deliverance—a sort of wallowing in one's futility, one's chaos. One expected only to survive. A common complaint in Kinshasa was that the men in the mansions, eating alone, were "not leaving enough crumbs": this matter of crumbs was the pressing grievance.

And to arrive at this idea of Congolese smallness is to gain a sense of the overwhelming crisis, of society's impotence—large ideas must live in smaller objects, acts, fantasies—and to see the urgency of the Chinese offer. The material world—the forest of things that the Congolese had inherited—decayed relentlessly. Society, internally ruinous, and reduced to ambience, was unable to build. The Chinese knew to build, and quickly; they had built before for Africans; their labor was cheap, their terms favorable. For thirty years the Americans, the West, had sustained Mobutu, but had built the people almost nothing. The Chinese, a last resort, seemed to offer to resolve the crisis—to renew the world, fulfill the fantasy. And already they were here; already they were at work—destroying Kinshasa's Boulevard, expanding its lanes and cutting down the ancient, broad trees on the sidewalks. Gone was the shade; the vendors could no longer squat over their wares. The people could no longer walk. The people were quiet. Such massive change seemed beyond them: a new destruction was being wrought; and the people were further severed, lost, hiding in the small and ephemeral.

The roads were now empty of people.

I had rarely traveled in the *ville* at night, and I was not accustomed to the sensations. In one section of the road, perhaps recently repaired, the streetlights made a repetitive flashing in the bus, over my lap—the experience, so familiar in a way, here seemed alien. The *ville* was almost totally desolate.

The Boulevard approached. The taxibus had at one point been full, but now Serge and I were the last passengers. The driver said something; Serge responded. Quickly their discussion became heated.

The driver pulled over and told us to get off.

"You had an argument?" I said, disbelieving.

"He won't take us any farther," Serge said.

Apparently no taxibus was running the length of the Boulevard that night. Serge had not known this; and he had become agitated.

It happened too quickly—we got out, and the bus was gone.

The Boulevard, spread out before us, was smoky. And instinctively we moved behind the trees on the side of the street. The first half of the walk was quiet, and brisk—I felt we would reach the commission in time. Then two gunshots rang out from deep within the *ville*. Serge stopped and held out his arm to block my path. The shots had been single—probably not to kill. We walked along the canal, where it was darker. Someone came up on us so silently that we leaped to one side. It was a pedestrian, in a fur-trimmed coat, like the Congolese often wear at night. We had startled him. Serge watched the man leave, and then looked again. I too felt we were no longer alone. Small bonfires appeared on the side of the road, giving sudden warmth. "Kata-Kata," Serge said. "We can still get a bus home." But in the distance we could see the venue—an area of brightness.

"Maybe a kilometer more," I said.

He agreed. "Inside we will be safe."

But the guards would not admit him. I hounded them, saying Serge was my cameraman. I pretended to lose my temper. They said no papers, no entry. But we knew that if Serge had been white it wouldn't have mattered. Serge pulled me aside. He was rubbing his hands over his head, looking distraught, expecting me to produce a solution. We were silent for some time, on the edge of the road. I could not imagine him having to return that way. Serge said the sooner he left the better. We made a feeble handshake, our palms only sliding—I watched him trudge into the darkness; he looked nervous, and I felt I was to blame.

Armed soldiers, UN, leaned against the compound's high walls. At the gate was a tank from whose hatch emerged a soldier who looked something like a centaur. Inside rows of cars were parked in the sand. The earth was washed-out, and even small stones cast shadows; the halogen lamps blinded when I looked up. Before me was the hall where the results would be declared. I was told the venue normally served as a school.

The hall was packed with journalists. Dignitaries trickled in, each outdoing the other in tardiness. We looked expectantly at the vacant microphone on the rostrum. The crowd made a low chatter. I had brought along a novel, but it was too hot to read. I began to sweat; my mouth went dry. It was like being in a minister's waiting hall—I felt returned to another Congo, a place without urgency. We seemed forgotten. I slipped into an agitated half slumber, my hands on my pockets, over my phone, my bag tight between my legs.

It was four hours after the scheduled start when the commissioner was ushered onto the stage.

Old-fashioned cameras whirred on both his sides. Parked outside the hall was a TV van—small satellite dish atop—transmitting live across the country. I took a seat close to an exit.

The commissioner, beneath his dark suit, had worn his tunic; and it was this sheer, collarless shirt of an abbot that more than the suit gave him protection and authority. He cleared his throat; the crowd hushed. His raspy voice echoed on the high ceiling. There was applause when he congratulated the people on the achievement of democracy, and on rising to meet the historic challenge. He then drew a piece of paper from his pocket and slowly unfolded it. In near-perfect silence he called out each province's name and, in the manner of the tedious radio broadcasts, the number of votes for each candidate; he stumbled while pronouncing the large figures. He kept us in suspense until the end. Kabila had won.

I stepped out of the hall and relayed the news to the editors in Dakar. I was again the AP's reporter of choice in Kinshasa by this time—the correspondents had stayed for the day of elections and then, the excitement over, had left for other countries. A flurry of activity broke out as I finished up my call. The compound's gates were flung open and, as a long burst of gunfire emanated from the street, the commissioner's convoy—five, six, seven black cars, skidding over the dirt—swept away. The crowd, which had surged forward, following the commissioner, suddenly fell back; gunfire responded from elsewhere in the darkness. The UN centaur pulled his tank's hatch over him. The gate slammed shut.

In the air a shrill humming noise grew progressively louder and ended with a thunderous crash a few feet from the compound: mortar bombs, launched high above us. A soldier yelled that no one should go indoors, so we stood with our bodies flat against the compound wall. Gunfire began to shell the wall's other side, sounding in our ears like hail. Then there was a shout to look up. We saw the figure of a man clamber over the roof's point and into a shadow.

The cry "Sniper!" created new panic. I ran with the others, half tripping, into the hall; the stage and rows of chairs were now empty. The bright lights made it impossible to see outside—one felt blind. And the crowd began an excited hubbub that was amplified by the hall's echoes. A soldier came in and tried to calm the group; but the noise turned into a din. Some of us went outside. We sat not far from the hall entrance, on a stretch of pavement under the building's eaves. It felt safer here. Before us were the compound's high walls, which I noticed were topped with broken glass, in maroon, purple, green: the colors of beer and soft drink bottles. And running around the compound, over these shards of glass, was thick barbed wire, twisted in large circles. Other journalists joined us on the pavement, some on the phone, some lighting cigarettes. A few preferred to sit inside their cars.

More troops arrived, with fresh cries. I became fatigued. The tank by the entrance was joined by another. I filed nonstop, via telephone; the AP wanted every last detail. The shooting that night, one sensed, had been less a surprise than a deception. No one knew for certain, but it seemed that Bemba's and Kabila's troops were in combat; only the next day would we know that soldiers loyal to the two leaders—all officially in the national army—had overrun Kinshasa.

The violence had paused. A group of photographers made their way to the gate, armed with large cameras. I joined them, tempted to peep out of the compound. There was nothing to see: it was too dark. What streetlights had been working seemed to have been shot out in the battle.

I called Serge at 3:00 a.m. He was still awake. I did not know whether to believe him that the shooting had never reached Victoire. In any case it seemed unlikely that I would be able to make it to Bozene that night.

The soldiers were, at intervals, allowing cars to leave. I moved around the crowd, scanning faces. Richard Bentley was there, looking collected, surrounded by a group of journalist friends who would no doubt sleep at his hotel suite. I skirted them, passed some other groups that also avoided my glances, and came upon two stringers—American and British—who looked equally lost. They asked if I might be willing to share the cost of a room at one of the big hotels. One of them had a car.

The soldier waved his arm. His mouth opened and closed, but I did not hear; our car shot out of the compound and hurtled down the street. The engine beat loudly. From a gap in the window a sharp wind hit my face.

I grabbed the handle above my window and looked out,

searching our surroundings for unusual movements. The buildings passed too quickly. Ours was the only car visible on the road. The American turned off our headlights, and I reclined in the backseat. My body was thrown from one side to the other.

The hotel, as we arrived, appeared as a large and silent block. It was in an area of the *ville* sheltered from the Boulevard. The sky was a faint rose color. We found the main doors barred by an iron grill. I shook them; a guard appeared and directed us to a side entrance. The lights in the lobby were out. There was no music. I passed tall potted plants that looked frail but had been polished. I relaxed. Even without the lights it was evident that this was an environment cared for, tended to; and soon we—unkempt, dirty, tired—would also be looked after, made part of this quietness.

I asked the receptionist, who wore a clean uniform, for a standard room. "We raised prices," he informed me. When? Since midnight, he said, returning to his register. He tore out the receipt. The stringers had moved to a narrow window in the lobby, where they had lit cigarettes, and leaned out in succession. They said they needed to calm their nerves. I left them for the room.

For many months I had wanted to live in the *ville*. When I had first arrived in Congo it had stunned me—the wide roads, the skyscrapers; it had seemed so peaceful and ordered compared with Victoire. But the transaction with the receptionist recalled, and in a way confirmed, my decision to not move. The transaction made plain to what extent my safety here, bought, was without compassion, and temporary. Such was the *ville*: bound by money, unwelcoming, and in a sense unoccupied, exterior to society. The poor saw it as a place to riot, as a route for escape to a better life; for the rich the *ville* was a shield, a way to keep distance from the menace of the shantytowns. It seemed the most modern part of the city, but the *ville* was in fact the most lawless: it belonged to expatriates, politicians, and *nouveaux riches*,

people to whom the law—the written law as well as those of the
streets, of the Donut Society—did not apply. The *ville* obeyed
only a most primitive law: force. That plant in the lobby had
given a false impression: its frailty I had instinctively taken as a
sign of protection. But to exist in the *ville* one needed iron grills,
security systems and guards with guns. The orderliness, the feeling of sanctuary: they had deceived.

My impulse was therefore to get away—and I began to think
to the morning, to my next flight.

I got into the elevator with two girls. There was a shudder, and
the elevator began to rise. I twitched to every click and movement of the machinery. *"Bonsoir,"* one of the girls said, in a sweet
voice, before looking at her companion. "Would you like to
spend the evening with my friend? I would take you myself, but
I have a *rendezvous."* The elevator doors rolled open with a roar
and before me was an open space, dimly lit.

The corridor was decorated with framed pictures of abstract
birds and ears of rabbits. The carpet was colored pale mustard.
Its floral motifs seemed to glow.

My key-card slotted clumsily into the socket; the lock clicked
and buzzed. "Aren't you going to be lonely?" the girl said, from
behind. I had not thought she would follow me. Her top was
tight; she looked timid. The handle felt large to my grip. I leaned
with my weight to open the door. I told her our bed was going to
be full that night.

This bed was large, plush, white. A quilt came down its sides
and touched the carpet. The bathroom smelled of disinfectant. I
fiddled with the taps. The tub was dry, of a cream color. And the
room's large window opened onto the Boulevard, whose towers
rose and seemed to touch the cover of dark clouds. The view was
vertiginous.

I tucked myself in, ruffling the cotton sheets against my neck.
My limbs slackened. My thoughts eased. The Boulevard seemed
distant. The stringers arrived before I was fully asleep, and I

rolled to the bed edge. Soon they snored, establishing a throbbing peace. I stared at the clock's green digits. I meditated on the evening. Gradually, the blinking of the digits became heavy to my eye; and at some point in the night they began to make a soft beating in my mind. The stringers didn't sleep soundly either. I got up to go to the bathroom. The carpet tickled my soles, and I felt the sensation run in my jaw, over my teeth. There was a scratching on the door. It repeated. I looked through the peephole and opened the door a crack. It was the timid girl. She had taken off her shawl, and thrown back her shoulders exaggeratedly. "I like your physique," she said, swaying.

The sun's golden glow fell on the curtains, which rippled from a slight opening in the window. I stepped to the view.

The city was utterly calm. Pillars of smoke billowed from places but I could not tell if they were due to the battle. In fact I was able to discern little about the urban expanse: the pedestrians seemed small, nearly absent. The shacks of neighborhoods were reduced to two-dimensional shiny roofs. I was too far away to hear the radios and pestles. The roads were filthy. I smelled an odor of citrus. Nothing corresponded: the room was a void and in it I felt severed. The city seemed grotesque, a noiseless machine moving urgently but without implication.

I spent the morning watching the street in front of the hotel; and just before noon, though the taxibuses had started to run, I hired a hotel taxi, a gray Mercedes, to take me to Victoire. The driver insisted I pay in advance. I sat in the back of the car, by a window, with one arm stretched over the length of the seat.

The day seemed to have begun with the typical fracas. On the Boulevard shops had shut, and outside a popular travel agency were haphazardly parked UN jeeps. But the roads were jammed as usual. Women walked in groups, bearing baskets of vegetables and sliced coconut on their heads. Children played with bicycle rims, propelling them forward with twigs. When the bureau called I was assured and brisk. "Nothing to report," I said. "I'm on my way home. Kinshasa seems calm—"

"What?" the editor said. "Who told you to go home?"

"The fighting is over."

"Do you have a flak jacket and helmet?"

"No."

"*Wait* a minute." He paused, muttering. "Don't you live away from town? What made you think you could just go? Why didn't you call us?"

"Man, I live in Victoire, not at the hotel. My money and passport are at home. What do I do if they shut down the roads?"

"The roads? Don't you get it, Anjan? What do we tell your mother, that they shut down the roads?" He was shouting now. "You have *no* idea what's going to happen in that city! There was a fucking battle last night! You should have stayed at that hotel!"

"Fine, all right—let me think," I said. "I'm in the car already." And I placed my phone beside me on the seat.

When we came to the turn for the Avenue des Huileries, which led to Victoire, I told the driver to keep going. "*Tout droit?*" His hands hesitated on the wheel. I made him go a mile or so and then turn, past the South African embassy, some distance away from the main road, toward the river, until we were driving past the low walls of the Indian margarine factory.

The factory belonged to the Rawji Group, the billionaire Indians. I had come here twice before, to do interviews for business stories. I did not know the owners particularly well—I was told they were wary of journalists. But they had operated in Congo for many generations, through the wars, coups and dictatorships; and they had much to lose from a prolonged battle: no business in Kinshasa matched this factory's scale and investment (its margarine was almost a necessity in Congo). I only wanted to stop for a few minutes—I thought it would be worthwhile to gauge the level of vigilance here.

The factory was set in a colonial-style enclave whose walls were covered in paintings of tubs of margarine; and after these large images, several times the size of a person, the premises took on a miniature quality, like the buildings on a movie set. The road by which I entered—on foot, because the factory guards blocked the taxi from coming in—was narrow, with a tight turn to the parking lot full of cars. The bosses had an area set apart, in the shade of some green corrugated plastic. Everything looked flimsy, of cheap material. The main administrative building was claustrophobic. Its glass windows were splattered with dry white paint. Outside, around the tar-black grounds, were isolated clusters of low buildings and small triangles of grass: decoration. The trees were desert palms that reached a little over one's head. And against the huge sky—the expanse of gray cloud made it seem vaster; I wondered if it had to do with our position in the Congo basin, a giant depression in the earth—everything in the enclave looked quaint.

I was just outside the main building, discussing the previous night's shootings with some factory middle management—they dallied about, without urgency; some were promising to dock the pay of laborers who had not reported for work that morning; and I was disarmed by their ease—when a shot sounded so close above my head that I instinctively fell to the ground. For some time I lay there, not daring to move. Then, keeping my palms flat on the cement, I turned only my head: the path was covered in flattened bodies. It was the first time in my life that I had so reacted—I found myself surprised to have in me this instinct, of the action movies, to fall.

We crowded into the main building, the Indians talking rapidly—the dialects mixed: Gujarati, Bhojpuri, Marwari. They cursed their luck, the soldiers, the Congolese. Some stared at the grass indifferently. I took a seat on a concrete sill and waited. Sometimes when a shot rang out I looked at the sky, as though expecting to see the bullet. And a young man who had so far been squatting came to sit on the sill beside me. He introduced himself as a clerk in the accounting department; then his expression became listless. The shooting meanwhile grew in frequency until it was constant, like at the venue where the election results had been declared.

"*Ho gaya.*" "It's happened," said the clerk. And now everyone, nodding, adopted this posture of knowingness—no one showed surprise. It was bravado; but the pretense, self-conscious and false as it was, seemed to signal that we were in a place of security. The fear began to subside. I listened to the Indians talk. And their mockery of the violence even started to be entertaining.

After half an hour or so most of the workers had dispersed. The fighting had not stopped, and I had thought they were stepping out temporarily. But no one returned. The cars were still in the lot. I asked the clerk what I should do, as a way to bring attention to myself.

He hesitated, then went to the back of the corridor and called someone. I waited at the sill, trying to listen in. When he returned it was with purpose in his stride; he said I should follow him out—the blasts sounded, unnervingly, just beyond the enclave—to a cement walkway along a row of bright yellow doors in a one-story building. I understood that these were the factory's guest quarters.

The clerk pushed open the last door; of lightweight wood, it flew open and banged into the wall. The room seemed like one of the temporary structures, imported whole, that one might find on a construction site. It had, by the door, a single bed. On the left was a bathroom. Before me, low on the wall, was a small air-conditioning unit. And alongside on a little table was a television. A small refrigerator was stocked with Coca-Colas. The clerk bent under the bed and found the cable for the internet. The stove even had a hot plate.

I said it looked fantastic.

He hummed in agreement. "*Bhagwan* saved you," he said, waving his hand at the sky. "He diverted you from that chaos." *Diverted, chaos*: I didn't expect such words from him; they sounded too bookish.

I saw him off at my door, where I stood awhile. The view over the walkway was of a few stunted palms lined in front of the main building. At my feet, lining the cement, were flowering shrubs, sparsely planted, behind which ran a network of thick black water tubes. The garden was like the rest of the factory's decoration—seemingly put there without consideration or care, out of some idea that plants and flowers were pretty.

I heard the adjacent door slam shut—and a paunched man came out, in singlet and shorts, carrying a computer in the crook of his arm, making straight for me. His feet, bare, landed on the cement with thuds. He looked extremely concentrated, and somewhat worried, as though he were about to deliver some difficult news. "Hello," he said. "You know CAD?"

I looked at him oddly. He then made a horrified expression, cringing as if he had made a grave error. "I'm sorry sir, I'm sorry," he said, taking his computer in hand. I told him I was only a guest, not a factory employee—he seemed relieved—but that I was stunned he could be programming at such a time. "What about that?" I said, pointing to my ear and then beyond the walls. He grimaced, but out of disbelief. "*That?*" And, now suddenly calm, as if I were an imbecile for asking, he said in a soft, melodious tone: "*That* will go on." He craned his neck to glance about us, as though to, for the first time, survey our surroundings. He turned, and I noticed he made a slight shrug; his door clicked shut.

I took a last look at the view. The room was icy to enter. I wrote a dispatch for the AP to say that the fighting had resumed. I showered, and sat on the bed, my back to the wall, and watched TV—strangely, I could find almost no broadcasts about the battle. The channels were full of commercials: shaky footage of hangers holding rows of jeans; ecstatic women twirling out of changing rooms, holding their buttocks. We were given a tour of Mr. Felix's house and shown his collection of shoes, his children, his waxed car and his wife—in that order. "Mr. Felix is a smart man," the narrator informed us, "he is reliable." It had seemingly not gone unnoticed that millions of people, confined to their homes, would be staring at their televisions. Congo's wealthy were taking the opportunity to promote themselves.

National television screened a heart surgery video: a pair of scissors cut a slit into some pink tissue. Forceps picked at the pieces of flesh. Blood seeped over the beating muscle. *Budup.* *Budup.* The scissors then cut another slit. Hands began to sew with a needle and thread. It was an advertisement for Kinshasa's Chinese hospital. Later the station ran old election campaign videos—profiles of politicians—and then a scene of Congolese aid workers in a dull room with foreign donors. The camera panned the room and zoomed in on a European. He bit his lips. He rubbed his nose and wiped his hands over his trousers. His eyes sometimes drooped. He looked this way and that; but the camera remained fixed, perhaps ordered to focus on the foreigners to show the meeting's importance. I became mesmerized by the slow, almost unmoving images. Never before had I such an opportunity to observe, so unhindered, the intricacies of a person's unconscious habits.

At about 8:00 p.m., dinner was delivered in a metal tiffin carrier, by a boy who was already at the end of the walkway when I answered his knock. He had brought chapatis, still warm, and a potato curry with coriander. Probably the clerk, I thought, though I had no way of knowing. I ate tentatively. And I got through about a fifth of the novel that I had tried to read at the election venue.

The setting should have seemed absurd; yet in the coolness, and after the neighbor's intense reaction, I too felt cut off from

the high-powered machine guns hammering the buildings outside. That seemed someone else's business; my business was
here; and it seemed possible, even easy, to become aloof like
the Indians. I found I could get used to the blasts as a kind of
background noise, and rather than waiting for it to stop I waited,
when it stopped, for it to pick up again.

 Before turning in I called Serge, to talk about coming to
fetch me: if the situation did not change I felt I could return the
next day. I also wanted Serge to share in my luck—I told him
about the room, the air-conditioning, the internet; I suggested
he spend the morning at the factory before we departed. But he
said the soldiers had set up barriers on all the main roads, and
there was now no way to pass between the *cité* and the *ville*. So I
would have to wait. "And the *ville* is not my place," he said. I felt
suddenly unnerved. "It isn't mine either, Serge."

The fighting escalated. The sounds became harder and more
powerful—now frightening. There were tanks on the road—
presumably the new machines Kabila had received some months
earlier from China. They were so close that I could hear their
engines heave; sometimes, above the enclave walls, I could see
a moving turret. Eight people had so far been killed in the violence, most of them during the previous day.

 The factory's location was unusual: not on the outskirts, as in
most cities, but in one of Kinshasa's wealthiest neighborhoods.
(The factory had been built in the 1930s; the city had grown
around it.) And around the corner from Bemba's residence, this
location put us at the center of the battle.

 The neighbor had presumably been instructed to share his
meals with me. When I opened my door that afternoon I found
at my feet two bowls covered in tissue paper, on which had been
placed some steel cutlery.

 I heard a heavy boom not far away—I looked out, and saw a

spiral of black fumes rise. The proximity was worrying. Kabila, I would learn, had shelled Bemba's house and helicopter. Bemba had been in the house at the time—with diplomats from the UN and American, French, British and Chinese embassies. They all had to be rescued in UN armored cars. The meeting had apparently unnerved the president: he had feared the foreigners were switching sides, that they were conspiring to remove him.

Concerned now about whether we were protected, and also about a rumbling noise that had persisted all night, seeming to come from within the enclave, for the first time I left the room. I made my way off the walkway and, keeping close to the walls, to the front gate. I crouched behind a cement parapet near the gate: the guards were in their glass-and-aluminum cabin, huddled over their radios. Propped up nearby was a Kalashnikov with a worn wooden butt. When they saw me they frantically began to wave and indicate that I should not approach.

In the other direction were the factory's installations. I passed the main building, where I stopped at a watercooler to fill a bottle to drink, and then the little triangular gardens, and proceeded along an empty road. There were no buildings here, no people. I came to an open pool, the size of my room, full of a black liquid—toxic effluent. Large metal pipes covered in a kind of aluminum emerged from it and led deeper within the enclave; I could not see their end. There was the throbbing noise of pumps, and an empty pulling sound—it surprised me that the machinery was still running.

It was in the middle of that night, my second at the factory and the third of the battle, that I began to become distressed. There was no obvious reason or trigger. I awoke in the middle of the night to the sounds of shooting, and immediately felt assailed by an anxiety.

Somewhere a mortar bomb fell and made a dull roar. It came back: the initial shock of the shots, their closeness. The illusion of safety had been shattered. I had realized we would soon be testing the infamous three-day rule, that on the third day of a lockdown the mobs became manic, uncontrollable. Several explanations for this had been proposed—hunger took over; or anger; some viral force emerged after three days. The rule had proven true over the years. And it began now to be mentioned on the radio. I imagined the enclave overrun with people; I noticed that my room's door, which did not fit properly within its frame, made a ceaseless light thudding with the shifting winds.

I had thought the factory would arrange to clean the room, but since the boy had dropped off dinner I had not seen a person. I still had the tiffin carrier, which smelled so powerfully of food that I put it next to the shower. Water dripped from a bathroom tap. I ran my hands over the walls, which were cold. The air-conditioning had ceased to be stimulating and was now a source of discomfort. I had not taken sufficient care with the room: the floor was everywhere stained with ugly brown patches from my bare feet collecting dirt and stepping into puddles.

The blasts now made a fickle confinement: though the battle remained always near, its distance shifted; so that the relief was always temporary, false—and one entered a state of continual stress.

A grasshopper had gotten into my room, or had perhaps always been present. In the fading light, against a wall, it showed its crouched form, its ribbed abdomen. It also seemed to wait.

I felt I slept numerous successive nights, each beginning with slumber and ending with alertness—to the ebonized vicinity, my capsule-sized room—and followed by the distressed realization that the sleep had been brief and the awakening rude. The body, too agitated, sometimes fell into a numbness.

By morning the continuity of the blasts had begun to create an irrational, possessing anxiety that could be set off by the most trivial sights: my unmade bed, water trembling in the bucket, slugs sliding over the wall outside the room. I could not see a bird; the small birds seemed to have all fled; I could no longer hear the chirps. I could think of nothing that reposed—my imagination seemed corrupt. The grass, the trees, the sky: all seemed tainted.

I began to make calls. The AP said it had no means to secure its journalists—the editor, sounding genuinely concerned, said I should try the embassies. I did not know many foreigners in Congo. I tried the UN, which said evacuating foreigners was not in its mandate. The Belgians asked if I was of European origin. Out of desperation I called Natalie. It was a difficult call—I was shrill, on the verge of breaking down. I cried out over the phone, screaming. But she showed genuine concern, and found for me the Canadian mission's phone number. The person there told me to call the Americans, who said they could do little for noncitizens. The British said the same. Only the French took down my phone number in case they passed near the factory. Everyone asked for my nationality; everyone seemed to be planning an evacuation. The pity I had felt for Serge at the venue I now felt for myself. Serge said the roadblocks were still up; he promised to come as soon as it became possible. The Indian embassy—I tried it last—did not answer my call. I knocked on the neighbor's door. He opened it, stretching his legs behind him, looking like someone on holiday.

He knew of the three-day rule. He said the enclave's walls would not be difficult to breach; and the factory's depots, stocked with foods and palm oil, were one of the city's prime targets.

All this he said without emotion. He seemed not to think—to have already removed himself from the context of the battle. And I learned why: he had known all along that he would escape.

The Indians were leaving that morning. The neighbor explained. Near the end of the enclave, a few miles away, was a port normally used to import factory raw materials. From there they would cross the river; a chartered Airbus would then fly them to Nairobi. The arrangements had been made by the Rawji Group and the Aga Khan, the leader of the Ismailis, a sect of Shiite Muslims who were powerful businessmen in Africa.

I asked the neighbor if I could join their plan. But he was impassive. "Can you just join like that?" he said. "You have to get permission. You need to reserve a seat, no?" Beginning to despise this man, and his detached way of speaking, and with heightened agitation, I asked how one could get permission— could he help me? "I don't know," he said, shaking his head. "Many families want to get on the boat. People are fighting for space. Do you know someone who can fight for you?"

It was to feel a kind of abandonment. I had exhausted every possibility. Perhaps in America and Dubai I still had relevance, but not here, in my room, in the enclave. The factory had become hostile. I packed my bags and stayed by my door, alert: my plan was to wait for the neighbor to leave his room and then to force myself on his evacuation party. The Indians could not refuse if I was standing in front of them—or so I thought.

But my safety, even then, would be uncertain: I had kept a gnawing secret from everyone. My passport was at Victoire. The UN or a government might have evacuated me without it, but the Aga Khan plan was private: travel papers would be needed at each border, even on the other side of the river. It would be legitimate for the Indians to claim I was a liability to the group. I did not know what I would then say, except perhaps to beg.

Through all this I was writing constantly. The correspondents had all left Kinshasa; when I looked for the news online I found mostly my own reports. There could be no thrill at this accomplishment. It only added a layer to my distress—a feeling of sweet terror.

After filing another dispatch, I went out, onto the cement walkway. I looked around. The shelling was still intense. I turned to the neighbor's door and knocked. I needed some reassurance; and my excuse, I thought, would be to ask for food that he was

going to leave behind. There was no response. I tried to listen
for sounds through the wood, but the ambient noise made that
difficult. I banged on the door with my fist. Still nothing. And
I noticed the absence of the low rumble. Yes, it had certainly
stopped.

The room no longer felt safe. I collected my bag and passed
by the main building, which was still deserted. I decided to go
to the gate. Again I crouched behind the walls. The guards were
by their radio. I ignored their signals for me to leave and ran
into their glass cabin. They seemed irritated, but accepted me.
And I preferred to wait here. I asked if they had seen the Indians leave. They became confused. Half the morning I spent in
their cabin, sometimes looking toward the guest rooms and the
enclave. Once I saw a figure in the distance, moving as though
on a bicycle. I raised an arm but it was too far. I did not shout.
And then, at around noon, there was news. The guards began
to chatter, and they turned the radio up. It was Radio France
Internationale—I struggled to hear, but then the words became
clearly audible. A Kabila spokesman was announcing that the
parties had reached a truce. *Cessez-le-feu. Cessez-le-feu.* Cease-
fire. The phrase repeated. I called the UN and confirmed it was
true. But the shooting continued around us. Perhaps the troops
had not been informed. Or they had decided to disobey the
order. The looting could have already begun. The mobs were perhaps already unstoppably making their way toward the factory. I
cringed. My phone was now ringing. It was Serge, telling me in
a high-pitched voice that he had gotten past the roadblock. He
had gotten past; I meditated on those words. I crouched deeper
within the cabin. It must have been twenty minutes before I
heard his sucking squeal sound above the shots. His figure,
across the road, was sprinting toward me. It was like a miracle.

The light in Kinshasa was pale, hazy. The little birds had returned to the trees and the electricity posts. My throat was parched. I felt in a trance as our taxi plowed forward through Kinshasa's streets. Serge had stayed the night at the factory, and in the morning—the city was calm—we decided to leave together. He called someone known to the family to pick us up; we could not trust the cars plying the roads.

The soldiers had destroyed bridges and water and electricity supplies. A building had a hole in it from a tank shell. At a roundabout we passed the dead bodies of young men, their blood over the tarmac.

I thought back to when I had first come to Congo, innocent. I remembered Lang, the mathematics professor. After I had told him I was leaving for Congo, at that same meeting, he had begun to search in his drawers for something. Muttering to himself, he shuffled through his papers. Finally he found it: a 1970s issue of *Rolling Stone* magazine. On the front page was a picture of students at UC Berkeley protesting against the Vietnam War. Lang had been among them. He had once resigned from a prestigious position at Columbia University for its treatment of war protesters. And Lang and I, besides mathematics, had often discussed our moral concerns. It was part of our bond—something that we had shared. He understood why I wanted to leave for Congo.

When he had given me the magazine, he had said: "We once used to go to the streets to fight for our rights, for peace, equality, women's rights, gay rights, the environment. But I don't see that anymore. I don't know if your generation really cares, or how much." He had seen that I was moving by my own convictions. I remembered vividly the moment I traded in my mathematics textbooks for his copy of *Rolling Stone*.

Over the course of the battle in Kinshasa I began to write for *The New York Times*. I had been one of the only journalists in the city, and they had needed someone in the violence for news. They had called me. The AP offered me jobs in Cairo, Johannesburg and Dakar.

The emptiness had been filled by fear. I had finally lived the story—lived some part of the sentiment of experiencing the war, and some part of the terror. The Congolese had become less foreign. From a life so far away from the Congolese, I had, in my way, come close to their experience. I felt I had approached them, and possessed some part of their distress.

I felt exhausted.

It was getting time to go home.

Bozene was empty, but for a few people who seemed to be running errands, replenishing supplies after the battle. The house was quiet. At the center of the dining table was a piece of clobbered metal. I asked what it was. The family did not respond. Nana led me to the bathroom, and showed me, on the wall, where the bullet had made a dent.

The silence was pierced by Bébé Rhéma's cries. She had returned from the hospital, almost cured of pneumonia. Jose was on his sofa, with Anderson, now in the president's party. Serge stayed awhile after dropping me off. The house's door was wide open for the first time that I could remember in weeks. Fresh air came in. The world outside was brightly lit. I took a place on the sofa and looked at the others—they were all staring at each other, wide-eyed, as if blind, and mute.

On one of my last mornings in Kinshasa, I sat on the edge of the river, watching the birds circle overhead and land among the tall reeds. Children could be heard talking. Fishermen in canoes slid along the still waters of a lagoon, carrying long poles and drawing in their nets, continuing their days in an even manner, with slow, calm movements, despite the raging chaos in the country.

On Bozene the Opposition Debout was nowhere to be seen. Flyers lay in tatters on the dirt roads. Activity at Victoire eventually resumed. Mothers began to search for food for their children. Husbands traveled into town to look for money. New businesses were started. New political parties were launched. People dreamed. The ambience resurged in the bars of Victoire. People found escape. But it all seemed a little more jaded—something vital had been diminished. The radios played the same lively music, unchanged despite all that had happened, making the music seem somehow dead. The churches gained more followers by transmitting the same messages of hope. The crumbling buildings had further deteriorated; on the broken cement were bright new edges that would soon be sullied by moss and grime.

On the way to the airport, the sounds were of people shouting. Metal hit metal. The driver accelerated through the slums. The roadsides were lined with bonfires giving off black smoke. And across the vast city these thick columns rose, and joined with the gray sky.

Acknowledgments

My parents, my dear sister, my publishers—Sonny Mehta, Gerald Howard, Ravi Mirchandani, and Chiki Sarkar—my agent, Robert Guinsler, and Jeffrey Gettleman.

Note on the Author

Anjan Sundaram is an award-winning journalist who has reported from Africa and the Middle East for the *New York Times* and the Associated Press. His writing has also appeared in *Foreign Policy, Fortune*, the *Washington Post, Los Angeles Times, Chicago Tribune, Telegraph, Guardian* and the *International Herald Tribune*. He has been interviewed by the BBC World Service and Radio France Internationale for his analysis of the conflict in Congo. He received a Reuters journalism award in 2006 for his reporting on Pygmy tribes in Congo's rain forest. He currently lives in Kigali, Rwanda, with his wife.